J2EE™ Design Patterns

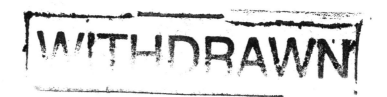

Other Java™ resources from O'Reilly

Related titles

Enterprise JavaBeans™
Java™ & XML
Java™ Cookbook
Java™ Enterprise in a Nutshell
Java™ I/O
Java™ in a Nutshell
Java™ Performance Tuning

Java™ Programming with
   Oracle SQLJ
Java™ Security
JavaServer™ Pages
Java™ Swing
Learning Java™

Java Books Resource Center

java.oreilly.com is a complete catalog of O'Reilly's books on Java and related technologies, including sample chapters and code examples.

OnJava.com is a one-stop resource for enterprise Java developers, featuring news, code recipes, interviews, weblogs, and more.

Conferences

O'Reilly & Associates bring diverse innovators together to nurture the ideas that spark revolutionary industries. We specialize in documenting the latest tools and systems, translating the innovator's knowledge into useful skills for those in the trenches. Visit *conferences.oreilly.com* for our upcoming events.

Safari Bookshelf (*safari.oreilly.com*) is the premier online reference library for programmers and IT professionals. Conduct searches across more than 1,000 books. Subscribers can zero in on answers to time-critical questions in a matter of seconds. Read the books on your Bookshelf from cover to cover or simply flip to the page you need. Try it today with a free trial.

J2EE™ Design Patterns

William Crawford and Jonathan Kaplan

O'REILLY®

Beijing · Cambridge · Farnham · Köln · Sebastopol · Tokyo

J2EE™ Design Patterns
by William Crawford and Jonathan Kaplan

Copyright © 2003 O'Reilly Media, Inc. All rights reserved.
Printed in the United States of America.

Published by O'Reilly Media, Inc., 1005 Gravenstein Highway North, Sebastopol, CA 95472.

O'Reilly Media, Inc. books may be purchased for educational, business, or sales promotional use. On-line editions are also available for most titles (*safari.oreilly.com*). For more information, contact our corporate/institutional sales department: (800) 998-9938 or *corporate@oreilly.com*.

Editor:	Mike Loukides
Production Editor:	Colleen Gorman
Cover Designer:	Hanna Dyer
Interior Designer:	David Futato

Printing History:

September 2003:   First Edition.

ISBN: 0-596-00427-3
[LSI]   [2011-02-11]

Table of Contents

Preface

So, you want to build enterprise applications?

Back in 1996, we were working on a web-based clinical data management system for a major Boston hospital. Java 1.0.2 had recently been released, and development tools were beginning to trickle onto the market. The Write Once, Run Anywhere promise of Java was beguiling, not in the least because we didn't have development environments that mirrored the deployment environments. And here was this object-oriented, strongly typed language with—even then—an excellent standard class library. It seemed like a perfect fit, at least in theory. In the end, the application sprouted several Java applets and an early, crude database-backed web site. Replacing Perl scripts with Java code required some fancy footwork, since none of the available web servers had any native Java integration. Performance was questionable, maintenance was iffy, and at a few points we found ourselves backtracking to Perl and C++. The application itself turned into a strange amalgamation of Perl CGI scripts, server-side Java applications (including part of a custom-built web server), HTML, and C++ CGI programs.

Our primary problem was that the necessary infrastructure for both developing and deploying the application just wasn't in place. Java's support for relational databases was primitive, and while the language has always supported certain operations as a web *client*, it wasn't until the Java Servlet API was introduced the following year that Java gained a standard, high performance mechanism for integrating into a web *server*. These limitations meant that while we could use Java for some of our development activities, those activities were sharply bounded. It also meant that we couldn't take much with us as we moved on to future projects with different environments and tool sets, all of which behaved more or less differently.

Now, Java has found its place in the enterprise world. Performance is competitive with any approach you care to name. The APIs that have been added during the subsequent four iterations of the language give Java broader native support for enterprise activities than any other language available. From a standing start when we first tried it in 1996, Java has become the lingua franca for server-side business programming. The cross-platform graphical user interface, which seemed to be the most promising aspect of Java, is only now beginning to take off in a real way, mostly in products focused on developers and system administrators. But Java has taken off behind the scenes for building e-commerce web sites, intranet business applications, and mission-critical distributed computing systems. Millions of people interact with enterprise Java every day, often without realizing it.

Even if we'd had the full resources of the modern Java environment available to us, success wouldn't be guaranteed. (Actually, the application in question worked out pretty well overall, but it's not an experience that we'd like to repeat.) Tools can be used poorly or inefficiently, and the sheer scope of the J2EE environment—which now includes thousands of classes—means that very few individual developers have built up a reservoir of experience in every area. J2EE has created standards and made implementation easier, but the fundamental design issues are still as relevant as ever. We just have more ways to tackle them and more tools to eliminate the grunt work. And, of course, a standard, consistent, widely deployed platform to build those solutions on.

This is a book about building effective applications for enterprise environments, using Java 2, Enterprise Edition (J2EE). This book is not about how to use the individual components of the J2EE specification, although we touch upon aspects of most of the components; a brief overview is provided below. Rather, this book is about the patterns that underlie effective software designs.

In addition to 12 combined years of experience building Enterprise Java systems, the authors, like the development community at large, have been the beneficiaries of over a decade of research and writing on object-oriented modeling, software design methodologies, and enterprise architecture. One of the most important ideas to gain prominence during this time is the *software design pattern*: a way of describing recurring solutions to common problems. This book is about the fusion of design patterns and enterprise design.

Audience

Readers should have a good working knowledge of the Java language itself. We don't expect that readers will be entirely fluent with J2EE, but we do expect a top-level knowledge of what's available in the J2EE technology stack (we include a brief overview in Chapter 1 for those who've been away, summarizing the problems that each technology solves). In the presentation tier section, readers will need some basic knowledge of Java Servlets and of HTTP and web protocols in general, but we explain some of the nuances as we encounter them. Since enterprise applications tend to be database-intensive, the business tier section (Chapters 6–10) makes frequent use of databases.

For a fast-paced primer on all the J2EE technologies, check out *Java Enterprise in a Nutshell* by William Crawford, Jim Farley, and David Flanagan, also from O'Reilly & Associates.*

Organization of This Book

This book provides developers with the patterns they need to build extensible, scalable, reliable systems with J2EE in a timely manner. Once you've finished reading it, you'll have an understanding of the primary J2EE patterns and how they relate to one another and to an application as a whole.

There are at least three ways to read this book. The simplest one is to start here and keep going until you hit the back cover. Another is to pick and choose: many chapters and sections of chapters are self-contained; if you're only interested in the business tier, you can focus on the second half of the book, and if you need tips on generating primary keys for database tables, Chapter 8 will see you through. Or, you can do it backwards by reading the four appendixes first. They'll give you a general outline of the different kinds of things patterns can do and how they can help you right now. Then head over to the appropriate chapters and read a bit more.

Chapter 1

Provides a brief introduction to design patterns and enterprise design. In addition to describing patterns themselves, we'll talk about how patterns help achieve four major design goals: extensibility, reliability, scalability, and timeliness. Although not necessarily all at once: we aren't miracle workers.

Chapter 2

Contains an introduction to the Unified Modeling Language, a standardized graphical approach to describing the purpose, structure, and processing of applications. We'll use UML throughout the rest of the book to describe individual design patterns. We've tried to make this introduction as complete as possible without taking several hundred pages, so you'll get a good idea of what's possible with UML and where you can go in order to learn more.

The rest of the book introduces a range of J2EE design patterns in the context of the design environments in which they are used. Rather than create a conventional patterns catalog, we've chosen to introduce these patterns in a narrative style, while keeping each section sufficiently distinct so that you can easily focus on the patterns themselves. The underlying themes of scalability, extensibility, and reliability flow through each chapter. Some of the chapters can stand alone: programmers working on the web tiers of an application do not necessarily need to know about patterns for MQ messaging systems, and vice versa. We do believe, however, that well-rounded

---

* Will suggests purchasing copies for friends, relatives, and loved ones.

developers will want to familiarize themselves with the whole package. We start with the presentation tier.

Chapter 3

   Outlines the general patterns involved in structuring the web-focused side J2EE applications, providing a framework for extensibility.

Chapter 4

   Continues the extensibility discussion, introducing additional patterns focused on creating more flexible presentation logic.

Chapter 5

   Looks at scaling the presentation tier, presenting strategies for improving resource management and general performance.

Next, we leave the presentation tier and move on to the business tier.

Chapter 6

   Introduces the business tier, focusing on the domain model for the application.

Chapter 7

   Provides patterns designed to create a more efficient and scalable interface between the presentation tier and the business tier—the former interacting with the user and the latter interacting with application data.

Chapter 8

   Focuses on the database, providing a set of patterns to implement persistence in your application.

Chapter 9

   Discusses ways to centralize present business logic to your application.

Chapter 10

   Discusses concurrency; in other words, the problems faced by any application in which two or more users might try to do the same thing at the same time.

Chapter 11

   Introduces a set of patterns for enterprise messaging systems.

Chapter 12

   Switches gears from the patterns chapters and introduces the concept of *antipatterns*: recurring worst practices in enterprise application development that must be avoided, if not at all costs, at least whenever possible.

We finish with a set of Appendixes, outlining each of the patterns presented in this book in a catalog format. The catalogs provide a quick reference to the various patterns in the book, as well as a way to efficiently explore potential solutions to current problems.

For Further Reading

Because design patterns are intrinsically all about documenting solutions, there is substantial literature on the topic. Here are a few other important titles in the patterns universe:

- *Patterns of Enterprise Application Architecture*, by Martin Fowler (Addison-Wesley). Java and .NET enterprise architecture from one of the leaders in the field.

- *Core J2EE Patterns*, Second Edition, by Deepak Alur, John Crupi, and Dan Malks (Prentice Hall PTR). Sun's contribution to the patterns literature.

- *Design Patterns*, by Erich Gamma, Richard Helm, Ralph Johnson, and John Vlissides (Addison-Wesley). The original software design patterns book, containing patterns useful for both enterprise and standalone development.

- *Pattern Oriented Software Architecture*, Volumes 1 and 2, by Frank Buschman et al (Wiley). Focuses on building larger architectures from scratch, outside the Java universe.

- *EJB Design Patterns*, by Floyd Marinescu (Wiley) Design patterns for EJB environments.

- *Bitter Java*, by Bruce Tate (Manning). A superb introduction to Java antipatterns.

On the Java side, O'Reilly's Java Series provides a series of titles focused on the underlying implementation technologies. In particular, we think this book is an excellent companion to:

- *Java Enterprise in a Nutshell*, Second Edition, by William Crawford, Jim Farley, and David Flanagan (O'Reilly). Everything you wanted to know about the J2EE APIs but were afraid to ask.

- *Java Enterprise Best Practices*, by the O'Reilly Java Authors (O'Reilly). Advanced techniques for the J2EE APIs.

And in addition:

- *Java Servlet Programming*, Second Edition, by Jason Hunter with William Crawford (O'Reilly).

- *Java Web Services*, by David Chappell and Tyler Jewell (O'Reilly).

- *Java Message Service,* by Richard Monson-Haefel and Dave Chappell (O'Reilly).

- *Enterprise JavaBeans*, Third Edition, by Richard Monson-Haefel (O'Reilly).

Conventions Used in This Book

The following typographical conventions are used in this book:

Italic
> Used for filenames, directories, emphasis, and first use of a technical term.

`Constant width`
> Used in code examples. Also used for Java class names and bean names.

`Constant width italic`
> Indicates an item that should be replaced with an actual value in your program.

`Constant width bold`
> Used for user input in text and in examples showing both input and output.

 Indicates a tip, suggestion, or general note.

 Indicates a warning.

Comments and Questions

Please address comments and questions concerning this book to the publisher:

> O'Reilly & Associates, Inc.
> 1005 Gravenstein Highway North
> Sebastopol, CA 95472
> (800) 998-9938 (in the United States or Canada)
> (707) 829-0515 (international/local)
> (707) 829-0104 (fax)

There is a web page for this book, which lists errata, examples, or any additional information. You can access this page at:

> *http://www.oreilly.com/catalog/j2eedp/*

To comment or ask technical questions about this book, send email to:

> *bookquestions@oreilly.com*

For information about books, conferences, Resource Centers, and the O'Reilly Network, see the O'Reilly web site at:

> *http://www.oreilly.com*

The authors maintain a home page for this book, at *http://www.j2eepatterns.info*. Another extremely valuable patterns resource is the patterns community at *http://www.java.net*.

Acknowledgments

The authors would like to thank everyone who took the time to read all or parts of the innumerable drafts of this book. In particular, we'd like to single out Ted Chen, William Connor, Liz Evans, Jim Farley, Eric Friedman, Phil Haigh, Dave Henry, Ron Hitchens, James "JC" Norman, Paul Tecca and last, but certainly not least, Dave Wood, who went through each chapter with a fine-tooth comb. We'd also like to thank all the writers, theorists, and programmers who have contributed to our understanding of both design patterns and enterprise architecture as a whole. All remaining misrepresentations, errors, and bad karma are, of course, our own.

At O'Reilly, Colleen Gorman did a fabulous job bringing it all together at the end of the development process. And of course, our editor, Mike Loukides, supported the project from its inception and gave us the freedom to put together the best book we could.

William Crawford

First off, I'd like to thank Jon Kaplan for working on this project with me, and Tracy Leeds Kaplan for letting him do it, even with the wedding falling right in the middle of the writing schedule. The result was a far better book that would have materialized otherwise.

I worked for two people during the course of this book, both of whom helped make it possible. Martin Streeter at Invantage and Howard Foster at Perceptive Informatics, Inc. both made sure that I had the time and support to bring the project to a successful conclusion. The extremely competent Perceptive engineering teams in Boulder, Birmingham and Boston also contributed greatly to the success of the project: it's all about environment.

Mike Loukides was very understanding when, after committing to deliver this book, my corporate world turned upside down when Invantage, Inc. became part of Perceptive Informatics. I hadn't planned on spending a cumulative month and a half in England during the first half of the year, and Mike demonstrated an almost god-like patience in addition to his other sterling qualities.

I wouldn't have gotten into this line of business in the first place without the help and support of my family, who stood by relatively patiently as computers turned into more computers. And, of course, many thanks to Rebecca Goetz (*http://rebecca-goetz.blogspot.com*) whose unflagging encouragement throughout the project was utterly irreplaceable: thanks for putting up with me, dear.

Jonathan Kaplan

I would like to thank my co-author Will Crawford and editor Mike Loukides for giving me a chance to work on this book. Will has shown me the ropes, guiding and advising me since even before day one. Mike has graciously put up with an endless number of mistakes, rewrites, and missed deadlines, and remained constructive and helpful all the while.

This kind of book is really a team effort, which came together with the tireless work of our technical reviewers, especially Dave Wood, and the dedicated team at O'Reilly. I would also like to thank my colleagues at Sun, for maintaining an environment so conducive to thinking about and building innovative software.

In the process of writing this book, I have benefited from the unending support of my family—my parents, grandparents, brother, and all the Leeds, who never lost faith, no matter how many times I said "just one more draft."

And last, but not least, I would like to thank my wife Tracy. Without her love, encouragement, and patience, none of this would have been possible.

—Cambridge, MA
August 2003

CHAPTER 1

Java Enterprise Design

Before we dive into specific patterns for enterprise architecture, we need to set the stage. In this chapter, we'll take a closer look at design patterns as a context, and then take an extremely quick tour through J2EE. Next, we'll explore the various tiers of an enterprise application, from the client up through the business logic and enterprise level services. We'll look at component-based design, and the four major themes that govern much of enterprise development: Extensibility, Scalability, Reliability, and Timeliness.

In the next chapter, we'll break off and concentrate on UML, the Unified Modeling Language, which provides a standard vocabulary to describe both design patterns and systems as a whole.

The rest of the book builds on the themes of good enterprise architecture practices and the design patterns that support them.

Design Patterns

A design pattern is a recurring solution to a recurring problem. From a programming perspective, a pattern *provides a set of specific interactions that can be applied to generic objects to solve a known problem.* Good patterns strike a balance between the size of the problem they solve and the specificity with which they address the problem.

The simplest patterns may be summed up in no more than a sentence or two. Using a database to store information for a web site is a pattern, albeit a fairly high-level and obvious one. More complex patterns require more explanation, perhaps including the use of modeling languages or a variety of other forms of longer description.

Design patterns originated outside the computer industry, originally showing up in conventional (as opposed to computer systems) architecture. Architects of buildings and architects of software have more in common than one might initially think. Both professions require attention to detail, and each practitioner will see their work collapse around them if they make too many mistakes.

The book to read, if you're interested in the architectural origins of design patterns, is *A Pattern Language: Towns, Buildings, Construction* by Christopher Alexander (Oxford University Press). Widespread acceptance of design patterns in software began with the publication of *Design Patterns: Elements of Reusable Object Oriented Software* (Addison-Wesley), by Erich Gamma, Richard Helm, Ralph Johnson, and John Vlissides, also known as the "Gang of Four."

Design patterns are discovered as much as created. Some of the most effective patterns emerged from two decades of object-oriented (OO) design theory and the fewer but highly intensive years of enterprise Java. In many cases, the challenge has been to move from best practices and gut feelings to clear, defined sets of activities that can form the basis for communication between developers. It's amazing how much easier it is to suggest that someone use an Actor-Observer pattern (which allows one piece of code to register interest in the activities of another and receive notifications of key events) than to explain how to implement an event model.

We hope that readers will have two reactions as they explore the patterns in this book. The first is to say, "That's cool" (or, if the boss is around, "That's useful!"). The second is to say, "So, what's the big deal?" Both reactions mean that we're doing our job—describing approaches that work. Design patterns in enterprise applications can be surprisingly simple on the surface. Of course, it's that generic aspect that makes them effective patterns in the first place.

Any developer who has built anything with J2EE, or even with significant components of J2EE, has probably discovered at least one or two of these patterns already. In fact, some of the patterns in this book originated before J2EE and influenced its development, and they can also be applied in other languages and environments. Using strong patterns makes for a better programmer, designer, or architect, regardless of the underlying language.

The Anatomy of a Pattern

Software design patterns represent a small fraction of the many types of patterns in the world. We mentioned already that design patterns started in the world of architecture. There are also business patterns, networking patterns, and even social patterns that describe how people should interact. So what makes a pattern a pattern?

To describe a general pattern, we'll take an example from city planning. Building a city is a lot like building a complicated application. There are buildings (objects) that encapsulate certain functions (police, fire, merchant banking, baseball stadiums, etc.). These buildings are largely independent, interacting only via the goods, services, and people (messages) that flow in and out of them on roads (interfaces). In a city, a design pattern might be "building in blocks."

There are several ways of describing a pattern, but they all have several aspects in common. The first part of the "building in blocks" pattern description is its *name*.

The name is important because it is a simple way for city planners to uniquely refer to the pattern. Any time one planner refers to "building in blocks," all the other planners should know what he is talking about. If the pattern has an alternate name—for instance, "grid layout"—it should be mentioned also.

The second part of the pattern description is the *goal*. This describes the problem solved by the pattern, or what we hope to achieve by implementing the pattern. The goal is sometimes described in terms of the *forces* that apply to the pattern. One of the forces acting on the "building in blocks" pattern is that it is difficult to navigate in a large city where the roads do not run parallel. Another is that buildings are easier to build when they are square, a process that requires perpendicular intersections.

The most important aspect of a pattern description is the *description* itself. This element tells how the pattern works. It is usually phrased in terms of *participants* (the objects that interact in the pattern). The description of a pattern summarizes the characteristics of the participants, as well as how they interact. Note that the participants must be generic enough that the pattern can be reused, but specific enough to solve a particular problem: a balance that changes depending on the goal of the pattern.

For "building in blocks," we would likely define buildings, streets, avenues, vehicles, and people as participants. People and vehicles interact by navigating between buildings on the streets, which are laid out in a grid. However, we can also treat this pattern as something more generic. Rather than describing buildings, pedestrians, streets, and so forth, we can talk about *components* (buildings) connected by *pathways* (streets) and navigated by *travelers* (people and cars). This allows us to apply the same pattern to the layout of an office (cubes, hallways, workers), or of a restaurant (tables, aisles, waiters), as well as the layout of a city.

Pattern descriptions typically have an implementation section. *Implementation* covers any specific information that goes into making a pattern work in practice. In software patterns, the implementation section is where you find actual code—or, at least, code fragments. The code is a sample implementation that demonstrates the central ideas of the pattern. For the "building in blocks" pattern, we might mention in the implementation section that streets are often named by numbers, while avenues are usually referred to by name. Since this pattern doesn't address the variety or ratios of building types a city might require, we wouldn't emphasize how many police stations and convention centers the city might need. That would be a different pattern.

Finally, it is often helpful to show cases where the pattern has been applied successfully. Not only does this information help readers decide if a pattern is applicable to their problem, it also provides a reference for finding more detailed information. New York City, Washington, D.C., and Philadelphia all use the "building in blocks" pattern. Most of Boston does not, and as a result requires the largest public works project in history to add more capacity to the roads.[*]

---

[*] See *http://www.bigdig.com/* for a detailed look at Boston's traffic woes and the world's largest refactoring activity.

Presenting Patterns

In this book, we take a somewhat unorthodox approach to working with design patterns. There are several books available, including the Gang of Four's, that present lists of patterns, sometimes organized according to a guiding principle or two. These are generally referred to as *pattern catalogs*. Rather than present another pattern catalog, we're going to discuss different aspects of J2EE development and introduce the patterns in context. The goal is to give the reader a set of patterns that build on each other. By presenting the patterns in the larger context of J2EE applications, we hope to foster a more complete understanding of effective Java Enterprise architecture.

For reference purposes, Appendix A contains an abbreviated form of a conventional pattern catalog, providing quick overviews of the problems dealt with by each pattern discussed in the book, and references back to the more detailed discussion.

J2EE

This book expects that you know the fundamental Java language and have some basic familiarity with the J2EE APIs. A J2EE environment differs from a Java 2, Standard Edition (J2SE) environment in that it offers a wider range of services than a standalone application could expect to find. J2SE is geared towards providing core language features (I/O, text manipulation, variables, object semantics), standard utility classes that apply in a variety of settings (collections, mathematics), and features required for building client applications (GUIs, and some basic enterprise integration, including access to databases and naming services).

The J2EE application model is built on a division of labor into various tiers. The client presentation in a web browser, applet, or Java application is separated from server side logic in a JavaServer Page or Java Servlet and the business logic in a database or Enterprise JavaBeans. The J2EE APIs are focused on implementing the interactions between tiers. The interfaces to each tier are standardized, allowing programmers with an understanding of the core J2EE concepts to easily apply their skills to any J2EE-based project.

The core of a J2EE application deployment is a J2EE-compliant application server. The application server supports hosting business logic components and web components, providing access to the full range of J2EE capabilities. Note that the J2EE API doesn't say very much beyond the essentials about how these servers should be designed, or how deployment, maintenance, and general administration should be conducted. The focus of the J2EE API, instead, is on programmatic interfaces and runtime behavior. This specialization can make it difficult to transfer administration skills from, say, IBM WebSphere to BEA WebLogic. Code, however, should transfer transparently. Figure 1-1 shows the canonical J2EE application model.

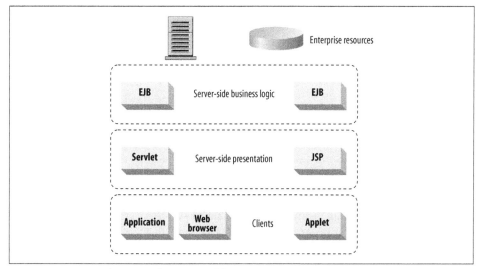

Figure 1-1. Canonical J2EE application model

Each J2EE API itself is simply a wrapper for a service provided by the J2EE container or by an external component within the enterprise. A full-scale J2EE environment could include one or more J2EE application servers hosting servlets and Enterprise JavaBeans, as well as an external transaction manager, an Oracle or DB2 relational database, and a messaging middleware system. Full J2EE platforms implement the following APIs:

Java Servlet API
> Allows a web server to process HTTP requests and return content to a client. The servlet code can make use of any other J2EE service in the process of fulfilling the request.

Java Server Pages
> These text files include fragments of Java code and are stored on a web server. A typical JSP consists of HTML with embedded Java code to customize the display according to the application's requirements. When a client requests a JSP, the server compiles the JSP into a Java Servlet and, if it has not already done so, executes the JSP and returns the results. Since JSPs are easier to write and modify than a Servlet, they are often used to create the HTML user interface for a web-based application.

Enterprise JavaBeans
> Allows the creation of server-managed distributed objects, representing the business data and logic behind an application. EJBs are divided into three categories: *entity beans* define the data structure for the application; *session beans* provide business methods that can manipulate entity beans and other resources; *message-driven beans* are similar to session beans, but they are triggered by the arrival of a message from a messaging middleware system. The EJB standard also

includes full support for transactions. Managing EJBs is one of the main duties of a J2EE server.

JNDI (Java Naming and Directory Interface)

Provides generic support for accessing directory services. In addition to providing a frontend to enterprise directory servers, such as LDAP-based employee directories, JNDI is used within the context of a J2EE application to identify resources such as Enterprise JavaBeans and database connections. By accessing all external resources via JNDI lookups, an application can be easily relocated or distributed.

JavaMail API

Enables support for generic point-to-point electronic messages. For all practical purposes, this means Internet email. JavaMail uses a generic architecture to support pluggable message transport and retrieval systems. The default installation from Sun includes support for SMTP, IMAP, and POP, and support for other protocols is available from a variety of third parties. While J2EE environments must provide an implementation of JavaMail, they do not need to provide any of the infrastructure for a particular transport mechanism.

Java Message Service API

Allows J2EE applications to integrate with Message Oriented Middleware (MOM) packages, such as Sonic Software's SonicMQ or IBM MQSeries. MOM packages allow messages to be routed between applications, providing delivery and quality of service guarantees that simple email cannot provide.

Java Transaction API

Allows applications to manage their own transactions. The Java Transaction API allows multiple components on different tiers and different servers to participate in a single, distributed transaction.

The J2EE standard also has a few additional features and requirements. It mandates interoperability with CORBA-based distributed objects. In addition, it requires support for the full J2SE API set, which provides the JDBC API for database access. Finally, it provides a standard, XML-based system of *deployment descriptors*, which describe the structure of a J2EE application (particularly EJB components and web applications), enabling faster deployment.

For tutorials and reference information on the individual APIs that make up J2EE, we suggest (with some admitted bias) *Java Enterprise in a Nutshell*, by Jim Farley, William Crawford, and David Flanagan. There are also a variety of books in the O'Reilly Java Series (and elsewhere) that do an excellent job of explaining each API in much more detail than we could do here.

You don't need to use every last J2EE API to build a J2EE application. While there is occasionally some confusion, an application is technically "J2EE" if it uses even one of the J2EE APIs. It's common to associate J2EE with Enterprise JavaBeans. This is particularly the case because EJBs, despite the name, are probably the most conceptually difficult J2EE component for programmers who started out with J2SE.

We can say that applications that use the full J2EE application model from HTML presentation through to an EJB-based business layer are "J2EE applications," while others simply "use J2EE technology," but the difference isn't something to waste much time on. The important thing is that you can use the mix of J2EE technologies appropriate for your application. Later in the book, we'll describe patterns geared toward effectively balancing the J2EE application model and real-world requirements.

Application Tiers

We've gotten all this way without defining enterprise applications. This is because they often defy simple definition. Enterprise applications range from mainframe-based transaction processing applications with aging green-screen terminals to phone systems, from traditional client/server to intranet web sites, and even to Amazon.com.

All enterprise applications are divided into *tiers*. These tiers are sometimes referred to as *components*, although this term is a little misleading; more than one component is frequently present on any given tier. A tier can be thought of as a collection of software with a particular scope of operation and a defined set of interfaces to the outside world.

Different people divide enterprise applications in different ways. The official J2EE application model, as discussed above, divides an application into a Client Presentation tier, a Server Side Presentation tier, and a Server Side Business Logic tier. Enterprise information systems, such as databases, constitute a fourth tier.

We call this the "official" model because it's what Sun's J2EE documentation proposes, but in reality, there's a lot of scope for individual choice. For example, when thinking about application tiers for this book, we came up with five layers:

Client Presentation tier
> Provides a user interface to the end user. The client can be "thin" (typically a web browser), "fat" (a full scale application), or something in between.

Server Side Presentation tier
> Provides the Client Presentation tier with the materials, such as HTML, required to produce the user interface.

Server Side Business Logic tier
> Includes the business methods sitting behind an application, performing actions like registering customers, taking orders, and managing shipping. These can often be thought of as the "verbs" of an application.

Server Side domain model
> Includes the data model used by the business logic tier, or the "nouns" of the application. The domain model includes entities like customers, orders, stock

records, and any other information that is manipulated in the course of the application's life.

Enterprise Integration tier
> Connects the application to other systems. This connection can take place via CORBA, web services, Message Oriented Middleware, email, or even sneakernet.

Notice that we've called two of these tiers "presentation" tiers. That's because both are responsible for creating the interface ultimately presented to the client. Different technologies are used to implement the client-side and server-side presentation tiers (HTML and JavaScript on the client side, Servlets, JSPs, and so forth on the server), but both are complementary.

These five tiers are certainly not canonical. Many applications don't include an Enterprise Integration tier, and many writers correspondingly don't treat it as a tier at all. The business logic and domain tiers are often combined. The persistence engine for the domain tier, typically a relational database, is often considered a separate tier because it is housed separately. We didn't list it that way because, in a perfectly compartmentalized application, the domain tier is the only part of the application that accesses the database layer.[*]

If we assume the client to be the "bottom tier" and the enterprise layer to be the "top tier," we can go on to say that tiers generally see higher tiers but not lower tiers. Furthermore, they should see as few other tiers as possible, using interfaces that are as tightly defined as possible. This makes it easier to modify one tier without affecting others. There are always exceptions to the order listed above. For instance, a fat client might skip the Server Side Presentation tier and interact directly with the business objects on the Server Side Business Logic tier via Enterprise JavaBeans. The same application may include a web interface where a Server Side Presentation tier component uses the same EJBs to create HTML.

Component-Based Development

We just mentioned that J2EE tiers are sometimes referred to, in error, as components. We shouldn't be too harsh, though, because it's a logical assumption to make and can even sometimes be true. A component is a self-contained piece of software with a known, well-defined interface that can be used by other pieces of software. According to this definition, a J2EE tier *is* a component, but it's a component that can be subdivided (at least hopefully!) into a number of subsidiary components, which in turn can be rearranged to modify the functionality of the software itself.

---

[*] This particular distinction is where a lot of people tend to play fast and loose, and often for good reason, since the domain tier can be most severe performance bottleneck in a large application. Much of Chapter 7 is devoted to addressing this issue. The database can also be seen as part of the Enterprise Integration tier, particularly if it plays host to a large quantity of application logic as well as raw data.

Characteristics of components

If areas of the program depend closely on each other, we say the components are *tightly coupled*. When one component is modified, its partner will usually need to be modified to match, and vice versa. For this reason, effectively sharing tightly coupled components can be a real challenge. When multiple developers work on these components, each developer risks breaking the entire application and the work of other developers. In the enterprise world, the situation becomes even murkier: individual applications can be components of large business process flows, and changing one small section can, in the worst possible case, cause entirely different applications to fail!

A component is *specialized* when it can only perform a specific task. While there is nothing inherently wrong with specialization, components that are specialized for a certain task are difficult to extend or reuse. To perform new tasks, the entire component must be copied before it can be changed. This divergence will cause maintenance headaches in the future, since updates will need to be repeated in several places.

Designing for change up-front can help solve these problems. Defining clear interfaces between components separates their interactions from individual implementations. As long as a component preserves its interfaces, it can change internally without breaking its partners. A component can even be replaced with an entirely different one, as long as the interfaces are the same. When components work together using these interfaces, they are said to be *loosely coupled*. Loosely coupled components can vary their implementation independently, which makes each part more likely to be reusable and easier to share.

To reduce specialization, larger components must be broken up into a collection of smaller ones. Code that is specific to a particular task should be separated out into a subcomponent, which *encapsulates* the task's functionality. This subcomponent can be modified and replaced independent of the rest of the application, promoting sharing and reuse.

In some ways, designing for extensibility may seem like a contradiction: expecting the unexpected. In fact, as a developer, you usually have some idea about where the software might evolve. This is often the case during iterative software development—you build a subset of the full product in each iteration, knowing in advance what features will be added by the time it is released. You can use this intuitive knowledge as a basis for making your software more extensible.

As software grows, however, it will probably be used in ways you never expected. Users will create new requirements on the program. If your design was not extensible, you will need to complicate it to meet these demands. Eventually, you will realize which areas of the program should have been extensible to begin with and rewrite large amounts of the program in order to retrofit them. The process of adding extensibility into an existing application is known as *refactoring*.

Core Development Concepts

When evaluating the end product of any enterprise development project, we can score it on four factors: Extensibility, Scalability, Reliability, and Timeliness. Different projects emphasize these factors to different degrees: NASA programmers will emphasize reliability above all else, giving appropriately short shrift to timeliness concerns. A startup may emphasize scalability and timeliness, with concerns over extensibility put off for the next release.[*]

Obviously, each of the four issues affects the others at some level. A highly extensible system might be made more scalable by plugging in higher performance components, and time spent up front building support for scalability will pay off in timely deployment of later versions. The important thing to know is that design patterns can improve performance in all four areas. In this book, we focus on extensibility and scalability in particular.

Extensibility

The one constant in software development is that requirements always change. With each version of a product, there are bugs to fix and ideas to develop into new features. These days, particularly in business programming, requirements often change between the time a product is designed and the time it is released. When requirements do change, software divides into two categories: the kind that can be easily extended and the kind that can't. Unfortunately, determining in advance which category your program fits into is difficult. If you were trying to extend a toaster, it might be easier to add the ability to toast bagels than bake cakes.

In general, the *extensibility* of software determines how easily changes can be accommodated. It is easy to say whether the program was extensible or not in hindsight, but for the program to be really useful, we must have a sense beforehand. In a first version, it is sufficient to show that a program avoids the most common extensibility pitfalls. Once a few versions have been released, empirical evidence provides a much clearer picture.

There are a few common reasons that programs are hard to change. One that occurs most frequently is the fear of breaking supposedly unrelated code. We've all been in the situation where a seemingly innocuous change to one object has caused another, seemingly unrelated part of the program to suddenly stop working. This kind of problem is usually discovered weeks later, and you get stuck revisiting several weeks worth of changes to find the single, obscure dependency you broke.

---

[*] Of course, there are other considerations that come into play on individual projects, such as manageability and usability, but we've found this set to be appropriate for our purposes.

As an application grows, the number of dependencies tends to go up, and consequently the amount of testing necessary after each change. Eventually, the fear of changing anything outweighs the benefits of new features, and development grinds to a halt. While this scenario sounds extreme, it is familiar to anyone who has worked on a large legacy application. In the enterprise environment the situation can get even worse, as changes to one application can affect entirely separate—but nonetheless related—systems. Imagine a financial system that starts requiring all transactions in Euros: if the purchasing computers aren't switched over at the same moment, chaos will ensue.

Even if you know all the dependencies, it can still be hard to change code. Changing one object's interface means not only changing that object, but also updating all the objects that rely on the interface. While providing backward-compatible interfaces is often a good compromise, this too becomes impossible after a few generations. In the end, someone gets stuck updating all the dependent classes—a tedious, thankless task, to say the least.

In short, be careful with dependencies. While objects must interact with each other in order for a program to do anything, the number of dependencies should be limited. In an extensible program, interfaces are kept as tight as possible to make sure objects only interact in well-known ways. Of course, there is a tradeoff here, as always. Components with rich interfaces can be more useful than components without them, but by their very nature, richer interfaces create tighter dependencies with other components.

Using clear interfaces separates an object's implementation from its interactions. This makes the specific implementation independent of the rest of the application, allowing implementations to be fixed, changed, or replaced at will. The application is no longer a single piece, but a collection of semi-independent components. Multiple developers can work on components without breaking, or even knowing about, the larger application. Components provide a certain functionality, which can be tested on its own and used in multiple applications. Multiple components can also be grouped into a larger entity that can itself vary and be reused. By using these larger components, an application can gain functionality without getting more complicated or sprouting more dependencies. In many ways, extensibility is simply a measure of how easy it is to understand the code. If the division of labor among components and the interfaces between them are clear, software is easy to extend. It can be worked on independently by a number of people without fear of interference, and new functionality does not further complicate the program.

Design patterns can help solve many extensibility problems. By documenting a particular aspect of architecture, a design pattern makes it easier to understand. Design patterns can be communicated to other developers, minimizing the risk that someone who does not fully understand the architecture will break other parts of the application. Most importantly, even the act of evaluating design patterns—whether they turn out to be applicable or not—forces developers to think out and articulate their design up front, often exposing flaws in the process.

Techniques for extensibility

Successful applications are constantly enhanced and extended, but these updates can come at substantial cost. Small design flaws in the original program are quickly magnified. All too often, the fix to one problem creates yet another problem that requires a new fix. These layered fixes make the code unwieldy and reduce opportunities for reuse. As more and more special cases are added, exhaustive testing becomes nearly impossible. Eventually, even adding a simple new feature becomes prohibitively expensive.

To make life even more complicated, these overgrown programs become increasingly difficult to understand. If learning one area of a program relies on learning five others first, it's unlikely that developers will be able to learn it fast. One person can reasonably build a text editor; however, he would have to be very dedicated to add a spellchecker, web browser, and other features. A clean, consistent base architecture allows many developers to contribute to the application.

The hallmark of extensible software is that it is designed to change. Whether you are working on an initial design or refactoring an existing one, there are several generic techniques that can make your designs more extensible:

Decoupling
> We have already talked a little bit about loose and tight coupling. In a loosely coupled system, components can vary independently. They can be prototyped, updated and replaced without affecting other components. Because of this, loosely coupled systems will generally be more extensible.

Centralizing
> When functionality is spread out over multiple components, making simple changes may require updating many parts of the code. It also makes the code harder to follow and therefore harder to understand and share. By gathering common functionality into central resources, the application becomes easier to understand, update, and extend.

Reusing
> Adding too much functionality to a single component specializes it. A specialized component cannot easily be adapted to perform other functions, so code must be duplicated. This duplication makes the code harder to maintain and update. A design in which common functionality is encapsulated in reusable components is more extensible, because larger components can be composed effectively from specialized existing components. Design patterns may well have their most profound impact in the area of extensible systems. We'll use all three of these approaches in the chapters ahead.

Scalability

When building desktop applications, you generally have the ability to define your platform, at least in broad terms. A word processor may have to deal with documents from 1–1000 pages long, but it won't have to deal with 1–1000 users editing the document at the same time. Assuming your test lab is outfitted realistically, it is possible to determine whether an application will perform appropriately. With one user, a program only needs to perform one task, or at most two or three related tasks, at a time. The time it takes to perform each task is a measure of the application's *performance*. Performance depends on the task itself and the speed of the underlying hardware, but that's about all.

Enterprise applications aren't that simple. The time it takes for a web server to process a request certainly depends on the performance of the server application and hardware, but it also depends on how many other requests are being processed at the same time on that server. If the application involves computing by multiple servers, the web server's speed will also depend on the speed of those other servers, how busy they are, and the network delays between them. Worst of all, the speed of transmitting the request and response—which is based on the speed of all the networks in between the user and the server—factors into the user's perception of how fast a transaction was processed.

While developers generally can't control network speed, there are things they can control. They can modify how quickly an application responds to a single request, increasing its performance. They can also vary how many requests a server can handle at the same time—a measure of the application's *scalability*.

Scalability and performance are intimately related, but they are not the same thing. By increasing the performance of an application, each request takes less time to process. Making each transaction shorter would seem to imply that more transactions could be performed in the same fixed time, meaning scalability has increased. This isn't always the case. Increasing the amount of memory used to process each request can increase performance by allowing the server to cache frequently used information, but it will limit scalability, since each request uses a greater percentage of the server's total memory; above a certain point, requests have to be queued, or the server must resort to virtual memory, decreasing both scalability and performance.

Scalability can be broadly defined as the ability of an application to maintain performance as the number of requests increases. The best possible case is a *constant response time*, where the time it takes to process a request stays the same regardless of the load on the server. Ideally, an enterprise application will be able to maintain a more or less constant response time as the number of clients reaches the standard load for the application. If a web site needs to serve 200 requests a second, it should be able to serve any one of those 200 requests in the same amount of time as any other request. Furthermore, that amount of time needs to be reasonable, given the nature of the application. Keeping the user waiting more than a half second for a page is generally not acceptable.

Linear scalability is when the time it takes to process n requests is equal to n times the time to process one request. So if one user gets a response in 1 second, 10 simultaneous users will each have to wait 10 seconds, as each second of processing time is divided 10 ways. Enterprise applications may hit linear scalability when under a particularly heavy load (such as after they have been linked to by *http://www.slashdot. org*). If the load on the server goes up to 400 users a second, the time required for each response might double from the 200 user level.

At some point, a program reaches its *scalability limit*, the maximum number of clients it can support. An application's scalability is usually a combination of all three factors: constant response time up to a certain number of clients (ideally to the maximum number of users the application needs to serve), followed by linear scalability degrading until the scalability limit is reached. Figure 1-2 shows a graph of performance versus number of clients, which is how scalability is usually represented.

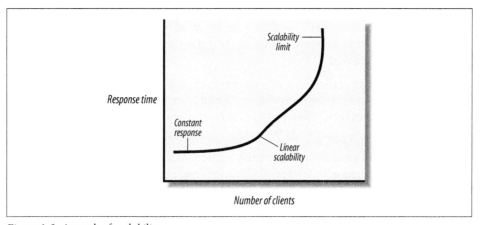

Figure 1-2. A graph of scalability

Building scalable systems almost inevitably involves a trade-off with extensibility. Sometimes breaking a larger component into smaller components, each of which can be replicated multiple times as needed, increases scalability. But more often, the overhead of communicating between components limits scalability, as does the increased number of objects floating around the system.

The design patterns in this book often focus on the interactions between application tiers. These interactions are where most scalability problems initially appear. Using effective practices to link these tiers can overcome many of the performance debts incurred by separating the tiers in the first place. It's not quite the best of both worlds, but it is usually a good start.

Of course, most systems do not need to be designed for unlimited scalability. In many cases—particularly when developing systems for use within a defined group of users (the case for most intranet applications)—only a certain number of clients need to be supported, and the trade-off between scalability and extensibility tilts toward the latter.

Design patterns support scalability in a number of ways, but primarily by providing a set of approaches to allow resources to be used efficiently, so that servicing n clients doesn't require n sets of resources. In addition, patterns can enable extensibility, and extensible systems can often use that extensibility to improve scalability by distributing operations across multiple servers, plugging in higher performance components, and even by making it easier to move an application to a more powerful server.

Reliability

Reliable software performs as expected, all the time. The user can access the software, the same inputs produce the same outputs, and the outputs are created in accordance with the software's stated purpose. Needless to say, complete requirements gathering is vital to ensuring software reliability, since without clear requirements there is no way to define what correct behavior actually involves. Requirements gathering is also important in figuring out what constitutes a reliable system: does the system need to stay up 99.999% of the time, or can it be taken down for maintenance for 2 hours a night?

Similar to scalability, a reliable system depends on the predictability of its underlying components. From a user's point of view, reliability is judged for the entire system, including hardware, software, and network elements. If a single component malfunctions and the user cannot access the application or it does not work correctly, the entire system is unreliable.

Corporate software projects are subject to specific quality requirements, and reliability is usually first among these. Most larger software teams have one or more people in a Quality Assurance role, or they make use of the services of a dedicated QA team or department. Larger projects, particularly in regulated industries such as health care, are subject to software validation processes and audits. A software audit can include every aspect of the development cycle, from initial requirements gathering through design, up to final testing and release procedures.

Design patterns can play a major role in ensuring reliability. Most of the patterns in this book are acknowledged, at least by some, as best practices within the industry. All of them have been applied countless times in enterprise application development projects. Design patterns can be validated at a high level and incorporated early on in the design process. This kind of planning makes the final validation process simpler, and generally produces code that is easier to audit in the first place.

Timeliness

The final goal of any software development project is a timely delivery of the finished software to the end users. At least, that's the way the end users generally see it! Design patterns might have less impact in this area than in the other three, although having a catalog of proven solutions to standard development issues can be a time-saver during the implementation phase.

The real time savings tend to come in subsequent release cycles and in projects that rely on an iterative development methodology. Since most patterns involve some sort of modular design, applications that use them will be easier to extend in the future, providing timeliness advantages to the next generation of software as well. Programmers can understand the structure of the application more easily, and the structure lends itself more readily to change: Version 2.0 can be made available much more readily than would otherwise be possible.

It is possible, of course, for patterns to negatively affect a project schedule. Solving a problem by writing code that conforms to a generic design pattern may take more time than solving the problem in a more direct fashion, although this investment is often recouped in later phases of the development process. But complex patterns can also introduce complexity where none is required. For enterprise applications, though, the balance tilts towards the patterns approach. Major systems are rarely, if ever, designed and implemented as one-offs: the ROI calculations at corporate headquarters assume that a project will be available through several years and likely through several new sets of features.

Later in this book, we discuss *refactoring*, the process of transforming existing software into better software by revisiting its various design assumptions and implementation strategies, and replacing them with more efficient versions. After learning an effective way to solve a problem, it is often tempting to race back to older code, rip half of it out, and replace it with a better implementation. Sometimes this philosophy leads to real benefits, and sometimes it leads to wasting time solving problems that aren't really problems.

Looking Ahead

This chapter provides the groundwork for understanding some of the primary issues in J2EE development and in enterprise architecture as a whole. In the chapters that follow, we'll look at the individual tiers within the J2EE model, and discuss patterns and approaches for designing and implementing them.

CHAPTER 2

The Unified Modeling Language

Before we dive into the design patterns themselves, it's worth stepping back and thinking about the framework they fit into. Design patterns are just one part of the much broader discipline of software engineering. Building any application involves requirements gathering, design, implementation, testing, and deployment. While design patterns provide developers with a library of proven techniques and allow teammates to apply labels to concepts, the patterns don't begin to address every aspect of enterprise development. Most importantly, perhaps, design patterns can't tell you where to apply a design pattern. That's why we have design.

Design patterns describe the implementation strategies for particular areas of the application, and even the overall design. Enterprise applications in particular need effective engineering practices, given their complexity and business importance. As object-oriented languages take hold in business environments, a need has emerged for a common language to discuss and describe object-oriented software, as well as the problems and business processes the software serves.

Software and process-modeling languages were created to meet this need for common vocabulary to describe software structure. The various leading modeling languages have blended together over the last few years into the Unified Modeling Language, generally abbreviated as the UML.*

UML supports all aspects of the software development life cycle, from requirements gathering to design to deployment. In particular, the UML can be extremely helpful in documenting the object structure underlying an application, known as the *domain model*; but UML models can represent use cases, class structures, program interactions, process flows, physical deployments, packages, and more. Often, simply creating UML diagrams uncovers subtle flaws in system design, saving huge quantities of effort later on in a project. For our immediate purposes in this book, the UML also

---

* Since UML is an acronym, convention is to use the acronym as you would use the full phrase. Hence "the UML" rather than simply "UML" in much literature.

provides an excellent way to describe design patterns, both in terms of class structures and program processes.

Thorough requirements gathering, design, and documentation are part of the overall pattern of effective enterprise development, and an understanding of UML is necessary in order to follow the current literature on both enterprise design patterns and best practices. We're not going to cover all of the UML in this chapter. The UML is a language in and of itself, and so far nobody has managed to write a comprehensive treatment that's less than 150 pages. However, we are going to attempt a relatively encompassing fly-over of the main features of the UML.

If you've ever used UML in real life, you can probably skip this chapter, although you might find the first few sections helpful. If your previous exposure to UML is minimal, make sure you at least read the sections on use cases, class diagrams, and interaction diagrams. Each section builds on the one before. For a longer (but still high-level) overview of the UML, check out *UML Distilled*, Second Edition, by Martin Fowler and Kendall Scott (Addison-Wesley), as well as the *UML User's Guide* and *UML Reference Manual*, both by Grady Booch, James Rumbaugh, and Ivar Jacobson, the creators of UML (also published by Addison-Wesley).

Origins of UML

Modeling languages for object-oriented software have been around since the 1970s and began to proliferate in the late 1980s. The profusion of modeling options caused problems, and no single approach managed to reach critical mass. Thus, while many approaches were helpful in the design process itself, no common vocabulary emerged. The debates between the practitioners of different modeling systems are sometimes referred to as the "method wars," which brings to mind some fairly amusing images of the goings-on at academic conferences in the late 1980s and early 90s.

The UML specification developed out of the method wars. Grady Booch, James Rumbaugh, and Ivar Jacobson emerged as the leading lights in the modeling movement. Booch's approach was design-oriented, while Rumbaugh's Object Modeling Technique was geared toward data analysis. Jacobson created the Object Oriented Software Engineering (OOSE) method, which focused on developing "use cases" to feed system design. Jacobsen is known as the Father of Use Cases.

In 1994, Rumbaugh joined Booch at Rational Software, and introduced Version .8 of UML in October. A year later Jacobson arrived at Rational, and the three focused on merging their different, yet largely complementary approaches into a single model. Booch, Jacobson, and Rumbaugh became known as the Three Amigos. The Software Development Life Cycle (SDLC) they developed at Rational is known as the Rational Unified Process, but the modeling language associated with it can be applied in any number of frameworks.

In 1996, in response to a request for standards proposals from the Object Management Group, Rational formed the UML Partners Consortium to gather support for the standard. UML 1.0 was submitted to the OMG in January 1997 as a suggested specification.

The consortium followed up with the UML 1.1 proposal, and in November 1997, the UML specification was accepted as a standard. Subsequent iterations have brought the UML to Version 1.4, and a substantially improved version, 2.0, is currently in the advanced preparatory stages. The rest of this chapter focuses on key elements of UML 1.4.

The Magnificent Seven

Remember that UML is not the be-all and end-all of software development methodology. It's just an extremely useful tool for communications between and within user groups, development teams, and deployment staff. It's possible to go overboard on modeling, particularly in areas that don't map directly to code, such as when building use cases during the requirements gathering phase.

UML is complex. The specification itself is dense, and as a result much of the available literature must address the complexities in detail. (Since this isn't a book on UML, we're saved from that particular fate.) The complexity can work for your project, but it can also result in massive expenditures of time and effort, particularly in "high ceremony" development environments that produce vast quantities of paper.* Most teams find a comfortable middle ground in which modeling, via UML or other methods, serves the team's underlying goals rather than becoming an end in itself.

The UML isn't the only tool that can be misused, of course. Design patterns can also be misapplied, making simple problems more complex than necessary, or encouraging code-first design-later development cycles as developers assume that the presence of patterns (with their promises of easy extensibility and maintenance) allow requirements to be dealt with as they come up.

To be useful, design patterns need to be expressed. While there are a variety of ways to do this, a UML diagram is part of most of them. The diagram can make broad concepts and implementation details clear in a language-independent way that doesn't require working through large chunks of sample code. There are relatively few programming patterns that don't lend themselves to some sort of UML representation.

Coupling modeling with design patterns has a number of advantages. The model provides context for choosing the right design patterns, although the presence of

---

* This is not a judgment against highly formalized development lifecycles. Depending on the project requirements and the team available, appropriate documentation can vary from the back of a few napkins (rare) to thousands of pages (equally rare).

effective design patterns will also, perhaps somewhat recursively, influence the development of the model. In most circumstances, the result is simpler, smaller, more manageable software.

Enterprise developers are faced with challenges in the area of software validation, particularly in industries that are highly regulated or in which systems are a major business asset.* Software validation efforts can be time-consuming and require clear documentation at the design and implementation levels—and in some cases, provable correctness. In these environments, proven patterns and documented design make it easier to create software that passes muster.

When introducing new developers to effective enterprise design, we like to combine the modeling approach of the Three Amigos and the patterns approach of the Gang of Four. We feel strongly that effective software engineering can't take place with just one approach or the other. Luckily, the two approaches are not contradictory, and we see no reason to separate them. Hence, the Three Amigos join up with the Gang of Four and become the Magnificent Seven. Or so we hope.

UML and Software Development Lifecycles

The typical software development process consists of several phases: requirements-gathering, high-level design, low-level design, coding and unit testing, integration testing, and deployment. Different methodologies divide these areas into different categories and subdivisions.

UML provides several diagram types that fit into each section of the Software Development Lifecycle (SDLC). Here's an overview of the diagram types we address in this chapter, in roughly the order they enter the development process:

Use case diagrams
> Used through the high-level design phase to identify common sets of activities that users of the system indulge in. Use case diagrams also describe the participants in each use case. Use cases are helpful when developing test plans.

Class diagrams
> Used as early as the high-level design process to define the domain model for the application: specifically, the relationship of data objects within the system, the relationships between them, and the operations that they can perform or that can be performed on them.

Interaction diagrams
> Sometimes used during the requirements gathering process but particularly used in high- and low-level design to show the interactions between objects in the

---

* This is an issue that is particularly near to Will's heart.

system. Interaction diagrams are also very helpful in the testing state when creating testing processes and procedures.

Activity diagrams

Used during requirements gathering and high-level design to further identify process flows within the system. Unlike program flow charts, activity diagrams include users and activities beyond the code itself, and allow clear delineation of the roles played by various participants.

Deployment diagrams

Used during the high-level design phase to indicate how a system will be distributed across physical resources, and during the deployment phase to document that configuration.

The rest of this chapter explores the diagram types in more detail.

Use Case Diagrams

A *use case diagram* is the highest level of abstraction available in UML. Use cases are collections of related activities that work toward a particular goal. They're part of the requirements gathering process rather than the design process itself, and can be as detailed or as generic as is necessary to communicate system requirements.

The challenge here is often to make the requirements accessible and useful to both the design team and the domain experts involved in the project. Depending on need, the size of the team and the preferences of those leading the development a project might have two or three use cases, or dozens, or even more, although there is generally a point at which the sheer volume of use cases grows unmanageable.

A "Buy Groceries" use case, for example, could consist of selecting food, checking out, processing a credit card, and bagging groceries. The use case can also incorporate internal variations, such as a declined credit card.

Use cases incorporate multiple *actors*, which may be humans or systems. The actors in the Buy Groceries use case could be the shopper, the checkout person, the grocery bagger, the inventory system, and the credit processor.

Like any UML diagram, use cases exist to convey information. A use case diagram can be a valuable communication tool, and the process of creating the use cases themselves almost invariably leads to better software and greater accountability. In addition to ensuring user needs are met, use cases help determine where a system is likely to need extension in the immediate future—information that can play a valuable part in the design process.

The ultimate consumer of the use case diagram is a human being; as a result, the diagram's goal is clarity, rather than precision. Some developers don't like using use case diagrams at all, preferring text, and some mix-and-match according to the needs of the current project. Use case diagrams at a high level are often used to quickly communicate the scope of a more detailed and nuanced textual discussion. In fact, UML use case diagrams alone are almost, but not quite, useless without the full textual use case sitting behind them.

In a diagram, a single use case is represented in the UML with an oval (see Figure 2-1). Detail is added by breaking each use case into a set of smaller use cases and adding them to the diagram. Actors are represented by stick figures. UML use case diagrams are not generally designed to demonstrate sequence. Activity diagrams, discussed later in this chapter, provide a more formalized mechanism for showing process, allowing use case diagrams to focus on goals.

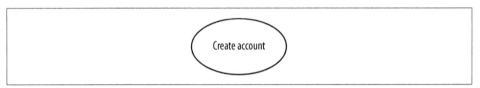

Figure 2-1. A simple use case

Let's look at a more complex set of use cases.

The project is a corporate web portal that will serve employees, customers, and partners. The task at hand is use registration for each type of user. Employees are assumed to be able to register themselves. Customers can, too. Partners can register themselves and get basic access, but need to be checked against a partner list before they can be granted full access. If the partner isn't on the list, a manager needs to authorize partner-level access for the user. We'll use this example (or variations) throughout this chapter.

To begin, we divide the problem into four basic use cases: Request Account, Define Partners, Approve Account, and Create Account. A simple UML diagram, as in Figure 2-2, shows the three actors that interact with the use cases.

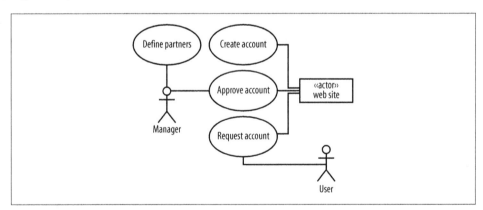

Figure 2-2. Use cases

The actors, represented by stick figures, are connected to the use cases they are involved with. The Manager and User actors are humans. The web site is not, so we represent it as a box. The box contains the notation «actor». This string, like all text encased in guillemots, is called a stereotype, and "overrides" the standard behavior of any shape in the UML. In this case, we identify a box (which usually indicates a class or an object—see Figure 2-2) to mark it as an actor. From a use case diagrams perspective, there is no difference between a stick figure and a stereotyped box, but using both forms lets us distinguish between people and systems.

It stands to reason that each user category has a different kind of account, since partners, customers, and employees have different data associated with them. Right now it doesn't matter whether we implement these accounts as three different classes (presumably descended from the same superclass), or as a single class with a wide variety of fields. From a use cases perspective, the process of requesting an account breaks down into three use cases. Each case is a subtype of the Request Account use case, and we represent it using the *generalization relationship*, identified by an open-headed arrow (Figure 2-3). We don't have to show every actor, as the diagram would rapidly grow cluttered.

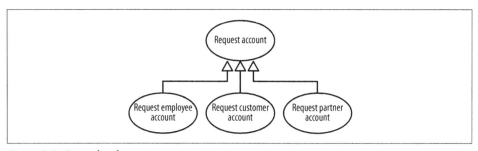

Figure 2-3. Generalized use cases

We can also use generalization on actors, so employees, customers, and partners can generalize to users.

When a use case includes multiple other use cases, an *include relationship*, indicated by a dashed arrow and an «include» stereotype, can be used to diagram the interaction. If a company assigns a value to a customer based on credit history and purchase history (for instance, in a loyalty program), the use case diagram for the activity might look like the one in Figure 2-4.

If a use case includes child use cases (in the example above the analysis use cases include the Assign Customer Value use cases) it might not be complete otherwise. The inclusion construct makes it easier to expand or contract use case diagrams according to varying requirements. A high-level diagram might simply include the Assign Customer Value use case, requiring the reader to investigate further in order to determine exactly what that particular use case consists of.

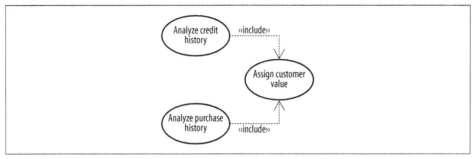

Figure 2-4. Included use cases

Use cases can also be extended by other use cases. In that kind of situation, a main use case declares one or more *extension points*. Extension points identify instances in the use case in which functionality from other use cases can be included. The extending use case declares the additional functionality and is connected to the main use case by an arrow and an «extends» stereotype. In Figure 2-5, an Authorize User use case declares an extension point for access approval. If the user being authorized is an employee or a partner, the use case can use the logic in the Employee Authorization and Partner Authorization use cases. Unlike use cases that incorporate other cases via the include functionality, the base use case should be complete whether or not any extensions exist.

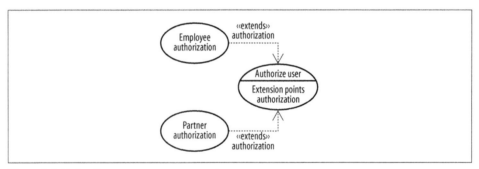

Figure 2-5. Extending use cases

Class Diagrams

Representing the domain model for an application is arguably the most important area of object-oriented modeling. *Class diagrams*, as a result, are the most widely used feature of the UML.

Class diagrams show the relationships between classes in a system. Since object-oriented design blurs the line between data objects and executable application logic, a UML class diagram documents both. UML actually supports both class diagrams and object diagrams. If you're reading this book, you're almost certainly familiar with the distinction between a class and an object: a *class* is a framework containing methods and data that can be instantiated into one or more *objects*, which contain actual data items. UML class diagrams show the relationship between the frameworks, and object diagrams show the state of a system with actual objects, containing actual values.

Although the names are the same, a class in a UML class diagram does not necessarily map to a Java class—although in more detailed, design-focused UML diagrams, they will. Class diagrams can be used to build conceptual pictures of an application's domain model, which can then be used to develop more specific system designs that eventually map into code.

It's nice to be as complete as possible when developing a class diagram, but it is by no means necessary. Generally, a modeler picks a level of completeness that corresponds with the current stage in the software design process. The highest level class diagrams ignore all private methods and internal data structures, focusing instead on the logical content of the objects.

The diagram in Figure 2-6 illustrates a single class, in fairly high detail. The first compartment of the box holds the class name. The second compartment identifies the fields within the class, and the third compartment includes the methods in the class. In UML terminology, these are referred to as the *attributes* and *operations* of the class, respectively. Each of the fields and methods has a visibility modifier: +, -, or # for public, private, and protected. A colon and a variable type to indicate the storage or return types can follow both fields and methods.

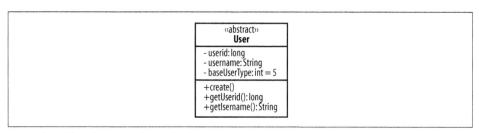

Figure 2-6. Class diagram of a single class

With the exception of the top compartment, each section is optional. Some modelers leave all three compartments in place for clarity, while other modelers omit the middle (fields) compartment if they are modeling at a high level.

In addition to the class name, the class name compartment contains the «abstract» stereotype, indicating that the class is abstract. Since stereotypes modify whatever follows them, we put the «abstract» stereotype above the class name rather than below.

Relationships Between Classes

Aside from detailing the attributes and operations of particular classes, UML class diagrams can also indicate the relationships between classes. The two basic associations possible between classes are a *dependency* and a *generalization*. Dependencies indicate that a class makes use of another class as part of a data relationship. Generalizations correspond to class inheritance, much as we saw for use cases. Figure 2-7 shows a set of classes for an implementation of our user registration scheme.

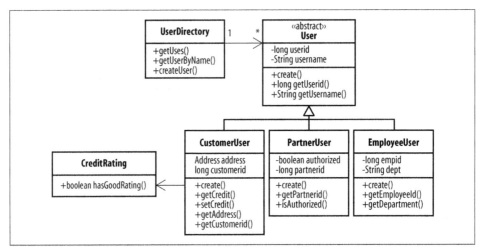

Figure 2-7. Basic class diagram

The diagram above shows two key aspects of the association between the UserDirectory and User classes. The first is the navigability of the relationship, indicated by the direction of the arrow. Drawing the arrow pointing from UserDirectory to User indicates that the UserDirectory has access to all associated User objects, but that User objects do not see the UserDirectory they are a part of. The diagram also indicates the multiplicity of the relationship between UserDirectory and User via the labels on each end of the association. The 1 next to UserDirectory indicates that for any given User object there is one UserDirectory, while the * on the User end indicates that there can be an unlimited number of users in a directory.

There is a generalization relationship between the User class and the CustomerUser, PartnerUser, and EmployeeUser classes that extend it. Each class defines distinct IDs for the user category as well as providing other relevant methods. The customer class has a relationship with a CreditRating object, which is not described in detail on the diagram. When refining the picture to move towards a more complete implementation, it makes sense to specify the kind of associations possible between a Customer and a Credit Rating.

Associations and dependencies can also be labeled. In addition, each class within the association can be assigned a particular role. The association name is printed toward the center of the association line, and the roles are listed on either side. General usage normally puts the name above the line and the roles below it. Figure 2-8 shows the `UserDirectory` and `User` relationship again, but the association has been named Directory Link and the two objects have been assigned the *directory* and *entry* roles within the association.

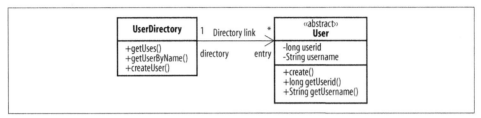

Figure 2-8. Labeled associations

Aggregation and composition

In addition to associations, UML provides constructs for representing aggregates and composites. Aggregates represent a "part of" relationship. While regular associations can be very loose, aggregates impose limits on the kinds of classes that can be included in the relationship, and the roles those classes can have. A customer may be associated with an order, but the order isn't necessarily part of the customer, and the order can be associated with other objects and maintain its relevancy even if the customer record is destroyed. At the same time, an order line item is part of an order, so a stronger relationship than a mere association can be drawn. A line item has no meaning outside of an order, so we can define an order as an aggregation of line items, plus other information.

In Figure 2-9, the `PartnerList` object is an aggregation of `Partner` objects. We use an open diamond on the parent side in order to indicate that it is an aggregate association, rather than a mere association.

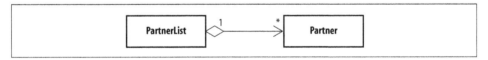

Figure 2-9. Aggregate association

UML defines an even stricter form of association, the *composite aggregation*, or simply *composite*. A composite relationship indicates that the subordinate objects are effectively part of the parent. When the parent object is copied, modified, or deleted, the subordinate objects should also be copied, modified, or deleted, as appropriate. The composite aggregation is indicated via a filled diamond on the association line next to the parent, as in Figure 2-10.

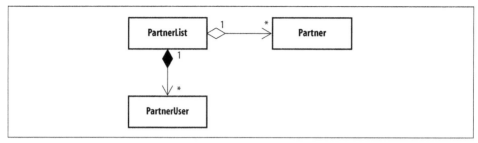

Figure 2-10. Composite aggregation

Figure 2-10 shows a PartnerUser class associated with the PartnerList via composite aggregation. If the PartnerList was simply an aggregation, each PartnerUser class could be associated directly with the relevant Partner class (which presumably contains information about the partnership relationship itself). In this case, however, the PartnerUser must be associated with the PartnerList instead, and it must use the PartnerList class to interact with the Partner data.

Describing Patterns with Class Diagrams

Throughout most of this book, we use UML class diagrams to talk about patterns; here's an example. Figure 2-11 shows an implementation of the Gang of Four Strategy pattern. The Strategy pattern allows a client (in this case, the StrategyRunner class) to perform an action using different approaches determined by plug-in classes that conform to a standard interface.

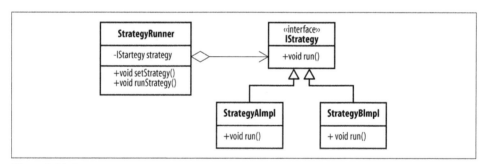

Figure 2-11. Strategy pattern

The StrategyAImpl and StrategyBImpl classes both implement the IStrategy interface, which includes a single method, run( ). At runtime, the application instantiates the appropriate strategy implementation and passes it to the setStrategy( ) method of the StrategyRunner, and then invokes the runStrategy( ) method. In real life, strategies could include persistence methods, cryptographic algorithms, message transports, or anything that might need to be done consistently in more than one way.

Objects

Class diagrams are static; they describe the relationship between classes but don't show the state of a system at a particular time. *Object diagrams* can be used both to model the potential contents of a system and to gain a "snapshot in time" of the data that currently resides within a system.

An object instance is represented as a box, just like a class, but the name is under-lined. Objects are labeled as *object name:class name*; the object name or class name may be omitted. Omitting the object name indicates that the name of the particular class instance is not relevant to the diagram.

The diagram in Figure 2-12 is fairly self-explanatory. The top compartment of the object contains the object name and class name, and the bottom compartments contain values for the fields. The lines between objects represent the associations. Associations do not need to be complicated. The presence of the objects themselves conveys most of the information about the types of associations that are permitted.

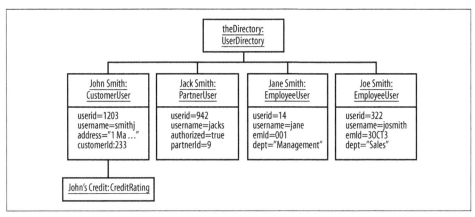

Figure 2-12. Object diagram

Packages

UML also provides a shape called a *package*. A UML package can be analogous to a Java package, or it can simply represent a group of classes with related functionality, regardless of underlying implementations. Creating packages within software projects is a good way to manage dependencies within applications, since the software can be dealt with in terms of the interfaces between packages rather than the interface between classes. This distinction makes it much easier to determine where changes to one area can affect others. Figure 2-13 shows a basic class diagram that documents the relationship between a Web Site, the Partnerships and Users domain objects, and three J2EE components. The servlets in the web site package depend on the J2EE servlets and JSP packages, as well as the JDBC package. They also depend on your own Partnerships and Users packages. The Users package also uses JDBC.

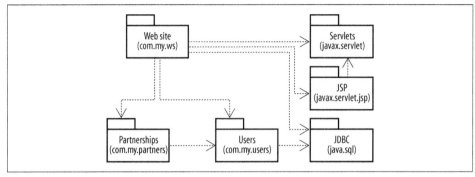

Figure 2-13. Class diagram with packages

Note that there are no cycles in this diagram (Package A depends on Package B, which depends on Package A). While there is nothing in the UML to forbid cycles, recursive package dependencies generally reveal design and maintenance problems. When dependencies between packages loop back on themselves, it's generally time to either change the software or change the diagram. Again, we don't need a one-to-one link between packages on a package diagram and packages in the way we think of them in Java. Java packages are primarily a mechanism for code organization rather than design, and they generally interlock more than the design level packages in our diagrams.

Packages can also be nested. This ability allows you to draw dependencies to either individual packages or to higher-level packages. Figure 2-14 shows the same package diagram as Figure 2-13, but it creates high-level packages for both the J2EE components and the application domain. Dependency arrows that cross over package borders connect single packages, while arrows from a package to an outer-level package show dependencies to the entire outer package. In this case, the code within the Web Site package is dependent on J2EE and the application domain, and the Users package within the application domain is dependent only on JDBC.

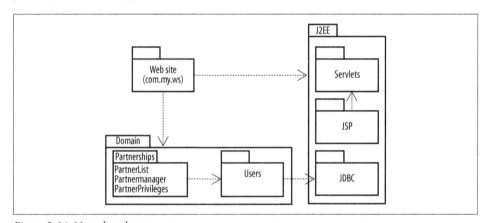

Figure 2-14. Nested packages

When we nest packages, we put the label on the tab, rather than in the main compartment. Within individual packages, we can list the interior classes (or embed full class diagrams, although that's unwieldy).

Interaction Diagrams

Class diagrams are not well suited to describing program flow. While modelers frequently use class diagrams to model aspects of systems that are oriented towards process instead of data, seeing the internal class relations does not always translate into a clear view of the underlying logic. All modeling systems have some mechanism for indicating the flow of control between multiple objects in the system. In the UML, these diagrams are referred to as *interaction diagrams*. There are two kinds of interaction diagrams: sequence diagrams and collaboration diagrams.

Sequence Diagrams

Sequence diagrams, which show the sequential interactions of a set of objects, are the most common kind of interaction diagram. They can be used for understanding the flow of control within an application (or more often, given the scale of the average enterprise system, within a component of the system).

Sequence diagrams consist of a row of boxes representing objects, generally placed from left to right in order of their appearance within the flow of control. These are the same boxes used for object diagrams with the labels underlined to indicate that they are objects rather than classes. A *lifeline* stretches down from each object. The lifeline begins when the object is created and ends when the object is removed. If the object is never removed, the lifeline continues to the bottom of the page.

Each lifeline contains one or more *activation boxes*. Activation boxes show that the object is actively processing, or blocking, while waiting for a response from further down the line. When modeling classes directly, activation boxes correspond to the duration of a method invocation on the object.

Figure 2-15 shows how an object representing the signup process for our hypothetical web site would go about creating a user account, associating it with a partner object, and requesting account approval from a manager. The sequence begins by calling a method on the web site signup object, which creates a user account. The newly created user account determines the level of access it is authorized to have, checking a partnership list and creating a new partner object if none is found. Creating a new partner kicks off an asynchronous request for a manager to review the new account.

The arrows connecting the activation boxes represent messages sent between the objects. These may be local method calls, remote object invocations, intersystem messages sent via SOAP or JMS, or any other kind of inter-object communication.

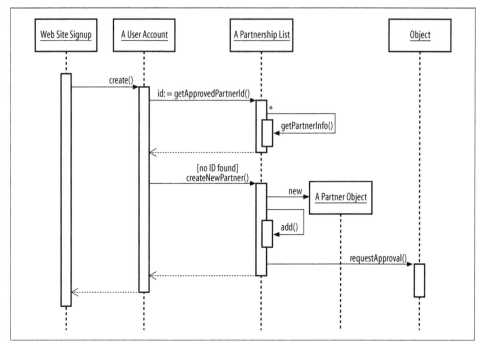

Figure 2-15. Sequence diagram

The solid arrow with the solid arrowhead represents a standard message, and the dashed arrow with an open arrowhead represents a message return. Standard messages imply a return; in many cases, you can leave the explicit return off the diagram entirely, reducing overall clutter. Finally, solid arrows with half of an open arrowhead (such as the one in the bottom righthand corner) represent asynchronous messages. Asynchronous messages, obviously, have no returns.

Each message can and should be labeled. At the minimum, the label will identify the type of message sent. Figure 2-15 labels messages with the name of the method invoked. When the message creates a new object, the message is labeled as "new."

Some messages include criteria surrounded by brackets. These are *conditions* that must be satisfied for the message to be sent. There is no specific format for conditions, but, obviously, they should be written so as to be readable.

Messages marked with an * are considered iterative. In Figure 2-15, the getPartnerInfo( ) method will be called repeatedly until all partner information has been received. Constraints on the message can be used to further tighten the loop.

Objects can send messages to themselves, a process that is akin to invoking a local method. In this case, the message arrow just doubles back towards the activation box, and a second activation box is added to the side of the first box.

Collaboration Diagrams

Sequence diagrams make the order of operations clear, but they don't lend themselves to particularly flexible layouts or provide a clear picture of the static relationships between classes or objects. Like sequence diagrams and object diagrams, *collaboration diagrams* are built around object boxes. As in sequence diagrams, objects are connected via messages, but lifelines are not used. Instead of tracking time from top to bottom, we assign a number to each inter-object message. In simple diagrams, the numbering sequence can be 1,2,3...n, which makes it easy to see where each message plays into the collaboration.

Messages in collaboration diagrams can also be numbered in outline form. When numbering messages in this way, the first message sent is numbered 1. The next message sent by the same object, after the completion of message number 1, is message number 2. However, if the recipient of message number 1 sends out an additional message in the course of responding to message number 1, that message is labeled 1.1. The first message sent by the recipient of 1.1 is 1.1.1, and so forth.

Figure 2-16 shows a collaboration diagram similar (but not identical) to the sequence diagram in Figure 2-15. The messages sent between objects are all procedure calls and are labeled with either the method name or the assignment performed. Some messages have conditions presented in square brackets, such as the [! approvedPartner] condition that launches an asynchronous request for approval to a manager object. In this diagram, the user object will be created anyway and the Manager object will presumably update it later, after manual approval.

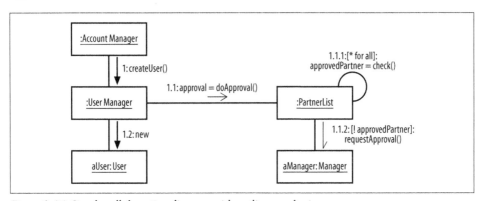

Figure 2-16. Simple collaboration diagram with outline numbering

This diagram also contains a loop-back in 1.1.1, represented by a line arching back into the object and a conditional beginning with an asterisk (*).

Activity Diagrams

Activity diagrams look like regular flow charts, and it's tempting to assume that's what they are. That would be a mistake: activity diagrams are both more and less than a regular flow chart. They're more flexible, since they provide clear support for parallel applications and for dividing different areas of the chart into different areas of responsibility. On the other hand, this flexibility means that it's harder to translate an activity diagram directly into program flow. Instead, an activity diagram is usually used to describe a use case in detail.

Activity diagrams, like most things, begin with a starting point, in this case drawn as a black circle. Diagrams move down the page, and an arrow connects each component. Activities are shown as lozenges. Decision points are shown as diamonds, and the conditions leading to each potential decision are shown as curly braces.

Activity diagrams support parallel operations via thick horizontal bars. Once an activity enters a bar, multiple activities can leave the bar. Another bar can be used to merge the activity once all the branches have been completed. It is not absolutely necessary to merge all of the parallel operations, but if you don't, each activity should be brought to a separate, explicit conclusion.

Finally, the end of the activity is shown as a black circle surrounded by a white circle. Figure 2-17 shows a complete activity diagram.

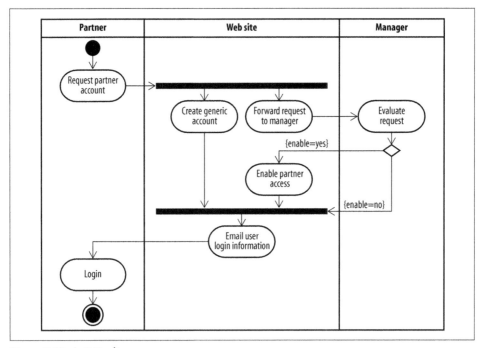

Figure 2-17. Activity diagram

The diagram in Figure 2-17 is divided into three parts, although this step is not required. Each of the parts is called a *swimlane*. A swimlane allows an activity diagram to be portioned according to the actor responsible for each section of the activity. In this case, the partner is responsible for requesting an account and logging in; the web site is responsible for creating accounts, forwarding approval requests, and emailing login information; and a manager is responsible for evaluating the request and deciding whether to enable partner access (if the manager decides not to, the web site emails the user with information about a generic account instead).

Deployment Diagrams

The final UML diagram type (for our purposes) is the *deployment diagram*. Deployment diagrams are used to show how individual components are distributed across multiple systems, and how those components interact. Servers are represented as three-dimensional boxes, and individual components are represented as rectangles with two smaller rectangles attached to the left side.

There are a few key types of associations possible within deployment diagrams. For example, lines between servers specify how components installed on each server communicate with each other.

Components can be connected via solid arrows to indicate persistent relationships. In Figure 2-18, the Swing Application and the Client Façade are joined at compile time. Dashed arrows indicate runtime connections such as those between the Client Façade and an EJB Session Bean, and between the session bean and a set of entity beans.

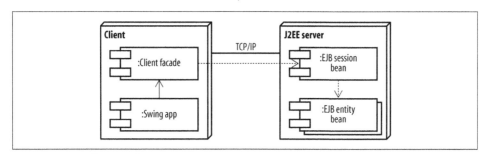

Figure 2-18. Deployment diagram

The entity bean in the diagram is shown in the stacked style to indicate that the system contains more than one instance of it.

CHAPTER 3

Presentation Tier Architecture

All applications eventually evolve
into operating systems.

We begin our discussion of enterprise applications with the presentation tier and a single question: how can we manage the evolution of our software? There's no simple answer. To successfully maintain software over the long term, we must create an architecture that allows the programmer to extend and rearrange the underlying components. The architecture needs to balance flexibility, extensibility, and performance.

In J2EE, the server-side presentation tier is responsible for most of an application's complexity. Since the presentation tier controls the user experience (and, by extension, the bulk of an application's feature set), it's often a magnet for change requests. The servlets, HTML, JSP pages, and other resources that make up the presentation tier tend to evolve like most pieces of complex software. User requests spawn new features, and new features create new code.

Since we know that software evolves, we can make our lives easier by planning for it up front. The *extensibility* of software determines how easily changes can be accommodated. Does a word processor need to be rewritten to add an email client? What about adding a spellchecker? An extensible program changes gracefully: adding and updating features has minimal impact on the rest of the program.

We sometimes know what features we'll be adding tomorrow, next week, next revision, and next year, and so we can create a software architecture with those directions in mind. But much of the time this foreknowledge is unavailable—or it turns out to be wrong. If we're going to assume that any application we build will be in use more than six months in the future, we need to bake extensibility right into the underlying architecture.

In this chapter, we look at patterns that affect the overall design of the presentation tier with an eye toward keeping it extensible. Here are the patterns we will discuss:

Model-View-Controller pattern
>   Provides an architecture for the entire presentation tier that cleanly separates state, presentation, and behavior.

Front Controller pattern
Demonstrates how to centralize access in a request-based environment.

Decorator pattern
Describes how to add functionality to a controller dynamically.

Server-Side Presentation Tier

Most developers think of a web browser as the presentation layer of J2EE. But the web browser isn't the whole story. J2EE supports many ways for users to connect: web browser, WAP-enabled phone, or web service, to name a few. These mechanisms have two things in common:

They have a client-server model. The clients, such as web browsers and cell phones, share the work of generating a presentation with a server. The server holds the server-side presentation tier, which typically generates marked-up data like HTML or XML. The client interprets the marked-up data and presents it to the user.

They are request-based. When the user wants to do anything, the client initiates a request to the server, and then waits for a response. The server processes the request and generates the appropriate response.

Enterprise developers usually don't have control over the client. Concentrate on what we can control: the server-side presentation tier. Figure 3-1 shows a typical setup for a server-side presentation tier in a web-based environment. The server is like a hotel's front desk, waiting for clients to call with questions (in the form of HTTP requests). The web server acts like a highly caffeinated receptionist, answering basic questions itself and directing complex requests to other interfaces—like the concierge or the plumber.

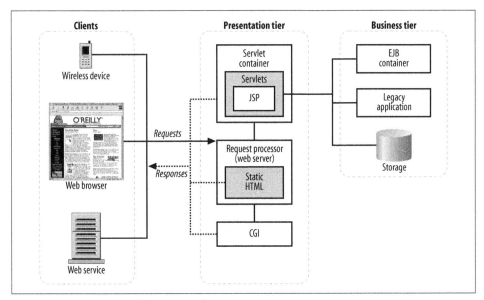

Figure 3-1. Components of the server-side presentation tier

Web servers support a number of interfaces for generating responses. For requests that always yield the same result, the server can create a response directly from a static HTML file. This option is obviously the most efficient, but it is the least flexible: any dynamic data must be generated by a plug-in to the web server itself. For more complicated requests, the server may use the CGI interface to execute an external program and use its results as the response. This method is more flexible, since programs can be added, removed, or changed without stopping the server. Unfortunately, it is inefficient, since it requires a new process for each request. The final option—the one implemented in J2EE—is to keep another process around that is always running. The web server can forward requests to this process at any time, without having to worry about startup costs. In J2EE, this process is the servlet container.

The next few chapters concentrate on life within the servlet container. We explore patterns for building extensible, efficient servlets and using the many related services provided by J2EE. But a presentation is only as useful as the data it presents; in Chapters 7 and 9, we discuss how to connect to business data. Later in the book, we focus on building the business tiers themselves.

Application Structure

It's never easy to start with a clean slate. Whether your application is big or small, the decisions you make at the beginning of the design process affect the application's entire lifetime. Wouldn't it be nice if there was a design pattern to define the overall shape of the presentation tier? The *Model-View-Controller* (MVC) *pattern* is just such a pattern.

The Model-View-Controller Pattern

As its name suggests, MVC breaks the problem of user interfaces into three distinct pieces: model, view, and controller. The *model* stores the application's state. A *view* interprets data in the model and presents it to the user. Finally, the *controller* processes user input, and either updates the model or displays a new view. By carefully dividing labor and controlling communication between these three pieces, we can achieve a robust, extensible architecture for the user interface and the application as a whole.

Figure 3-2 gives an overview of the communications within the MVC architecture. While MVC was originally designed for graphical environments—in which the user acts directly via a mouse or keyboard—over time, it has been adapted for use in other areas of programming.

The MVC paradigm extends quite naturally to enterprise software, where the "user" may be a web browser or web server. Since the presentation tier is request-driven, the "user" can be any request originator. A controller (for example, a web server) handles the request. The model, then, is the business data, and the view is the response that is finally generated. An MVC application is made up of a set of models, views, and controllers that handle related requests.

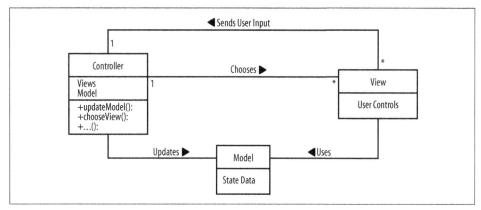

Figure 3-2. Overview of the MVC pattern

A controller is the first point of contact for a request. Its job is to coordinate request handling, turning user input into model updates and views. The controller acts as a supervisor, planning what changes need to be made and what view needs to be shown, then calling the chosen model and view to execute the actual plan. An application may have multiple controllers, each responsible for a certain area of the application. By coordinating the response to the user's requests, controllers manage the overall flow of the application.

The model stores application state. Application state is data stored anywhere: databases, JavaBeans, files, network services, or just in memory. The model's job is to manage access to this state, providing the controller and view with a uniform interface. The model does not, however, simply copy data obtained from other sources. It is an abstraction of the data, and may implement and enforce rules on how data is accessed or combine multiple fields of data into a single logical field. Since multiple views and controllers access the model at once, the model might also be aware of transaction and threading issues. The model is a good place to spend some design time, and we cover it in depth in Chapters 6 through 10.

The view reads data from the model and uses the data to generate a response. The view itself is a stateless component that simply transforms values from the model into a format that clients will find useful. Of course, just because its job is simple doesn't mean the view isn't complicated. As we will see in Chapter 4, a view is often made up of a number of sub-views, each of which transforms different data in the model.

The key to the MVC pattern is that each component is simple and self-contained, with well-defined interfaces. Because of these interfaces, components can vary independently and are therefore easier to share and reuse.

Using MVC in J2EE

To start thinking about J2EE in terms of the MVC pattern, let's walk through a standard J2EE interaction. Imagine a web page that allows a user to sign up for a mailing list. The user enters her first name, last name, and email address into a form. When she clicks Submit, our application adds her address to the list and reports whether the submission was successful. Since the form itself never changes, it is stored as a normal HTML file, as shown in Example 3-1. To handle the form submission, we will build a simple application, dividing the presentation into model, view, and controller.

Example 3-1. subscribe.html

```
<!DOCTYPE HTML PUBLIC "-//W3C//DTD HTML 4.01 Transitional//EN">
<HTML>
  <HEAD>
    <TITLE>Subscribe!</TITLE>
  </HEAD>
  <BODY>
    <FORM action="/servlets/ListController" method="get">
        First Name: <INPUT type="text" name="first"> <br>
        Last Name: <INPUT type="text" name="last"> <br>
        Email Address: <INPUT type="text" name="email"> <br>
        <INPUT type="submit" name="Subscribe!">
    </FORM>
  </BODY>
</HTML>
```

To some degree, J2EE has MVC concepts built-in. We generally build the presentation tier from three main components: servlets, JSP, and JavaBeans. The model—in the form of JavaBeans and Enterprise JavaBeans—provides access to the data in the business tier. The controller is generally some set of servlets and supporting classes that process input and control navigation. Finally, the view is usually implemented as JSP pages and static HTML. Unfortunately, in the J2EE context, the line between view and controller is easy to blur, as we will see when we discuss presentation tier antipatterns in Chapter 12. Figure 3-3 shows how the MVC components can be used to respond to a request.

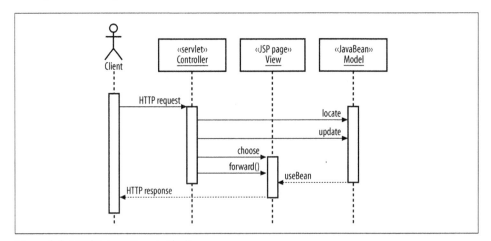

Figure 3-3. MVC interactions in J2EE

In the next sections, we discuss the JavaBean data model, servlet controller, and JSP view in depth. For readers unfamiliar with the J2EE presentation tier, it's a quick tutorial.

The data model

Before we can define the views and controllers that operate on the data model, we must know something about the model itself. First and foremost, the model is a part of the business tier, and it represents the interface between the underlying business data and all possible presentations. The design of the model is therefore datacentric, since it is based on the underlying data and not necessarily the needs of a specific presentation.

In the J2EE world, models are generally JavaBeans, or the similarly named but functionally distinct Enterprise JavaBeans. Like MVC, JavaBeans were originally used in GUIs, but were adopted later for more general use. They provide a generic individual component for use within a larger framework. A JavaBean contains a set of properties, and the JavaBeans specification provides rules about the types and names used for setting and retrieving these properties. The framework, knowing only those rules, can interact with the data the bean represents. The bean itself is responsible for the details of retrieving the information, and can abstract the grubby specifics away from the application.

The rules for writing a JavaBean are intentionally loose: a bean must provide a constructor that takes no arguments; it must not have any public variables; and any access to bean state should take place through getXXX( ) and setXXX( ) methods. Note that there are no requirements to subclass a certain class or implement a particular interface and no restrictions on providing additional methods or constructors. In fact, the requirements to not have public variables and to provide accessor methods are generally good programming practice anyway, and existing classes can often be converted to JavaBeans by simply renaming the getter and setter methods.

For our purposes, we divide a model object into two parts: *accessor methods* are the getter and setter methods used to change the underlying model, such as the methods to add items to a shopping cart; *business methods* are other methods that operate on the model data, such as the method to calculate sales tax or process a purchase. Conveniently, any object that can be described this way also fits the definition of a JavaBean, so we will generally use the terms model object and bean interchangeably.

We are ignoring the problem of finding and instantiating our beans—no easy task, especially where EJBs are concerned. We come back to this issue when we talk about the controller, and in Chapter 9. For now, we assume our model can just as easily be a simple front end to a database, an EJB, or an adapter for a legacy application.

For this example, we will use a very simple bean as the model. Our MailingBean stores all the data about a user needed to subscribe to a particular mailing list. This means storing the user's first name, last name, and email address. These fields are available through six accessor methods: getFirst( ), setFirst( ), getLast( ), setLast( ), getEmail( ), and setEmail( ). The bean also contains a single business method, doSubscribe( ). When this method is invoked, the bean attempts to add the address specified in the email field to the list. If it fails, it will return false and provide a more detailed error message, accessible via the getErrorString( ) accessor. The interface to our bean is shown in Example 3-2.

Example 3-2. MailingBean interface

```
public interface MailingBean {
    // first name
    public String getFirst( );
    public void setFirst(String first);

    // last name
    public String getLast( );
    public void setLast(String last);

    // email address
    public String getEmail( );
    public void setEmail(String email);

    // business method
    public boolean doSubscribe( );

    // subscription result
    public String getErrorString( );

}
```

We're not going to discuss how the bean actually works, since we spend plenty of time in later chapters describing the many methods for connecting to and using business data. For now, it is sufficient to know that we can get a new instance of a MailingBean by calling MailingBeanFactory.newInstance( ).

The controller servlet

Now that we have our data model set, we can move on to the controller. Imagine a user fills out the form from Example 3-1 and clicks Submit. In the first step, the user's web browser generates an HTTP GET request for */servlets/ListController*, with the data filled into the query string. The request URL looks like:

```
http://my.server.com/servlets/ListController?first=Jay&last=Test&email=jay%40test.com
```

Since this is a user interaction, we would like the request to go to a controller in order to coordinate a response.

In J2EE, the controller should be implemented as a servlet. While it is technically possible to use a JSP page as a controller, the programming freedom offered by servlets provides a better match.* There are many possible designs for this servlet, some

---

* Of course, this can be an arbitrary distinction. Since a JSP is compiled into a servlet before execution, we can write identical code that would be contained in any given servlet as a JSP page. However, we try to avoid this approach, since it makes the control logic too fragile: changes can be made by corrupting a single file with a text editor, rather than requiring a rebuild of Java classes.

of which we will explore when we talk about the Front Controller and Service to Worker patterns. From our current perspective, the job of the controller is to:

1. Read the request.
2. Coordinate access to the model.
3. Store model information for use by the view.
4. Pass control to the view.

The servlet's doGet( ) method provides us all the information we need to perform these tasks. We can retrieve information from the request, including the *first*, *last*, and *email* parameters submitted via the form. Additionally, we can locate or create JavaBeans for our model using the appropriate API, such as JNDI for EJBs. Once the beans are located, we can update the model using their accessor and business methods. We can also make the beans available to the view. Finally, when we're finished, we can transfer control to the view.

For the first step—reading the request—the servlet API provides us with an HttpServletRequest object. The servlet container creates this object based on data from the web server. When a servlet's doGet( ) method is called, it is passed an instance of HttpServletRequest. One of the main functions of this object is to make the request parameters available to the servlet. To retrieve a parameter, we use the getParameter( ) method, passing it in the name of the field as defined in the HTML form. In order to read the email address parameter, we use the code:

```
String email = request.getParameter("email");
```

The second step requires working with the model. The exact methods of interacting with the model vary based on the details of the model and what exactly the servlet is trying to do. When working with a JavaBean based model, the servlet typically creates a new bean using a factory, or locates an existing one via a lookup service like JNDI. In this case, we will use the previously mentioned factory:

```
MailingBean mb = MailingBeanFactory.newInstance( );
```

Once the bean exists, it can be manipulated. Here, this means setting the values of various fields and then calling business methods to interact with the actual mailing list software. For example:

```
mb.setEmail(email);
```

The third step is to store model information for use by the view. To do this, we need to communicate data between our controller servlet and the view, a JSP page (see the sidebar, "Servlet/JSP Communication"). In this example, we simply store a reference to our MailingBean in the request scope, so it can be manipulated by the view. To do this, we use another method of the HttpServletRequest object, setAttribute( ):

```
request.setAttribute("mailingbean", mb);
```

Along with the bean itself, we use a string key. This key is important, because it will be used by the view to identify the bean in question.

Servlet/JSP Communication

Most J2EE applications make extensive use of servlets and Java Server Pages, dividing functionality between the two technologies. In general, we will try to avoid putting code into JSP, instead developing servlets, JavaBeans, and JSP custom tags where significant logic is needed. In order to do this, we will frequently need to exchange data between the different components.

The J2EE environment supports a generic scoping mechanism, allowing different pieces of an application to interchange data. Conceptually, each scope works like a simple hash table, in which objects can be inserted and retrieved along with a string key.

J2EE provides four separate scopes:

Application scope

> Shared between all servlets, JSP pages, and custom tags within a J2EE application or within the whole container if no applications are defined. These values are only reset when the J2EE container is stopped or the application is unloaded. The programmatic interface to the application scope is the `ServletContext` object.

Session scope

> Stores information for the life of an HTTP session. There is a separate session object per user, and sessions generally persist for the life of a user's interaction with the system or until they are manually reset. Session scope is accessed via an `HttpSession` object. It's worth noting that there's nothing in HTTP itself about keeping track of a user's session; the Servlet API implementation builds on top of the HTTP standard to provide this functionality. Session scope is often overused, leading to the Overstuffed Session and Leak Collection antipatterns (described in Chapter 12).

Request scope

> Used to store data that only persists for the life of a request, and is removed once the response is sent. Request scope data is stored as attributes of the `ServletRequest` object, so objects stored in request scope survive through calls to `include` and `forward`.

Page scope

> Used in JSPs and custom tags. Data stored in the page scope is available for the entire processing of a single JSP page, including all its custom tags. Data in page scope can be treated as a local variable.

Storing a bean in application scope is appropriate if the value is common to all servlets, and also for storing data for longer than one HTTP session. Examples in which application scope is useful include storing global configuration information that can be changed for the whole site at once, or storing data about how many times users have logged in over the life of the application. Session scope is a good place to store user information, such as preferences. Request scope is ideal for sending data that may change from request to request, particularly for transmitting data that is only needed to generate the next view.

Once control passes to the view, the controller has done its job. We transfer control using the servlet's RequestDispatcher object, which is used to forward requests within the server. Using the RequestDispatcher, we can send requests to multiple servlets, JSP pages, or even static HTML pages without the client's involvement. We simply provide a URL to the request dispatcher, and use the forward( ) method to transfer control :

```
RequestDispatcher dispatcher =
    getServletContext( ).getRequestDispatcher("/success.jsp");
dispatcher.forward(request, response);
```

Our complete ListController servlet is shown in Example 3-3. It performs the steps described above; additionally, it chooses a view based on the results of the MailingBean's business method.

Example 3-3. The ListController servlet

```
import javax.servlet.*;
import javax.servlet.http.*;
import java.io.IOException;

public class ListController extends HttpServlet {
    public static final String FIRST_PARAM = "first";
    public static final String LAST_PARAM = "last";
    public static final String EMAIL_PARAM = "email";
    public static final String MAILINGBEAN_ATTR = "mailingbean";

    public void init(ServletConfig config)
    throws ServletException {
        super.init(config);
    }

    public void destroy( ) {
    }

    // handle get requests
    protected void doGet(HttpServletRequest request,
                        HttpServletResponse response)
    throws ServletException, IOException {
        // read the paremeters from the request
        String first = request.getParameter(FIRST_PARAM);
        String last = request.getParameter(LAST_PARAM);
        String email = request.getParameter(EMAIL_PARAM);

        // get the mailing list bean for this list
        MailingBean mb = MailingBeanFactory.newInstance( );

        // set the parameters into the bean
        mb.setFirst(first);
        mb.setLast(last);
        mb.setEmail(email);
```

Example 3-3. The ListController servlet (continued)

```
        // store a copy of the bean in the request context
        request.setAttribute(MAILINGBEAN_ATTR, mb);

        // perform the business method
        boolean result = mb.doSubscribe();

        // choose a page based on the result
        String nextPage = "/success.jsp";
        if (!result) nextPage = "/failure.jsp";

        // transfer control to the selected view
        RequestDispatcher dispatcher =
            getServletContext().getRequestDispatcher(nextPage);
        dispatcher.forward(request, response);
    }
}
```

JSP: The view

Once the controller has finished actively processing the request, we turn things over to the view. For a web-based presentation tier, the view is anything that writes to the HTTP response. It can be a servlet, a JSP, or even a regular HTML file. We will focus on JSP pages, since they map very well to our idea of a view: they have just enough logic to turn data stored in a JavaBean into an HTML display. Using a servlet as a view tends to create a maintenance nightmare, since each change requires a recompilation and redeployment.

The view, as we've mentioned, is stateless. Each time it is called, it must read the model data and format it as an HTML page. Our JSP page consists of normal HTML with various JSP directives interspersed. The JSP is automatically compiled into a servlet, which generates the response from a combination of the static HTML in the file and the results of processing the various JSP directives.

The view must be able to read its data from the model. Since the controller has already stored our model as a JavaBean in request scope, retrieving the model can be done with a single JSP directive:

```
<jsp:useBean id="mailingbean" scope="request"
            class="mvcexample.model.MailingBean" />
```

This simple directive looks in the current request for an instance of class MailingBean with key "mailingbean". Since this key matches the bean that was added by the controller, our bean should be found. It is now available with the ID "mailingbean" to the jsp:getProperty and jsp:setProperty directives. In order to dynamically include the user's email address, we can use the directive:

```
<jsp:getProperty name="mailingbean" property="email"/>
```

Note that the spelling and capitalization of the property element must match the spelling and capitalization of the bean method exactly, with the first letter in lowercase.

Our JSP page will simply generate a text message based on whether the MailingBean's business methods succeed or fail. When the request fails—for instance, because the email address is not valid—the JSP page we will use looks like the one in Example 3-4. We will use a similar one for success. While it would be quite easy to provide a JSP page that handles both success and failure, we have chosen to preserve the role of the controller by allowing it to choose the output page.

Example 3-4. failure.jsp JSP page

```
<%@page contentType="text/html"%>
<jsp:useBean id="mailingbean" scope="request"
            class="MailingBean" />
<html>
<head><title>Subscription Results</title></head>
<body>
<br><br>
Dear <jsp:getProperty name="mailingbean" property="first"/>,
<br><br>
We're sorry, the address
<jsp:getProperty name="mailingbean" property="email"/>
could not be added to the list.<br><br>
The problem was:
<jsp:getProperty name="mailingbean" property="errorString"/>.
</body>
</html>
```

Using the Model-View-Controller pattern provides an overall structure for web applications in J2EE. While the idea of using JavaBeans as a model, JSP for the views, and servlets for the controller is not a requirement, it is a good rule of thumb. It's far more important to understand how the separation between the model, view, and controller makes an application extensible and maintainable.

 In Chapter 12, we discuss the Magic Servlet and Compound JSP anti-patterns, which should help you recognize when the MVC separation is not being maintained and learn how to fix it.

Building a Central Controller

As an architecture, MVC is a good start and suitable for many applications. But sometimes more advanced processing is called for, so it's time to start filling in the holes in the MVC architecture, starting with the controller. Not only is the controller the first point of contact for requests, it is also the place where we have the most programming and design freedom. Unlike the model, which is shaped by the underlying data, the controller is designed from start to finish as a part of the presentation tier. And unlike the view, which is stateless and generally focused on presentation, we are free to perform as much complicated logic as we like.

The MVC pattern does not specify how many controllers there should be. In our previous example, we built a controller that handled the input from a single screen. In order to extend our application along those same lines, we would have to add new screens and an equal number of new controllers. Alternatively, we could build a single, omniscient controller. This controller would know about every possible request and how to generate a response to each.

Since we are interested in building extensible software, it's obvious that neither of these solutions is exactly right. Building an entire new controller for each screen does not just mean lots of classes, it makes the application harder to extend. If we wanted to build a logging mechanism, for example, we would have to add logging code to each controller separately. In fact, there are lots of things we might need to do for every request: implement navigation, maintain session information, and gather statistics, to name a few. Adding each of these functions to a mix of static HTML, JSP, and servlets is a time-consuming and error-prone process.

We encounter similar problems when using a single controller. While it would be easy to add common functions, the controller must also contain the specific functions for each page. This situation is not very extensible. To add new functionality, we probably need to recompile and redeploy the entire controller (and retest, and redocument...).

A pair of patterns helps balance these two approaches. The Front Controller pattern advocates building a single controller that performs common functions on each request, but delegates other functions to a page-specific controller. The Decorator pattern then shows how to dynamically expand the front controller.

The Front Controller Pattern

The front controller provides a single location that encapsulates common request processing. Figure 3-4 shows an overview of the Front Controller pattern, which looks very similar to our example from the Model-View-Controller pattern.

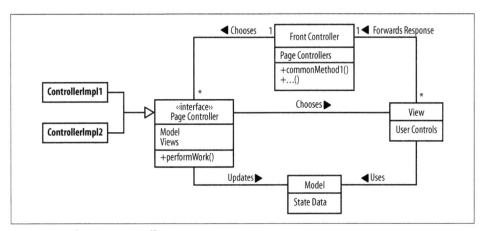

Figure 3-4. The Front Controller pattern

The main participant in the Front Controller pattern is the controller itself. Its job is fairly simple: perform common tasks, and then forward control on to a page-specific controller. While the front controller processes every request, it does not contain the code needed to handle all cases. The specific functions of updating the model and choosing the view are delegated to a page-specific controller.

The page controller performs the model updates and view selection exactly like the controller in the Model-View-Controller pattern described previously. Page controllers may be entire separate servlets, but often they are implemented as much simpler classes based on the GoF Command pattern (see the sidebar, "The Command Pattern"). In this design, many different kinds of page controllers share a simple common interface, and are often referred to as "actions."[*]

The Command Pattern

Actions are a good example of one of the most useful GoF patterns, the Command pattern. Each *command* is a single object that encapsulates some sort of request—for example, adding a row to a database, or saving a file to disk. Within a given context, many commands share a common, simple interface. Each command might consist of a constructor and a performUpdate( ) method. Internally, the command object stores arguments passed into the constructor, and then applies the actual change when performUpdate( ) method is called.

Commands are powerful for three main reasons. The first is their inherent reusability: a command that performs a specific update based on a simple interface can be reused any time that update needs to be made. For instance, if two applications both need to add users to the same database, the same action can be used in both places.

Commands can also be stored. Since a command encapsulates all the data for a given request, it can be created and initialized at one point and applied at another. For example, a web application might store all of its database updates and then send them to the server as a big group.

Commands can also support undoable operations. Since commands store all the data necessary for a particular request, it is often possible to add an undo method to the interface. If we get halfway through our database update and realize something is wrong, we can easily go through our commands backwards, with each command undoing whatever changes it made.

Since the front controller chooses the page controller, it is ultimately responsible for choosing the correct actions and views. In the Service to Worker pattern in

---

[*] Developers familiar with the Struts framework will recognize this concept of actions as similar, if not identical, to the Struts concept of an action. Actions are also similar to Java Server Faces event listeners.

Chapter 4, we will build a complicated controller that handles navigation, taking lots of different information—the request, user name, etc.—into account when choosing actions and views. A simple front controller, however, only intercepts requests, sending them to their original destination after performing common actions.

Using a front controller incurs certain costs. Since its code is executed in every single request, it goes without saying that the implementation must be as efficient as possible. In most systems, the web server or other framework provides optimized methods of performing certain functions, such as logging and user management. Using the built in versions is usually more efficient than if we implemented them ourselves, but the tradeoff, of course, is in functionality. Often a mixed strategy, like a very simple front controller that leverages or adds to built-in functionality, is the best approach.

The Front Controller Servlet

In a web application, the front controller is almost always implemented as a servlet. While it is technically possible to use a JSP page, it's usually a bad idea—JSP pages should not be used to implement complicated logic. A second, more compelling option is to use a servlet filter as the front controller. We discuss this option below.

In this example, we extend our MVC example with a simple front controller to provide security management through a login function. Our front controller will be implemented as a request-intercepting servlet. If the servlet determines that a user has not logged in, it forwards the user to a login page. Once the user has logged in, requests are forwarded to the elements we developed in the MVC example, which act as page controllers. The interactions between these components are shown in Figure 3-5.

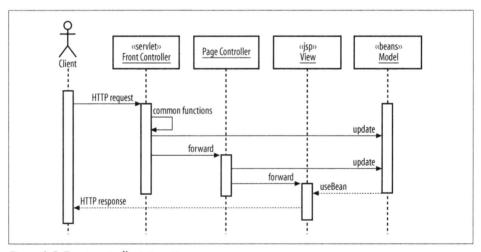

Figure 3-5. Front controller interactions

Our front controller servlet actually looks almost exactly like the `ListController` we built in Example 3-3. Like the list controller, it accesses a JavaBean—in this case, the `UserBean`, which stores username and password information:

```
public interface UserBean {
    // the usename field
    public String getUsername();
    public void setUsername(String username);

    // the password field
    public String getPassword();
    public void setPassword(String password);

    // business method to perform login
    public boolean doLogin();
    public boolean isLoggedIn();
}
```

The front controller also chooses between views. If the user has not yet logged in, *login.jsp*, shown in Example 3-5, is displayed. If the user has logged in, the request is forwarded to the original target.

Example 3-5. login.jsp

```
<%@page contentType="text/html"%>
<jsp:useBean id="userbean" scope="session"
            class="UserBean" />
<html>
<head><title>Login</title></head>
<body>
<br><br>
<form action="/pages/subscribe.html" method="get">
Username: <input type="text" name="username"
                value=<jsp:getProperty name="userbean"
                                    property="username"/>>
<br>
Password: <input type="text" name="password"><br>
<input type="submit" value="Log In">
</form>
</body>
</html>
```

Example 3-6 shows the front controller itself. Note how it uses the session scope to store the user's login information, so the information persists across all requests from the user.

Example 3-6. The FrontController class

```
import javax.servlet.*;
import javax.servlet.http.*;

public class FrontController extends HttpServlet {
    public static final String USERNAME_PARAM = "username";
```

Example 3-6. The FrontController class (continued)

```java
    public static final String PASSWORD_PARAM = "password";
    public static final String USERBEAN_ATTR = "userbean";
    public static final String CONTROLLER_PREFIX = "/pages";

    public void init(ServletConfig config)
    throws ServletException {
        super.init(config);
    }

    public void destroy() {
    }

    protected void doGet(HttpServletRequest request,
                         HttpServletResponse response)
    throws ServletException, java.io.IOException {
        // the default next page
        String nextPage = request.getRequestURI();

        // strip off the prefix
        nextPage =
            nextPage.substring(CONTROLLER_PREFIX.length());

        // find userbean from session
        HttpSession session = request.getSession(true);
        UserBean userBean =
            (UserBean)session.getAttribute(USERBEAN_ATTR);

        if (userBean == null || !userBean.isLoggedIn()) {
            // read request parameters
            String username =
                request.getParameter(USERNAME_PARAM);
            String password =
                request.getParameter(PASSWORD_PARAM);

            // if it doesn't exist, create it
            if (userBean == null) {
                userBean = UserBeanFactory.newInstance();
                session.setAttribute(USERBEAN_ATTR, userBean);
            }

            // record username and password values
            userBean.setUsername(username);
            userBean.setPassword(password);

            // atttempt to login
            boolean result = userBean.doLogin();

            if (!result)
                nextPage = "/login.jsp";
        }

        // transfer control to the selected page controller
```

Example 3-6. The FrontController class (continued)

```
        RequestDispatcher dispatcher =
            getServletContext( ).getRequestDispatcher(nextPage);
        dispatcher.forward(request, response);
    }
}
```

If the user is already logged in, the request is forwarded immediately to the requested URL—but with the prefix stripped off. We'll discuss why this is necessary in a minute.

Deploying the front controller

Since we are creating an intercepting filter, we want all requests—whether for static HTML pages, JSPs, or servlets—to go to our controller when they first come into the system. There is one gotcha here: requests generated with the forward( ) method of the RequestDispatcher must not go to the front controller. If they do, we have created an infinite loop.

Unfortunately, avoiding this loop is not as straightforward as you might think. The RequestDispatcher generates requests exactly as if they came from outside the system. If we simply deploy our controller to intercept all requests, it will not work; it will cause a loop. Instead, we must create a convention: any URL beginning with */pages* will invoke the controller. When the controller does a forward, it simply removes the prefix, meaning that any page can be accessed by simply putting the prefix in front of it. In Example 3-5, the form action is */pages/subscribe.html*. Therefore, if the login is successful, the response will be generated by */subscribe.html*. We can achieve the same effect by choosing an extension instead of a prefix. In that case, */subscribe.html.act* might map to */subscribe.html*.

The final step in deploying the controller is to edit the server's *web.xml* file to make sure the controller is called for any request beginning with */pages*. We can accomplish this with the deployment section shown in Example 3-7.

Example 3-7. Front controller deployment information

```xml
<?xml version="1.0" encoding="UTF-8"?>

<!DOCTYPE web-app
    PUBLIC "-//Sun Microsystems, Inc.//DTD Web Application 2.3//EN"
    "http://java.sun.com/dtd/web-app_2_3.dtd">

<web-app>
  ...
  <servlet>
    <servlet-name>FrontController</servlet-name>
    <servlet-class>FrontController</servlet-class>
  </servlet>
  <servlet-mapping>
    <servlet-name>FrontController</servlet-name>
```

Example 3-7. Front controller deployment information (continued)

```
    <url-pattern>/pages/*</url-pattern>
  </servlet-mapping>
...
</web-app>
```

This method is fairly complicated and somewhat kludgey. Fortunately, a more elegant solution is in the works. Instead of using a servlet as a front controller, a servlet filter can intercept requests and invoke actions in much the same way as a servlet. We talk more about filters in the next section, but for now it is sufficient to note that one of the new features in the Servlet API Version 2.4 extends the functionality of filters to allow fine-grained control of request interception. Using the REQUEST context allows us to filter only the original request, not forwards and includes—meaning we could use "*" as a URL pattern without worrying about infinite loops.

The Decorator Pattern

The Decorator pattern combines multiple small components into a single piece. *Decorator* is a term used by the GoF to describe what is basically a wrapper: a class that contains a single child and presents the same interface as that child.

The decorator "decorates," or adds a piece of functionality, to its child. When a method is called on the decorator, it does its own preprocessing, then calls the corresponding method on the child. The result is an extended response, just as if the original component had the decorator code built into it. Since the decorator presents the same interface as the child, code that relies on the child does not even need to know that it is using a decorator and not the child itself.

Decorators contain only a single child, but they can be chained. A *chain* of decorators consists of multiple decorators, each decorating the original object at the end of the chain. It is the responsibility of each decorator to call the methods of the next object in the chain. In this way, multiple levels of decorators can be added to the same target object. Figure 3-6 shows a chain containing two decorators. Note that both decorators present the same interface, Component, as the target.

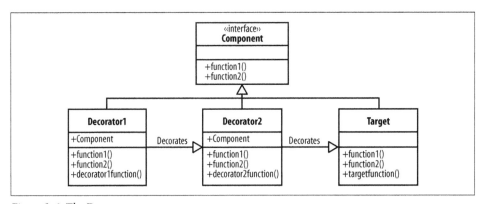

Figure 3-6. The Decorator pattern

The major restriction on a decorator is that it only decorate a single component. This detail is important, since it guarantees that decorators may be configured into chains of arbitrary length.

While it is convenient to dynamically add and remove decorators, doing this too much can significantly increase complexity. Decorators are designed to be independent of each other and of the target, but in practice this is rarely the case. Dependencies and ordering assumptions can cause difficult bugs when a decorator is missing, or if decorators are added in the wrong order.

Decorating the Front Controller

In J2EE, decorators have many uses. In the business tier, wrappers help us access beans remotely and implement security, among other things. In the presentation tier, they help us dynamically extend both views and controllers. We are going to look at one key application of decorators: dynamically extending the front controller.

The problem with front controllers is that they tend to get complicated. Imagine we have a front controller that controls logging, the LoggingController. If we want to add optional debugging code, we could modify the servlet's doGet( ). We would then have a second controller, the DebuggingLoggingController. If we wanted logging only in certain cases, we might need four different controllers. Building, deploying, and testing all these combinations can become a nightmare.

By chaining different combinations of decorators on the front controller, we can quickly add and remove features from the controller. And by using decorators, we can effectively decouple all these different functions.

Implementing a decorating filter

J2EE supports decorators natively: the Java Servlet API, from Version 2.3, provides a powerful filter mechanism. These filters decorate requests to the J2EE server, allowing preprocessing of the request and postprocessing of the result. Filters can also be chained arbitrarily. Most importantly, they can be added and removed from any page or set of pages at runtime.

A filter decorates a request made to the servlet container. Decorating a request is actually quite simple: instead of calling a servlet's doGet( ) or doPost( ) method, the servlet container calls the filter's doFilter( ) method. The filter is passed the request, the response, and an object of type FilterChain, which can be used to call the next filter in the chain. A given filter reads whatever part of the request it wants, generates whatever output it wants, and uses the FilterChain's doFilter( ) method to invoke the next filter in the chain. If there are no more filters, the target servlet's doGet( ) or doPost( ) method is called.

The filter may preprocess the request before calling the next element in the chain, or postprocess data that has been returned by filters later in the chain. This kind of processing is useful for tasks such as decrypting a request as it is received and then encrypting the response before it is sent out. The filter may also choose *not* to run the next filter in the chain (for example, in order to create a security filter that refuses access to some resources). Figure 3-7 shows the interactions that occur when two decorating filters are chained together.

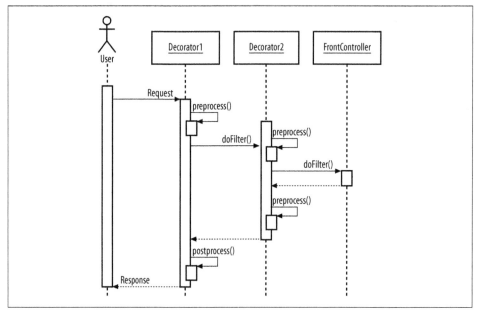

Figure 3-7. Using a decorating filter

Let's look at a simple filter that prints out some debugging information about the request it receives. The RequestInfoFilter is shown in Example 3-8. For each request, this filter prints out information about the desired URL and all the request parameters.

Example 3-8. A simple debugging filter

```
public class RequestInfoFilter implements Filter {
  // describes the filter configuration
  private FilterConfig filterConfig = null;

  // nothing to do in the constructor
  public RequestInfoFilter( ) {}

  // just store the FilterConfig
  public void init(FilterConfig filterConfig) {
    this.filterConfig = filterConfig;
  }

  public void doFilter(ServletRequest request,
                       ServletResponse response,
                       FilterChain chain)
```

Example 3-8. A simple debugging filter (continued)

```
  throws IOException, ServletException {
    ServletContext sc = filterConfig.getServletContext( );

    // preprocess the request
    HttpServletRequest hrs = (HttpServletRequest)request;
    sc.log("Request Attributes:");
    sc.log("Method: " + hrs.getMethod( ));
    sc.log("QueryString: " + hrs.getQueryString( ));
    sc.log("RequestURL: " + hrs.getRequestURL( ));
    sc.log("RequestURI: " + hrs.getRequestURI( ));
    sc.log("PathInfo: " + hrs.getPathInfo( ));
    sc.log("Parameters:");

    // enumerate all request parameters
    for (Enumeration e = request.getParameterNames( );
         e.hasMoreElements( ); ) {
      String name = (String)e.nextElement( );
      String vals[] = request.getParameterValues(name);

      StringBuffer out = new StringBuffer( );
      out.append(name + "=");

      // each parameter may have multiple values
      for(int i=0; i < vals.length; i++) {
        out.append(values[i]);
        out.append(",");
      }

      // remove the trailing comma
      sc.log(out.substring(0, out.length( ) - 1);
    }

    // invoke the next filter in the chain
    chain.doFilter(request, response);
  }

  // called when the filter is deactivated
  public void destroy( ) {}
}
```

We can use a different kind of decorator to allow more advanced filters. The FilterChain object's doFilter( ) method takes an instance of the ServletRequest and ServletResponse classes. In our filter, we can decorate the request and response objects, providing versions to extend the functionality of the core request and response, and pass those decorated requests and responses into the doFilter( ) method. Later filters and the eventual target treat the decorated request and response as they would the original.

Version 2.3 of the Servlet API provides classes for decorating the request and response: the ServletRequestWrapper, ServletResponseWrapper, and corresponding HttpServletRequestWrapper and HttpServletResponseWrapper. The constructors for these classes take an instance of the request or response class in their constructor. They present the full request or response interface, implementing all methods by forwarding to the original request or response. By subclassing these objects, we can easily modify their behavior to store and modify data generated later in the request processing.

Wrapping the request and response allows us to build a variety of powerful filters. To compress the output of a page, a filter can wrap the response with a ServletResponseWrapper that compresses its ServletOutputStream. Encrypting filters can be built the same way, along with decrypting filters that decrypt the request on the fly. Example 3-9 shows a filter that translates pages with the header variable "XML-Encoded" from XML to HTML using a predefined XSLT Transformation file.

Example 3-9. An XSLT filter

```
public class XSLTFilter implements Filter {
 private FilterConfig filterConfig = null;

 public XSLTFilter() {}

 public void init(FilterConfig filterConfig) {
  this.filterConfig = filterConfig;
 }

 public void doFilter(ServletRequest request,
                      ServletResponse response,
                      FilterChain chain)
  throws IOException, ServletException {

  ServletContext sc = getFilterConfig().getServletContext();
  sc.log("XSLTFilter:doFilter():start");

  // wrap response
  XSLTResponseWrapper xsltResponse =
   new XSLTResponseWrapper((HttpServletResponse)response, "/SimpleTransform.xsl");

  HttpServletRequest httpRequest = (HttpServletRequest)request;

  // forward to next filter
  chain.doFilter(httpRequest, xsltResponse);

  // write actual response
  xsltResponse.writeResponse();
  sc.log("XSLTFilter:doFilter():end");
 }

 public void destroy() {
 }
}
```

The filter itself is simple. It wraps the original response with an instance of the XSLTResponseWrapper and passes it on to the rest of the chain. When the chain returns, it calls the writeResponse() method to postprocess the result.

The complexity of this filter lies in the response wrapper. By default, the response may be sent over the network to the client incrementally, as it is generated. Since postprocessing does not do us much good if the response has already been sent, we are left with two options: manipulating the response as it is generated, or collecting and storing the data in the stream and processing it all at once.

Whenever possible, it is better to manipulate the stream as it comes in, saving the overhead of storing the data. This approach is ideal for applications that only require sequential access to the data: compression, encoding, and other techniques that are designed to work on streams of data.

Unfortunately, XML processing requires random access to the data, so we will have to store it ourselves. The CacheOutputStream, shown in Example 3-10, performs this function. Once all the data has been written to the CacheOutputStream, it can be retrieved as an InputStream.

Example 3-10. The CacheOutputStream

```
// a Utility class to adapt a ByteArrayOutputStream
// to be a subclass of ServletOutputStream
class CacheOutputStream extends ServletOutputStream {
  private ByteArrayOutputStream bos;

  public CacheOutputStream( ) {
    bos = new ByteArrayOutputStream( );
  }

  public void write( int b ) {
    bos.write( b );
  }

  public void write( byte[] b, int offset, int len) {
    bos.write( b, offset, len );
  }

  public byte[] toByteArray( ) {
    return bos.toByteArray( );
  }
}
```

The response wrapper overrides the getOutputStream( ) and getWriter( ) methods of the original to return a CacheOutputStream. Example 3-11 shows the actual wrapper.

Example 3-11. The XSLTResponseWrapper

```
public class XSLTResponseWrapper
extends HttpServletResponseWrapper {

  // the original response
  private HttpServletResponse orig;

  private PrintWriter writer;
  private ServletOutputStream stream;
```

Example 3-11. The XSLTResponseWrapper (continued)

```java
// the name of the XML transform filter
private String transform;

// whether the output page is XML
private boolean isXML = false;

// store the transform file and original request
public XSLTResponseWrapper(HttpServletResponse response,
                           String transform)
{
  super(response);
  orig = response;
  this.transform = transform;
}

// create the output stream - if the response is
// encoded, store it for transforming later, otherwise
// just use the default stream
public ServletOutputStream createOutputStream()
throws IOException
{
  if( this.containsHeader("XML-Encoded") ) {
    isXML = true;
    return new CacheOutputStream();
  } else {
    return orig.getOutputStream();
  }
}

// return the output stream - fail if getWriter() has
// been called previously
public ServletOutputStream getOutputStream()
throws IOException
{
  if( stream != null ) return stream;

  if( writer != null )
    throw new IOException("getWriter() already called");

  stream = createOutputStream();

  return stream;
}

// return a Writer - fail if getOutputStream() has
// been called previously
public PrintWriter getWriter() throws IOException {
  if( writer != null ) return writer;

  if( stream != null )
    throw new IOException("getOutputStream() already called");

  writer =  new PrintWriter(
```

Example 3-11. The XSLTResponseWrapper (continued)

```
        new OutputStreamWriter(createOutputStream( )));
    return writer;
  }

  // called by the filter to do the actual XML transformation
  // returns immediately if the data was not XML
  public void writeResponse( ) throws IOException {
    if( !isXML ) return;

    ServletContext sc = filterConfig.getServletContext( );
    sc.log("XSLTFilter:writeXML");

    if( stream == null )
      throw new IOException("No stream to commit");

    InputStream is =
      ((CacheOutputStream)stream).getInputStream( );

    // do the actual transform
    try {
      DocumentBuilderFactory dbf =
          DocumentBuilderFactory.newInstance( );
      DocumentBuilder db = dbf.newDocumentBuilder( );

      // read cached response data
      Document doc = db.parse(is);

      // apply the transform
      TransformerFactory tf = TransformerFactory.newInstance( );
      StreamSource stylesheet =
          new StreamSource(sc.getResourceAsStream(transform));
      Transformer transformer = tf.newTransformer(stylesheet);
      DOMSource source = new DOMSource(doc);

      // send results to the original output stream
      StreamResult result =
          new StreamResult(orig.getOutputStream( ));

      transformer.transform(source, result);
    } catch( Exception ex ) {
      sc.log("Error Transforming", ex);
    }
  }
}
```

The code must enforce that only one of those methods may be called for each response. Also, this wrapper chooses at runtime whether to store the data. If the response is not XML encoded, the data is passed directly to the client. Therefore, we must set the XML-Encoded response header before generating any output.[*]

---

[*] This isn't a standard HTTP header, but one we've defined for our own application.

Deploying decorating filters

Decorators can be dynamically added and removed. Like servlets, filters are configured in the *web.xml* file. They are deployed against a target, which may contain wild cards. As we mentioned earlier, unlike servlets, filter patterns are not looked at in include and forward calls, so there is no problem of recursion. If we have a global filter we can simply deploy it for all requests, with the following entry in *web.xml*:

```
<filter>
 <filter-name>RequestInfoFilter</filter-name>
 <filter-class>RequestInfoFilter</filter-class>
 </filter>
<filter>
<filter-mapping>
 <filter-name>RequestInfoFilter</filter-name>
 <url-pattern>/*</url-pattern>
</filter-mapping>
```

By adding multiple entries in this way, we can easily chain filters. The filter chain is built dynamically at request time. By changing the target URL—say, to apply to only */page/**—we can have filters on just the front controller. We can even put filters on individual pages by specifying the URL of the page controller—say, */page/XMLPage*. Since all filters that match are composed into a chain, a different chain would be built for *XMLPage* than the front controller itself.

Other decorators

Of course, filters are not the only kind of decorators in J2EE. In implementing our filters, we used wrappers for the servlet request and response, which are another example of decorators. Other kinds of decorators can be found in every layer of J2EE.

While decorators represent a fairly simple way to extending an object's functionality, aspect-oriented programming (AOP) is a programming methodology centered around dynamically extending objects. An aspect in AOP represents a common concept that cuts across multiple classes, like the idea of logging. An *aspect* encapsulates the code to perform an action (like logging) as well as the targets it applies to (the front controller) and the conditions under which it should apply (whenever a get request is received), all in one construct. Whenever its conditions are met, the code in an aspect is executed. In simple cases, like logging, an aspect works a lot like a decorator. But aspects provide many sophisticated ways of specifiying conditions, such as determining when one method is called from within another, which make them far more powerful (and complicated) than decorators.

In this chapter, we looked at three design patterns that help create an extensible presentation tier. The Model-View-Controller pattern gives an architecture for enterprise applications that separates the application into functional pieces with clear interfaces. The Front Controller pattern extends this architecture, describing a central controller that performs common functions on each request. Finally, the Decorator pattern shows how to dynamically add functionality to the front controller. Used together, these patterns create an extensible foundation that we will expand on throughout the rest of this book.

Advanced Presentation Tier Design

The patterns discussed in the previous chapter give a broad framework for the presentation tier. Now it's time to dive into the details. This chapter looks at more advanced design patterns for the presentation tier, with a specific question in mind: how can we build reusable components?

Reusable components are something of a holy grail for programmers. Many developers and companies believe that programs, like cars or computers, ideally should be assembled from off-the-shelf pieces. There are many advantages to a component-based development model. Shorter development time is one. Lower price is another: reusing a component spreads the development costs out over time, and also reduces the risk of bugs, since the component has already proved itself in previous uses. When the risk of bugs is lowered, testing can focus on new code, further reducing costs and time.

With all these advantages, why aren't more developers building applications from off-the-shelf components? One explanation is economic: so far, no one has been able to build a successful business model around software components.[*] But more often than not, the reason is that designing reusable components takes time and effort. Reusable components require up-front design, not after-the-fact retrofitting. The interfaces and dependencies for each component must be clearly defined. Interfaces must be kept simple and dependencies to the bare minimum. A component with clear, simple interfaces is easy to test, replace, repurpose, and reuse.

This chapter focuses on patterns for breaking the presentation tier down into small, reusable components. We will look at these patterns:

Service to Worker
> Describes how to divide a controller into reusable navigation and actions.

View Helper
> Shows how to encapsulate related functions in a view into a single, reusable object.

Composite View
> Separates the view into multiple subviews.

---

[*] This problem may soon be solved with the rise of web services.

Reuse in Web Applications

Reusability is a driving factor in object-oriented languages, including Java. Java is full of built-in frameworks meant to promote reuse. JavaBeans provides an explicit component model, while Swing and AWT both provide reusable widget libraries. Throughout the software industry, the adoption of object-oriented programming languages in the 90s led to across-the-board development of a number of frameworks for reuse.

Sadly, there is no standard component framework in the relatively young field of J2EE web applications. While the JavaBeans component model is often used to communicate model data, there is no universal mechanism for reusing parts of views or controllers. Until quite recently, web application developers have had to build their own framework or settle for applications that were not intrinsically reusable. This problem has been recently recognized, and frameworks such as Struts* have gained popularity as a solution (see the sidebar "Frameworks and Patterns"). These frameworks allow controllers and views to be developed using standard interfaces and connected in standard ways.

Frameworks and Patterns

Most web application frameworks implement at least the MVC pattern, and many even claim to be "pattern-based." In general, frameworks force applications written to them to conform to certain patterns. Recognizing these patterns can be a big help in designing applications that work well in a given framework. Here's a look at two popular frameworks and the patterns they implement:

- Jakarta Struts is probably the best-known web application framework. It is based on what they call a "Model 2" approach, an implementation of MVC in which you write the model and view components, and Struts provides the controller. The Struts controller is based on the Service to Worker pattern, featuring a front controller, a dispatcher configured via XML files, and a code framework for embedding application logic into *actions*. Struts also provides a number of utility classes and tag libraries, including Tiles, an implementation of the Composite View pattern.

- JavaServer Faces (JSF) is a new web application framework from Sun. The primary goal of JSF is to provide a UI framework for web applications, allowing the development of custom, reusable UI widgets that maintain state across requests. As such, JSF is centered around the Composite View pattern, and includes an extensive tag library for developing and using these components. JSF also provides a simple implementation of the Service to Worker pattern, including a front controller, an XML-configured navigation handler, and support for actions.

---

* An impressive list of open source frameworks is available at *http://www.waferproject.org*.

Extending the Controller

In the last chapter, we discussed how to best add features to a front controller. The main problem was that adding new features directly to the controller specializes it. A specialized controller quickly becomes unwieldy, with lots of code for each specific page. Every time we wanted new functionality, we had to rebuild, retest, and redeploy the entire controller. To solve this problem, we looked at the Decorator pattern, which allowed us to dynamically add functionality to the front controller.

With decorators in place, common functions such as security are separated from the front controller. But the controller is still responsible for managing page navigation as well as instantiating actions. Since the set of pages and the set of available actions are likely to change, a tight coupling between them and the front controller is a bad idea. Similar to decorators, we would like to separate the specialized bits of the code for actions and navigation into their own classes and leave the major objects—like the front controller—to act as frameworks.

Here's an example. Imagine a simple, multistep form, such as an online mortgage application.* If each page in the form contained embedded references to the next page, it would be very difficult to change the page order. Each affected page, as well as those that came before and after it, would need to be modified to reflect the change. Even worse, these pages could not be reused. If the first page of our mortgage application took basic name and address information, we might want to use the same view in a credit card application. Unfortunately, we can't, since the first mortgage page contains a reference to the second mortgage page: there's no way to direct it to the credit card application instead. This inflexibility stems from the tight coupling of views to controllers.

To build a flexible application, we need to decouple the pages and controllers. We need the flexibility to add, remove, and reorder pages, reusing them at will. Ideally, we want to do all of this at runtime, while preserving the view-controller separation. The Service to Worker pattern can help us.

The Service to Worker Pattern

The *Service to Worker pattern* is based on both the Model-View-Controller pattern and the Front Controller pattern. The goal of Service to Worker is to maintain separation between actions, views, and controllers. The *service*, in this case is the front controller, a central point for handling requests. Like in the Front Controller pattern, the service delegates updating the model to a page-specific action called the *worker*. So far, Service to Worker is the same as the Front Controller pattern.

* Yes, we know that in reality these are anything but simple!

In the Service to Worker pattern, an object called the *dispatcher* performs the task of managing workers and views. The dispatcher encapsulates page selection, and consequently, worker selection. It decouples the behavior of the application from the front controller. To change the order in which pages are shown, for example, only the dispatcher needs to be modified.

The Service to Worker pattern is shown in Figure 4-1. It looks like the Front Controller pattern, with the addition of the dispatcher.

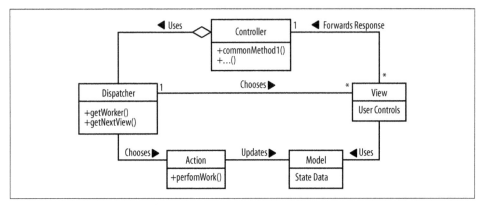

Figure 4-1. The Service to Worker pattern

The controller provides an initial point of entry for every request (just like in the Front Controller pattern). It allows common functionality to be added and removed easily, and it can be enhanced using decorators.

The dispatcher encapsulates page selection. In its simplest form, the dispatcher takes some parameters from the request and uses them to select actions and a view. This type of simple dispatcher may be implemented as a method of the front controller. In addition to the requested page, the dispatcher often takes several other factors into account when choosing the next view, the current page, the user permissions, and the validity of the entered information. This type of dispatcher is implemented as a separate class, and ideally, it is configurable via a file at runtime.

The dispatcher uses a set of actions to perform model updates. Each action encapsulates a single, specific update to the model, and only that update. An action might be something as simple as adding a row to a database table, or as complex as coordinating transactions across multiple business objects. Because all navigation is encapsulated in the dispatcher, the actions are not responsible for view selection. As in the Front Controller pattern, actions are usually implemented as an instance of the GoF Command pattern.

The end result of the Service to Worker pattern is an extensible front controller. The controller itself is simply a framework: decorators perform common functions, actions actually update the model, and the dispatcher chooses the resulting view.

Because these pieces are loosely coupled, each can operate independently, allowing extension and reuse.

Service to Worker in J2EE

As an example of Service to Worker, let's think about a *workflow*.* A workflow is a sequence of tasks that must be performed in a specific order. Many environments have workflows, such as the mortgage application we discussed earlier and the "wizards" that guide a user through installing software.

Our workflow is very simple, and it is based on our previous examples. It consists of three web pages: one asking the user to log in, another setting a language preference, and a third displaying a summary page. This workflow is shown in Figure 4-2.

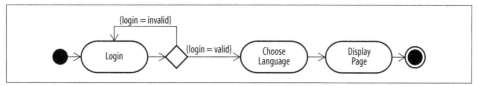

Figure 4-2. A simple workflow

While it would be easy enough to build this workflow based on the Front Controller pattern, we would like the result to be extensible. We want to be able to add pages and actions without changing the front controller. Ideally, we would like to specify our workflow in XML, so we could change the order of pages without even modifying the dispatcher. Our XML might look like:

```
<?xml version="1.0" encoding="UTF-8"?>
<workflow>
    <state name="login" action="LoginAction"
            viewURI="login.jsp" />
    <state name="language" action="LanguageAction"
            viewURI="language.html" />
    <state name="display" action="RestartAction"
            viewURI="display.jsp" />
</workflow>
```

The dispatcher, then, is a simple state machine. When a request is submitted, the dispatcher determines the current state of the session and runs the corresponding action. If the action succeeds, there is a transition to the next state. Once the state is determined, control is forwarded to the associated view.

---

* This example is based loosely on a proposed workflow language for the Struts framework, part of the Apache project. More information is available from *http://jakarta.apache.org/struts/proposal-workflow.html*.

The interactions in a J2EE Service to Worker implementation are shown in Figure 4-3. To explain all these pieces, we'll work backward, starting with models and views and ending with the front controller.

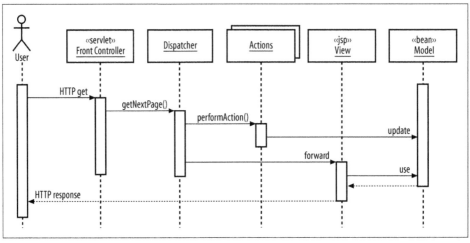

Figure 4-3. J2EE Service to Worker implementation

Models and views

The models and views in the Service to Worker pattern remain more or less unchanged from the MVC and Front Controller patterns. As in Chapter 3, our model is the UserBean. The interface has been extended slightly from earlier examples to include a "language" attribute:

```
package s2wexample.model;

public interface UserBean {
    // the username field
    public String getUsername();
    public void setUsername(String username);

    // the password field
    public String getPassword();
    public void setPassword(String password);

    // the language field
    public String getLanguage();
    public void setLanguage(String language);

    // business methods to perform login
    public boolean doLogin();
    public boolean isLoggedIn();
}
```

The views are simple JSP pages that read the model data from our UserBean. Our login page is virtually unchanged from the earlier example. Example 4-1 shows the login page.

Example 4-1. login.jsp

```
<%@page contentType="text/html"%>
<jsp:useBean id="userbean" scope="session"
             class="s2wexample.model.UserBean" />
<html>
<head><title>Login</title></head>
 <body>
  <br><br>
  <form action="/pages/workflow" method="post">
   Username:<input type="text" name="username"
   value=<jsp:getProperty name="userbean" property="username"/>>
   <br>
   Password: <input type="password" name="password">
   <br>
   <input type="submit" value="Log In">
  </form>
 </body>
</html>
```

The only thing to notice here is that our form action is now */pages/workflow*. This will be the target of all our links, such as those in the second page, *language.html*. Since this page does not require any dynamic data, it is stored as a plain HTML file, shown in Example 4-2.

Example 4-2. language.html

```
<html>
<head><title>Language Selection</title></head>
 <body>
  <br><br>
  <form action="/pages/workflow" method="get">
   Language: <select name="language">
             <option value="En">English</option>
             <option value="Fr">French</option>
             </select>
   <br>
   <input type="submit" value="Continue">
  </form>
 </body>
</html>
```

Actions

Actions, as we mentioned earlier, are implemented as instances of the command pattern. All of our actions will share a simple interface:

```
public interface Action {
    public boolean performAction(HttpServletRequest req,
                                 ServletContext context);
}
```

This interface gives each action full access to the request, as well as the servlet context, which includes the HTTP session. Each action reads a different set of parameters from the request. The action then updates the model data, which is accessible through either the request or the session. If the performAction( ) method returns true, the dispatcher knows to move on to the next state. If not, the same state is repeated.

Example 4-3 shows the LoginAction, which is called with input from the login page. This action is also responsible for creating the initial UserBean if it does not exist.

Example 4-3. LoginAction.java

```
package s2wexample.controller.actions;

import s2wexample.controller.*;
import s2wexample.model.*;
import javax.servlet.http.*;
import javax.servlet.*;

public class LoginAction implements Action {
    public static final String USERBEAN_ATTR = "userbean";
    private static final String NAME_PARAM = "username";
    private static final String PASSWORD_PARAM = "password";

    public boolean performAction(HttpServletRequest req,
                                 ServletContext context) {
        // read request parameters
        String username = req.getParameter(NAME_PARAM);
        String password = req.getParameter(PASSWORD_PARAM);

        // find the UserBean, create if necessary
        HttpSession session = req.getSession( );
        UserBean ub = (UserBean)session.getAttribute(USERBEAN_ATTR);
        if (ub == null) {
            ub = UserBeanFactory.newInstance( );
            session.setAttribute(USERBEAN_ATTR, ub);
        }

        // try to login, return the result
        ub.setUsername(username);
        ub.setPassword(password);
        return ub.doLogin( );
    }
}
```

The dispatcher

Dispatchers, like actions, come in many flavors. There may be a single master dispatcher or different dispatchers for different parts of an application. Usually, there is one default dispatcher and a few more specialized ones to handle special cases like wizards. In any case, we will define a simple Dispatcher interface to allow uniform access to all the possible dispatchers:

```
public interface Dispatcher {
    // called after initialization
    public void setContext(ServletContext context)
        throws IOException;
    // called for each request
    public String getNextPage(HttpServletRequest req,
                              ServletContext context);
}
```

The dispatcher must build and store a simple state machine for each user. As requests come in, the dispatcher retrieves the current state and uses it to determine the correct action to run. If the action succeeds, it displays the view associated with the next state.

Our dispatcher must also process the XML state data. When we see an action attribute, we will convert it to a Java class by loading the class named *name*Action, where *name* is the value of the action attribute.

Internally, we will use simple Java objects to model the states of the workflow. The WorkflowDispatcher is shown in Example 4-4.

Example 4-4. WorkflowDispatcher

```
 package s2wexample.controller;

import javax.servlet.*;
import javax.servlet.http.*;
import java.io.*;
import javax.xml.parsers.*;
import org.w3c.dom.*;

public class WorkflowDispatcher implements Dispatcher {
    // tags expected in the XML
    private static final String WORKFLOW_TAG = "workflow";
    private static final String STATE_TAG = "state";
    private static final String NAME_ATTR = "name";
    private static final String ACTION_ATTR = "action";
    private static final String VIEW_ATTR = "viewURI";

    // where to find action classes
    private static final String ACTION_PREFIX =
        "s2wexample.controller.actions.";

    // the internal model of a workflow state
    class State {
        protected String name;
        protected Action action;
        protected String viewUri;
    }
```

Example 4-4. WorkflowDispatcher (continued)

```java
    // the current state and state list
    private State[] states;
    private int currentState;

    // called by the controller after initialization
    public void setContext(ServletContext context)
        throws IOException {
        InputStream is =
            context.getResourceAsStream("/LanguageWorkflow.xml");
        try {
            states = parseXML(is);
        } catch(Exception ex) {
            throw new IOException(ex.getMessage());
        }
        currentState = 0;
    }

    // choose the next state
    public String getNextPage(HttpServletRequest req,
                              ServletContext context) {
        State s = states[currentState];
        // increment the state only if the action suceeds
        if ((s.action == null) ||
            s.action.performAction(req, context)) {
            if (currentState < states.length - 1) {
                s = states[++currentState];
            } else {
                currentState = 0;
                s = states[currentState];
            }
        }

        return s.viewUri;
    }

    // parse a state XML file
    private State[] parseXML(InputStream is) throws Exception {
        DocumentBuilderFactory factory =
            DocumentBuilderFactory.newInstance();
        DocumentBuilder builder = factory.newDocumentBuilder();
        Document doc = builder.parse(is);

        // find the workflow element
        NodeList workflows = doc.getElementsByTagName(WORKFLOW_TAG);
        Element workflow = (Element)workflows.item(0);

        // find all the states
        NodeList states = doc.getElementsByTagName(STATE_TAG);
        State[] stateList = new State[states.getLength()];

        // read state information
        for(int i = 0; i < states.getLength(); i++) {
```

Example 4-4. WorkflowDispatcher (continued)

```
            stateList[i] = new State( );

            Element curState = (Element)states.item(i);
            stateList[i].name = curState.getAttribute(NAME_ATTR);
            stateList[i].viewUri = curState.getAttribute(VIEW_ATTR);

            // convert actions names into class instances
            String action = curState.getAttribute(ACTION_ATTR);
            if (action != null && action.length( ) > 0) {
                Class c = Class.forName(ACTION_PREFIX + action);
                stateList[i].action = (Action)c.newInstance( );
            }
        }

        return stateList;
    }
}
```

The front controller

Last but not least is the front controller, which is more of a framework than a container for actual application logic at this point. The controller's job right now is to manage dispatchers, using them to choose the next view. Once the view is chosen, the front controller passes control to the view, and the front controller's job is finished. Example 4-5 shows our front controller servlet.

Example 4-5. FrontController.java

```
package s2wexample.controller;

import javax.servlet.*;
import javax.servlet.http.*;
import java.io.*;
import s2wexample.model.*;

public class FrontController extends HttpServlet {
    private static final String DISPATCHER_ATTR = "Dispatcher";
    private static final String DISPATCHER_PREFIX =
        "s2wexample.controller.";

    public void init(ServletConfig config) throws ServletException {
        super.init(config);
    }

    // process get requests
    public void doGet(HttpServletRequest request,
                      HttpServletResponse response)
    throws ServletException, IOException {
        process(request, response);
    }

    // process post requests
```

Example 4-5. FrontController.java (continued)

```java
    public void doPost(HttpServletRequest request,
                       HttpServletResponse response)
    throws ServletException, IOException {
        process(request, response);
    }

    // common processing routine
    public void process(HttpServletRequest request,
                        HttpServletResponse response)
    throws ServletException, IOException {
        HttpSession session = request.getSession( );
        ServletContext context = getServletContext( );

        // get the last element of the request in lower case
        String reqPath = request.getPathInfo( );
        reqPath = Character.toUpperCase(reqPath.charAt(1)) +
            reqPath.substring(2).toLowerCase( );

        // find the dispatcher in the session
        Dispatcher dispatcher =
            (Dispatcher)session.getAttribute(reqPath +
                                             DISPATCHER_ATTR);
        // if no dispatcher was found, create one
        if (dispatcher == null) {
            String className = reqPath + "Dispatcher";
            try {
                Class c = Class.forName(DISPATCHER_PREFIX +
                                        className);
                dispatcher = (Dispatcher)c.newInstance( );
            } catch(Exception ex) {
                throw new ServletException("Can't find class " +
                                           className, ex);
            }

            // store the dispatcher in the session
            dispatcher.setContext(context);
            session.setAttribute(reqPath + DISPATCHER_ATTR,
                                 dispatcher);
        }

        // use the dispatcher to find the next page
        String nextPage = dispatcher.getNextPage(request, context);

        // make sure we don't cache dynamic data
        response.setHeader("Cache-Control", "no-cache");
        response.setHeader("Pragma", "no-cache");

        // forward control to the view
        RequestDispatcher forwarder =
            request.getRequestDispatcher("/" + nextPage);
        forwarder.forward(request, response);
    }
}
```

Notice that the front controller manages dispatchers in the same way that the dispatchers manage actions. Dispatchers are mapped based on the requested URL. Since all our views used the path */pages/workflow* in their requests, the front controller maps these requests to an instance of the WorkflowDispatcher class. As a result, the same application could use many different dispatchers for different parts of the web site. In practice, the mapping between URLs and dispatchers is usually done with an XML file, just like for actions.

Using the Service to Worker pattern, the controller has been divided up into a set of reusable components: a front controller, dispatchers, and actions. Adding a new page is dynamic: you simply create the view JSP and corresponding action class and add it all to an XML file. To add, remove, or reorder pages, we only need to change the XML.

The Service to Worker pattern, as we have presented it, is quite flexible. The simple navigation model of our example, however, is only really appropriate for workflows. Even branches to the linear flow of pages are not covered. We won't cover all the possible dispatchers and actions here. Both the Jakarta Struts project and Sun's J2EE sample applications contain more advanced implementations of the Service to Worker patterns, and they are a good place to look for more information.

Advanced Views

Until now, we have treated the view as a black box, assuming that a single JSP page will convert our model data into HTML to send to the user. In reality, this is a tall order. Large JSP pages with lots of embedded code are just as unwieldy as a large front controller. Like the controller, we would like to break the view into a generic framework with the specialized pieces separated out.

The challenge is to break up the view within the restricted programming model of JSP. Remember that one of our goals was to minimize embedding code in our JSP pages, since it blurs the line between the view and the controller. Thus, we will avoid the kinds of classes and interfaces we used to solve the same problem in the controller.

Fortunately, JSP gives us a different set of tools to work with: JSP directives and custom tags. We will use both of these extensively in the next two patterns to help separate the view into reusable components.

The View Helper Pattern

One mechanism for reducing specialization in views is a *view helper*. A view helper acts as an intermediary between the model and the view. It reads specific business data and translates it, sometimes directly into HTML, and sometimes into an intermediate data model. Instead of the view containing specialized code to deal with a particular model, the view includes more generic calls to the helper. Figure 4-4 shows how a view uses helpers.

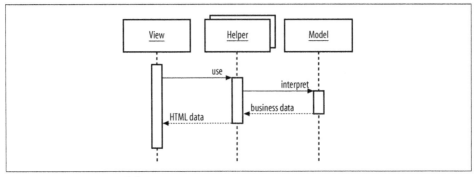

Figure 4-4. A view using helpers

View helpers increase reusability in two ways: by reducing the amount of specialized code in a view, helpers make views more reusable; and, since a helper encapsulates a specific kind of interaction with the model, helpers can be reused themselves.

Implementing a View Helper

When you think about view helpers in JSP, custom tags should immediately pop to mind. Conceptually, custom tags fit the bill—they adapt Java objects into JSP markup. Moving code embedded in JSP into custom tag classes reduces coupling, since the tag defines a clear interface independent of the underlying objects. And since tags are grouped into libraries by function, they are inherently quite reusable themselves. While it is easy to think of all custom tags (or even all tags) as view helpers, they are not the same thing. A view helper is a tag, or set of tags, that translates model data into a convenient form for the view.

A view helper may read business data in many forms, including JavaBeans, Enterprise JavaBeans, direct database access, or access to remote web services. For our example, let's look at the last of these: accessing a remote web service.

Really Simple Syndication (RSS)[*] is an XML format that is the de facto standard for web sites to exchange headline information. RSS files are generally available via public HTTP from most news sites, at the very least. Example 4-6 shows a slightly simplified RSS file for a made-up news page, *PatternsNews*. (For simplicity, we have stuck to the 0.91 version of RSS. The current version, 2.0, is far more complicated.)

Example 4-6. PatternsNews.xml

```
<?xml version="1.0" encoding="iso-8859-1"?>

<!DOCTYPE rss PUBLIC "-//Netscape Communications//DTD RSS 0.91//EN"
                 "http://www.scripting.com/dtd/rss-0_91.dtd">

<rss version="0.91">
  <channel>
```

---

[*] RSS is an actively evolving standard. For a good introduction and history, see *http://backend.userland.com/rss*.

Example 4-6. PatternsNews.xml (continued)

```
    <title>Patterns news</title>
    <link>http://www.patternsnews.com</link>

    <item>
      <title>Local pattern-creators honored</title>
      <link>http://www.patternsnews.com/stories?id=0001</link>
    </item>
    <item>
      <title>Patterns solve business problem</title>
      <link>http://www.patternsnews.com/stories?id=0002</link>
    </item>
    <item>
      <title>New patterns discovered!</title>
      <link>http://www.patternsnews.com/stories?id=0003</link>
    </item>
  </channel>
</rss>
```

We would like to read RSS files and include their headlines on our own web site. In order to do this, we will build a view helper that makes the RSS data available as a JSP custom tag. Figure 4-5 shows the pieces we will build.

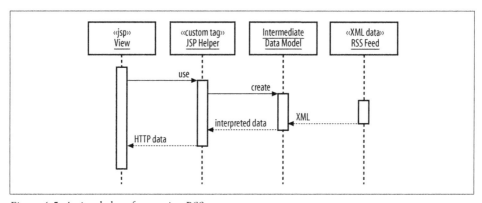

Figure 4-5. A view helper for parsing RSS

Parsing the RSS

For starters, we need to parse the RSS into a Java format that we can use. To do this, we create an RSSInfo class that parses RSS files and stores them as Java objects. We won't go into the specifics of how the parsing works, since the innards look a lot like the DOM-based XML parser we built for the last example. Example 4-7 shows the interface to the RSSInfo class.

Example 4-7. The RSSInfo interface

```
public interface RSSInfo {

    // channel information
    public String getChannelTitle( );
```

Example 4-7. The RSSInfo interface (continued)

```
    public String getChannelLink( );

    // item information
    public String getTitleAt(int index);
    public String getLinkAt(int index);
    public int getItemCount( );

    // parse the RSS file at the given URL
    public void parse(String url) throws Exception;
}
```

The RSSInfo object represents an intermediate data structure: it is not exactly the underlying data, but also not exactly what we are using in the application. Building an intermediate data model may seem inefficient, but it can help significantly in reusability. Since the RSSInfo class is independent of any type of display mechanism, it can be used in many contexts: JSP custom tags, servlets, web services, etc. If the parsing was implemented directly as custom JSP tags, the logic would have to be duplicated.

Using the RSS: Custom tags

Now that we have a generic method for parsing RSS, we would like to use it in a JSP environment. We could store the RSSInfo object in the session and access it directly using JSP directives. While this option is quite flexible, it embeds a fair amount of logic for iteration and such in the JSP.[*] This logic would have to be rewritten for each page that used the RSS parser. As another option, we could create a custom tag that read the RSS and returned a preformatted table. This method has the advantage of being easy, since only one line of JSP is needed to include all the headlines. Unfortunately, it would mean including our page styles in the custom tag, and we would be unable to reuse the tag on a different page.

The best solution in this case is a hybrid: we will design custom tags to parse and iterate through the RSS data, and expose JSP scripting variables with the relevant values. This solution allows us the flexibility to format the output any way we want, while performing the heavy lifting in the custom tag logic. To format the RSS data as a table, for example, we would like to have our JSP look something like Example 4-8.

Example 4-8. JSP custom tags in action

```
<%@page contentType="text/html"%>
<%@ taglib prefix="rss" uri="/ReadRSS" %>
<html>
<head><title>RSS Results</title></head>
<body>
```

---

[*] Version 2.0 of the JSP spec adds an expression language and standard tag library, which greatly reduce the need for embedded scripts in these situations. This does not, however, provide an excuse for manipulating ill-suited business objects directly in JSP.

Example 4-8. JSP custom tags in action (continued)

```
<rss:RSSChannel URL="http://www.patternsnews.com/patternsnews.xml">
 <b><a href="<%= channelLink %>"><%= channelName %></a></b>
 <br>
 <table>
  <rss:RSSItems>
   <tr><td><a href="<%= itemLink %>"><%= itemName %></a></td></tr>
  </rss:RSSItems>
 </table>
</rss:RSSChannel>
</body>
</html>
```

Here, our view helper consists of two custom tags. The first, RSSChannel, takes a URL corresponding to an RSS file and downloads and parses that file using the RSSInfo class. It exposes the channel title and channel link information in two scripting variables: channelTitle and channelLink. The second tag, RSSItems, performs a similar task, repeating its body for each item in turn and exposing the itemTitle and itemLink variables. The helper (the tags) is therefore responsible for creating and interpreting the intermediate data model (the RSSInfo).

The RSSChannel tag source is shown in Example 4-9.

Example 4-9. RSSChannelTag.java

```
import javax.servlet.*;
import javax.servlet.jsp.*;
import javax.servlet.jsp.tagext.*;

public class RSSChannelTag extends BodyTagSupport {
    // scripting variable names
    private static final String NAME_ATTR = "channelName";
    private static final String LINK_ATTR = "channelLink";

    // the input parameter
    private String url;
    // the RSS parser
    private RSSInfo rssInfo;

    public RSSChannelTag( ) {
        rssInfo = new RSSInfoImpl( );
    }

    // called with the URL parameter from the tag
    public void setURL(String url) {
        this.url = url;
    }

    // used by the RSSItemsTag
    protected RSSInfo getRSSInfo( ) {
        return rssInfo;
    }
```

Example 4-9. RSSChannelTag.java (continued)

```
    // parse the RSS and set up the scripting variables
    public int doStartTag( ) throws JspException {
        try {
            rssInfo.parse(url);

            pageContext.setAttribute(NAME_ATTR, rssInfo.getChannelTitle( ));
            pageContext.setAttribute(LINK_ATTR, rssInfo.getChannelLink( ));
        } catch (Exception ex) {
            throw new JspException("Unable to parse " + url, ex);
        }
        return Tag.EVAL_BODY_INCLUDE;
    }
}
```

The RSSItems tag is slightly more complicated, since it implements the IterationTag interface. It loops through the item data, setting the itemTitle and itemLink variables with every pass. RSSItems also uses the findAncestorWithClass( ) method to locate the RSSInfo object that was stored by the parent. The RSSItemsTag source is shown in Example 4-10.

Example 4-10. RSSItemsTag.java

```
import javax.servlet.*;
import javax.servlet.jsp.*;
import javax.servlet.jsp.tagext.*;

public class RSSItemsTag extends BodyTagSupport implements IterationTag {
    // the names of the scripting variables
    private static final String NAME_ATTR = "itemName";
    private static final String LINK_ATTR = "itemLink";

    // keep track of looping
    private int counter;
    // the stored RSS data, obtained from enclosing tag
    private RSSInfo rssInfo;

    public RSSItemsTag( ) {
        super( );
        counter = 0;
    }

    // find the RSSInfo from the enclosing tag and set the
    // initial values of the scripting variables
    public int doStartTag( ) throws JspException {
        if (rssInfo == null) {
            RSSChannelTag rct =
                (RSSChannelTag)findAncestorWithClass(this, RSSChannelTag.class);
            rssInfo = rct.getRSSInfo( );
        }

        pageContext.setAttribute(NAME_ATTR, rssInfo.getTitleAt(counter));
        pageContext.setAttribute(LINK_ATTR, rssInfo.getLinkAt(counter));
```

Example 4-10. RSSItemsTag.java (continued)

```
        return Tag.EVAL_BODY_INCLUDE;
    }

    // after each pass, increment the counter if there are still items left
    // refresh the scripting variables at each pass
    public int doAfterBody() throws JspException {
        if (++counter >= rssInfo.getItemCount()) {
            return IterationTag.SKIP_BODY;
        } else {
            pageContext.setAttribute(NAME_ATTR, rssInfo.getTitleAt(counter));
            pageContext.setAttribute(LINK_ATTR, rssInfo.getLinkAt(counter));
            return IterationTag.EVAL_BODY_AGAIN;
        }
    }
}
```

With the custom tags, we have built a reusable view helper. The helper encapsulates a general mechanism for RSS parsing in an intermediate class, RSSInfo, and interprets the data using JSP custom tags. We could add other helpers, such as those to use the RSSInfo object in a web service. View helpers add a slight overhead to request processing. But the benefits, in terms of extensibility and reuse, tend to far outweigh these costs. By encapsulating common functionality, view helpers provide a simple way to organize otherwise complicated data access. We see an analogous pattern from the business object perspective when we look at the Session Façade pattern in Chapter 9.

Composite View

Views tend to have a lot of repeated elements. This isn't a bad thing—a good user interface requires consistency. If the general presentation or the navigation were different from screen to screen within an application, the user would be very confused indeed.

Think about the structure of web sites. Many sites follow a basic pattern, like the one shown in Figure 4-6: the content of the page is surrounded by a header on the top (usually with ads), a navigation area on the left, and a footer on the bottom. This consistent layout makes navigation within a site easy, and allows people unfamiliar with a new site to understand it quickly.

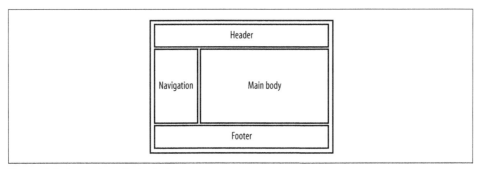

Figure 4-6. A generic web site design

Ideally, we would like the page's code to reflect this high-level organization. We should be able to specify the structure of the page in one generic template, and then vary the content on a per-application and per-page basis. Further, we should be able to apply this concept recursively, allowing each of the areas in our page to separate themselves into template and content. The Composite View pattern supports both of these requirements.

The Composite View pattern

The *Composite View pattern* is based on the GoF composite pattern. The idea is fairly simple: treat the objects as a tree structure, in which parents expose the same interface as their children. When this concept is applied to a view, it means thinking of each page as composed of a number of elements. Each of the elements may be a leaf, which displays an actual widget to the screen. An element may also be a container, which contains multiple elements as children. The children of a container may be leaves, or other containers, resulting in the tree-like structure. Figure 4-7 shows the participants in a Composite View.

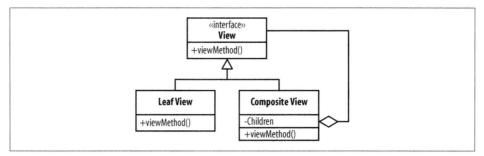

Figure 4-7. Classes in the Composite View pattern

The Composite View pattern is a staple of most graphical systems. In Java's Swing, for example, the user interface is built as a set of panels. Each panel contains any number of components, as well as other panels.

View represents a common interface implemented by both leaves and containers. There are varying opinions on how rich this interface needs to be. Obviously, it must contain methods like draw( ), which are required by both leaves and containers. Methods that are specific to containers, like adding and removing children, could go either way. We could treat a leaf as a container with no children, thus allowing containers to export exactly the same interface as the leaves they contain (like in the Decorator pattern). Or we could put the container-specific interfaces only in the composite classes, saving overhead. In a system like Java, where runtime type-checking is relatively cheap, the container methods are usually restricted to the container, but either choice is valid.

The `LeafView` and `CompositeView` objects implement the `View` interface. Leaves always display directly to the output. A composite must coordinate the display of all its subcomponents, as well as any rendering it might do itself.

In some systems, the ordering of subcomponents within a composite is not important, but in displays it usually is. In a graphical application, there's frequently some concept of "layout"—a richer syntax for how components are arranged within a container. The layout might include the sizes and shapes of various components, for example. To be truly flexible, our solution needs to abstract layout within a container from the components themselves, a feat accomplished with a template.

A template allows us to specify the high-level layout of a page, based on a generic set of components. The layout can be reused on different sets of components, allowing the view to vary dynamically. By modifying the template, we can make changes to the global layout in one central place. And templates may themselves contain other templates and components.

In the same way that the Service to Worker pattern divided the controller into reusable dispatchers and actions, the Composite View pattern divides the view into reusable components. These components contain clear interfaces, so they can be shared, substituted, and extended at will.

Implementing composite views

The view tier in a web application has built-in support for a basic level of composition. Both JSPs and Servlets are used as views, but they can also be containers. The JSP include directive and the matching `RequestDispatcher.include()` method for servlets allow for the embedding of any other JSP page, servlet, or even static web page.

While the servlet include mechanism is quite flexible, the JSP include directive is not. Including a page requires embedding its URL into the parent page, creating a tight coupling between the parent and the child. We want to avoid this coupling, so that we can reuse the parent page on different sets of children.

In this example, we build the JSP custom tags to support the notion of containers. One tag defines a container and one defines an element in a container. The `container` tag determines the name of the container and and the container maps that label at the back end to support the include tag. The `include` tag works like the normal JSP include tag, except that instead of specifying a URL, we specify a label, and the container maps that label to different URLs depending on the page being viewed. An `include` tag is always nested within a `container` tag. Example 4-11 shows how a container might be used to create a layout similar to that in Figure 4-6.

Example 4-11. MainTemplate.jsp

```
<%@page contentType="text/html"%>
<%@ taglib uri="/container" prefix="cv" %>
```

Example 4-11. MainTemplate.jsp (continued)

```
<cv:container name="main">
<html>
<head><title><cv:include label="title" /></title></head>
<body>
<table width="100%" height="100%">
<tr><td><cv:include label="header" /></td></tr>
<tr><td><cv:include label="body" /></td></tr>
<tr><td><cv:include label="footer" /></td></tr>
</table>
</body>
</html>
</cv:container>
```

We populate the template with an XML file. It maps the "title," "header," "body," and "footer" labels to different URLs, depending on what screen is being shown. To do this, we will create an XML document similar to the one we used for workflows. Example 4-12 shows how this format could be used for the "main" container.

Example 4-12. Views.xml

```
<?xml version="1.0" encoding="UTF-8"?>

<views>
    <view name="page1" template="MainTemplate.jsp">
        <container name="main">
            <include label="header" url="Header.html" />
            <include label="footer" url="Footer.html" />
            <include label="body" url="page1.html" />
        </container>
    </view>
    <view name="page2" template="MainTemplate.jsp">
        <container name="main">
            <include label="header" url="Header.html" />
            <include label="footer" url="Footer.html" />
            <include label="body" url="page2.html" />
        </container>
    </view>
</views>
```

We now have a view element for each page in the application that specifies the template to be used. Each view consists of one or more container elements. The name attribute of a container matches the name attribute specified in the container tag in the JSP. While this might seem overly complicated, it has the advantage of supporting nesting. As long as container names are unique within a given page, as many containers as desired can be put into a single view.

When including form elements in an HTML page, it is often necessary to supply a name to each element. This name must be unique within the page to allow proper processing when the request is received. If form elements are nested in a composite view, there is a potential to use the same form element name multiple times.

In this example, each page lists *MainTemplate.jsp* as its view, but specifies different values for the "body" include. When the cv:include tag is encountered in the JSP above, it substitutes the appropriate URL from the XML file.

Reusing the front controller and dispatcher

To support this at the backend, we will extend our earlier Service to Worker example. We will use the same front controller class but create a new dispatcher, the CompositeDispatcher. The composite dispatcher parses the XML file and stores view information in a View object. Example 4-13 shows the View object's interface.

Example 4-13. The View interface

```
public interface View {

    // get the url for a given container and label
    public String getURL(String container, String label);

    // check if there is a record for the given container
    public boolean hasContainer(String container);

    // get the template this view uses
    public String getTemplate();
}
```

Once again, we won't go into the messy details of storing View information or parsing XML. Once the XML is parsed, the CompositeDispatcher stores each view indexed by name in a HashMap called "views." When a request comes in, it expects the page name in a request attribute. The dispatcher simply looks up the appropriate view object and stores it in the request so that the container tags can use it. The getNextPage( ) method of this dispatcher looks like this:

```
    public String getNextPage(HttpServletRequest req,
                              ServletContext context) {
        String page = (String)req.getParameter(PAGE_ATTR);
        View v = (View)views.get(page);
        if (v == null) {
            v = (View)views.get(DEFAULT_VIEW_NAME);
        }

        req.setAttribute(VIEW_ATTR, v);
        return (v.getTemplate( ));
    }
```

Building the custom tags

Once again, JSP custom tags prove to be a powerful and efficient mechanism for extending the view. In this case, using tags in combination with a dispatcher simplifies them even further. Our first tag, the ContainerTag, simply looks up the appropriate container in the View object provided by the dispatcher. If the container exists, it is stored for use by the ContainerIncludeTag. If it does not, the entire contents of the container are skipped. Example 4-14 shows the ContainerTag source.

Example 4-14. ContainerTag.java

```java
import javax.servlet.jsp.tagext.*;
import javax.servlet.jsp.*;
import javax.servlet.*;
import java.io.*;

public class ContainerTag extends TagSupport {
    // the session key for the view object
    private static final String VIEW_ATTR = "view";

    // the name of the container
    private String name;
    // the view object, for use by ContainerIncludeTag
    private View view;

    // determine if the named view exists
    public int doStartTag() throws JspException {
        view = (View)pageContext.getRequest().getAttribute(VIEW_ATTR);

        if (!view.hasContainer(name))
            return SKIP_BODY;

        return EVAL_BODY_INCLUDE;
    }

    // get the stored view
    public View getView() {
        return view;
    }

    // used by the JSP tag to set the name
    public void setName(String value) {
        name = value;
    }

    // get the name of this container
    public String getName() {
        return name;
    }
}
```

The `ContainerIncludeTag` simply uses the stored `View` object to map the include parameters into URIs. It then uses the JSP-provided `pageContext` object to include the view's content. Example 4-15 shows the `ContainerIncludeTag`.

Example 4-15. ContainerIncludeTag.java

```java
import javax.servlet.jsp.tagext.*;
import javax.servlet.jsp.*;
import javax.servlet.*;
import java.io.*;

public class ContainerIncludeTag extends TagSupport {
    // the label of this include
    private String label;

    // get the view object from the parent tag
    // map the given name to a URL and include it
    public int doEndTag() throws JspException {
        // find the parent tag
        ContainerTag ct = (ContainerTag)findAncestorWithClass(this, ContainerTag.class);
        View v = ct.getView();

        // get the view URL
        String viewURL = v.getURL(ct.getName(), label);
        if (viewURL != null) {
            try {
                // include it
                pageContext.include(viewURL);
            } catch( Exception ex ) {
                throw new JspException("Unable to include " +
                                       viewURL, ex);
            }
        }
        return EVAL_PAGE;
    }

    // used to set the name from the JSP tag
    public void setLabel(String value) {
        label = value;
    }
}
```

Using templates

Just like in the Service to Worker example, the XML file format and implementation we have shown here is simplified. There are lots of possible extensions to this basic concept that can make templates a more convenient and powerful tool. One simple extension is to allow values to be substituted directly from XML attributes rather than from a file. For instance, in order to add titles to our web page in the previous example, we would rather not include a whole file with just the title in it. Instead, in the *Views.xml* file, we specify something like:

```xml
<include label="title" text="Page 1" direct="true" />
```

The `<cv:include>` tag reads the direct attribute and substitutes the string `"Page 1"` instead of including an entire page.

When developing a web application, using composite views promotes consistency in the user interface and reusability for views. As with decorators, composite views can cause trouble when they are deeply nested or have too many dependencies.

In this chapter, we looked at three patterns that promote reuse in the presentation tier. All three use the same divide-and-conquer strategy, separating large, specialized components into smaller, resuable pieces. The Service to Worker pattern encapsulates model changes in reusable actions and navigation in a replaceable dispatcher. The View Helper pattern shows how to add reduce specialization in views by delegating tasks to a reusable helper, and the Composite View pattern divides the view into reusable containers and leaves.

CHAPTER 5

Presentation Tier Scalability

Many developers believe design patterns and scalability do not go hand in hand. They argue that patterns add layers to an application, so the server must perform more operations and use more memory to handle each request. The extra operations slow response time down, and the increase in memory means fewer clients can be supported per server. By itself, this is a fair assessment, and if no two requests were alike, it might be the end of the story.

In an enterprise application, however, many clients need to access similar data. On a site that publishes stock quotes, for example, the server may respond to thousands of requests a minute for the same stock. If the price of the stock changes every five minutes, it would be massively inefficient to contact the stock market for each request. Even in an online bank, where every user wants to view personal data, resources such as database connections do not need to be recreated for every request.

Often, we can sacrifice some speed up front for better performance in the average case. While the first request for a particular stock quote or the first connection to a particular database might require a lot of work, subsequent requests will be much faster. It is fair to say the system's scalability will increase: we can support more requests in the same amount of time.

In this chapter, we look at three patterns that increase the scalability of the presentation tier using variations of this concept:

Asynchronous Page
  Shows how to cache data, such as stock prices, and use it to generate dynamic pages.

Caching Filter
  Can be used to cache entire dynamic pages after they are generated.

Resource Pool
  Describes how to create a "pool" of large or expensive objects that can be loaned out as needed, saving instantiation costs.

Scalability and Bottlenecks

Before we jump into the patterns, let's take a minute to discuss what we mean by a *scalable* system. Think of a web-based system as a request processor. Requests come in from the clients, and the clients wait until results are generated. Everything in between—whether it's simply returning the contents of a static file or generating a fully dynamic page—is the actual processing.

For a request processor, scalability is related to the number of requests that can be processed simultaneously. In a simple sense, scalability might be the ability to "survive" a certain number of hits at the same time, eventually delivering a proper response to each one, but we know from experience that this is not really the case. If a news site gets 10,000 simultaneous hits and responds to each of them within 3 seconds, we might say the site scales adequately, if not exceptionally. But if the same site gets 100,000 simultaneous hits, responding to each one within three minutes would not be acceptable.*

A better definition of scalability is a system's ability to grow in order to handle increased demand. Obviously, no single server can be expected to handle an infinite number of requests. In a scalable system, you have options when a single server has reached its maximum capacity. In general, you can:

- Buy a faster server
- Buy more servers

While it may seem obvious that a faster server can handle more requests, it is not always the case. Imagine a bank that stores its total assets in a single record, which must be updated every time money is deposited or withdrawn. If the record can only be updated by one request at a time, the maximum number of transactions will be limited by the time it takes to write this record. Increasing the speed of the server's CPUs might help a little, since the asset total could possibly be updated faster. But the overhead of allowing multiple CPUs to communicate—more processes contending for access to the single resource—could mean that adding CPUs actually decreases overall speed! A single point that limits the scalability of the entire application (like our total asset record) is known as a *bottleneck*.

Potential bottlenecks multiply when you start using multiple servers. Imagine a distributed version of our banking application, with a total asset counter on its own dedicated server. Each request processor will send a message to this server every time money is deposited or withdrawn. Clearly, scalability of this system is still limited by the time it takes to update the total asset counter. But the network between the

---

* For developers, acceptable scalability might be related to what's going on behind the scenes: a dynamic page won't be expected to return as quickly as a static page. Users don't share this nuanced view.

request processors and account server might also limit scalability, as well as the time it takes to translate data to and from a format that can be sent over the network.

In practice, scalability requires tradeoffs. One such tradeoff is between a few large systems and many small systems: many smaller systems are usually cheaper, but the communication can limit scalability. There is also a tradeoff between caching and memory use. Using a large cache may mean that more requests can be served from the cache, and the system therefore will be much faster. However, it also means the memory for the rest of the system is limited, so requests that are not served from the cache may be even slower. The art of building a scalable application is in eliminating unnecessary bottlenecks while balancing code complexity and resource allocation.

Content Caching

One of the best ways to increase scalability is through caching. Caching static pages is a well established practice on the web, and dedicated web caches are taking their place with routers and switches as standard equipment in the data center. A web cache maintains copies of the most frequently requested files, which allows it to serve those requests quickly, without involving the real web server. Most caches rightly ignore dynamically generated pages, as there's no way to efficiently determine whether any two requests should receive the same response (or, for that matter, whether the web server needs to process the request for other reasons).

To create a high performance J2EE environment, we need to bring the benefits of caching to the dynamic components of the presentation tier. In this section, we'll look at two approaches to this problem: caching the input used to generate the dynamic content, and caching the generated content itself.

Caching Content Components

The traditional communication model for web applications is *synchronous*. In other words, clients make requests for URLs and wait until they receive a web page in response. Given the nature of this exchange, it is easy to see why most application logic is implemented in a synchronous manner. As requests come in, the various parts of the response are calculated and correlated, and then the final response is generated. The problem with this approach is that it can be quite inefficient.

In Chapter 4 we discussed a method of adding remote news feeds to a page by building a simple RSS parsing mechanism. Our approach was synchronous: when a request came in for a page containing a news feed, a JSP custom tag read and parsed the remote data and then formatted it for display. If we scale this approach up to the point where we have multiple servers each talking to multiple feeds, we might end up with something like the situation shown in Figure 5-1.

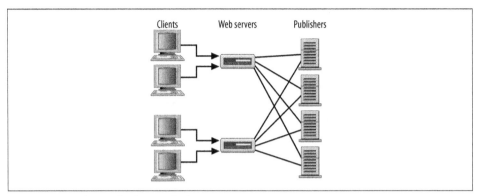

Figure 5-1. Reading multiple news feeds

This approach is inefficient for a number of reasons. Contacting every publisher on every request wastes bandwidth and saturates the publishers' servers. Requests would also be quite expensive in computer resources, since the feed needs to be parsed and translated into HTML on every request. Caching the data on each server should significantly increase the number of clients that can be supported.

While caching represents a significant win for scalability, it does not exploit the fact that news feeds only update intermittently. Having a cache requires a caching policy; for instance, the data could be updated on every tenth request, or every ten minutes. Keeping the data up-to-date still requires each web server to contact the publisher frequently, wasting bandwidth and potentially CPU time. It also means rereading and reparsing the data separately on each server. A better solution would be one where the data was only transmitted when it changed. Figure 5-2 shows the same system using a publish-subscribe model. A single machine, the application server, subscribes to a number of news feeds. When new data becomes available from a particular feed, the data is parsed and sent to all the individual web servers.* Because the data is only sent from the publisher to the subscriber as needed, we say this solution is *asynchronous*. Often, an asynchronous solution requires far less bandwidth than a synchronous one, since data is only sent to the many web servers as needed.

The Asynchronous Page Pattern

The benefits of asynchronous communication are not new. Messaging in particular has been a major component of enterprise backends for a long time. The Java Message APIs and the recent addition of message-driven JavaBeans have solidified the place of asynchronous communication in the Java enterprise architecture. While no standard is currently in place, asynchronous web services are starting to crop up. However, with the exception of a few "push-based" (another term for publish-subscribe) content

---

* We'll discuss publish-subscribe in other contexts and in more detail in Chapter 11.

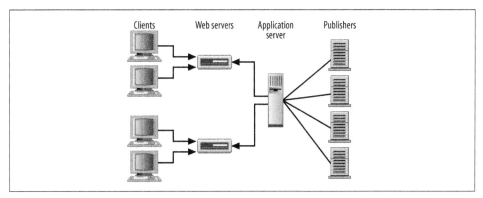

Figure 5-2. A publish-subscribe model

providers, asynchronous communication has never taken off at the client tier because the standard clients—web browsers—do not support publish-subscribe systems.

The lack of browser support for push-based systems does not mean asynchronous communication has no place in a web-based world. It can still be a powerful tool for improving scalability by reducing the work required to handle each transaction.

The *Asynchronous Page pattern* takes advantage of asynchronous retrieval of remote resources to improve scalability and performance. Rather than waiting for a request for a stock quote, for example, a server may accept all stock quotes as they are generated. When a request comes in for a particular quote, the server simply replies with the data it has already received.

Figure 5-3 shows the interactions in the Asynchronous Page pattern. In general, there is a single subscriber that listens to feeds from a number of publishers. As data is updated, the subscriber updates the models of the dependent web applications. When requests come in, the responses incorporate the latest values that have been published.

It's important to note that the interface between the publisher and the subscriber does not need to be push-based. Although it is ideal for the publisher to directly notify the subscriber when there are changes to the data, it is also reasonable to have the subscriber poll the publisher at regular intervals.

The amount of work involved in updating the model can also vary. In some cases, the raw data read from the publisher may be inserted directly into the model unmodified. The pattern is more beneficial, however, when the subscriber processes the data, reducing the work for all the various models. A common tactic is to remove the dynamic page altogether, replacing it with a static page that is simply rewritten each time data is published.

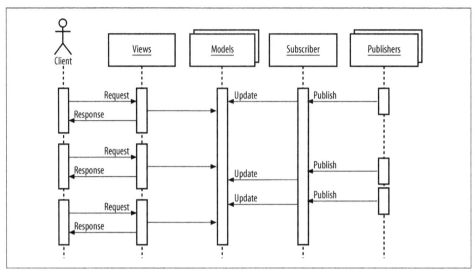

Figure 5-3. Asynchronous Page interactions

Implementing the Asynchronous Page pattern

Let's update our earlier RSS-parsing example to use the Asynchronous Page pattern. Remember, RSS is a standard for sharing news feeds between web sites. It's an XML-based format, and we want to present it as HTML.

Originally, we created a class and two custom tags to flexibly parse RSS. The RSSInfo class reads and parses the RSS from a given URL. Based on this class, we created two tags. The first, RSSChannel, takes a URL as an argument and reads the remote data. Within the RSSChannel tag, two scripting variables store the name of the channel and its link. The RSSItems tag may be nested in an RSSChannel tag. The RSSItems tag iterates through each item in the channel, storing its title and link in scripting variables.

Our problem is that the RSSChannel tag is actually reading the data from the remote source. It would be more efficient if the data were stored locally, and only updated as needed. Unfortunately, RSS does not provide a subscription mechanism, so we must poll the remote data. Rather than go through that process at each read, we want a dedicated mechanism to do the polling and update the local copy. The dedicated mechanism will allow us to read the data from a single, central source, and then distribute it to the actual request processors if it is changed.

In this example, we will add a single class, the RSSSubscriber. RSSSubscriber allows subscriptions to be added to different RSS URLs. Once a subscription is added, a separate thread polls the URL at a specified interval. If the URL is changed, the new data is added to a local cache. All requests after the original are served from this cache. An implementation of the RSSSubscriber class is shown in Example 5-1.

Example 5-1. The RSSSubscriber class

```java
import java.util.*;
import java.io.IOException;

public class RSSSubscriber extends Thread {
    private static final int UPDATE_FREQ = 30 * 1000;

    // internal representation of a subscription
    class RSSSubscription implements Comparable {
        private String url;
        private long nextUpdate;
        private long updateFreq;

        // sort based on next update time
        public int compareTo(Object obj) {
            RSSSubscription rObj = (RSSSubscription)obj;
            if (rObj.nextUpdate > this.nextUpdate) {
                return -1;
            } else if (rObj.nextUpdate < this.nextUpdate) {
                return 1;
            } else {
                // if update time is the same, sort on URL
                return url.compareToIgnoreCase(rObj.url);
            }
        }
    }

    // a set of subscriptions, sorted by next update time
    private SortedSet subscriptions;
    private Map cache;
    private boolean quit = false;

    // singelton subscriber
    private static RSSSubscriber subscriber;

    // get a reference to the singleton
    public static RSSSubscriber getInstance() {
        if (subscriber == null) {
            subscriber = new RSSSubscriber();
            subscriber.start();
        }
        return subscriber;
    }

    RSSSubscriber() {
        subscriptions = new TreeSet();
        cache = Collections.synchronizedMap(new HashMap());
        setDaemon(true);
    }
```

Example 5-1. The RSSSubscriber class (continued)

```
// get an RSSInfo object from cache, or create a new
// subscription if it's not in the cache
public RSSInfo getInfo(String url) throws Exception {
    if (cache.containsKey(url)) {
        return (RSSInfo)cache.get(url);
    }

    // add to cache
    RSSInfo rInfo = new RSSInfo( );
    rInfo.parse(url);
    cache.put(url, rInfo);

    // create new subscription
    RSSSubscription newSub = new RSSSubscription( );
    newSub.url = url;
    newSub.updateFreq = UPDATE_FREQ;
    putSubscription(newSub);

    return rInfo;
}

// add a subscription
private synchronized void putSubscription(RSSSubscription subs)
{
    subs.nextUpdate = System.currentTimeMillis( ) +
                        subs.updateFreq;
    subscriptions.add(subs);
    notify( );
}

// wait for next subscription that needs updating
private synchronized RSSSubscription getSubscription( ) {
    while(!quit) {
        while(subscriptions.size( ) == 0) {
            try { wait( ); } catch(InterruptedException ie) {}
        }

        // get the first subscritpion in the queue
        RSSSubscription nextSub =
            (RSSSubscription)subscriptions.first( );

        // determine if it is time to update yet
        long curTime = System.currentTimeMillis( );
        if(curTime >= nextSub.nextUpdate) {
            subscriptions.remove(nextSub);
            return nextSub;
        }

        // sleep until the next update time
        // this will be interrupted if a subscription is added
        try {
            wait(nextSub.nextUpdate - curTime);
```

Example 5-1. The RSSSubscriber class (continued)

```
            } catch(InterruptedException ie) {}
        }
    }

    // update subscriptions as they become available
    public void run( ) {
        while(!quit) {
            RSSSubscription subs = getSubscription( );

            try {
                RSSInfo rInfo = new RSSInfo( );
                rInfo.parse(subs.url);
                cache.put(subs.url, rInfo);
            } catch(Exception ex) {
                ex.printStackTrace( );
            }

            putSubscription(subs);
        }
    }

    public synchronized void quit( ) {
        quit = true;
        notify( );
    }
}
```

Our new RSS subscription mechanism runs on a single host, but it is easy to see how it could be extended to multiple servers. In any case, it supports more simultaneous requests by having a dedicated thread for updating and parsing requests. Except for the initial request for a given subscription, no thread ever has to block on reading or parsing the remote data. It is effectively done in the background.

To use the RSSSubscriber, our custom tag simply calls getRSSInfo( ) for the URL it is passed. getRSSInfo( ) will read the data from the cache when possible and create a new subscription when it is not. Example 5-2 shows the custom tag class.

Example 5-2. The RSSChannelTag class

```
import javax.servlet.*;
import javax.servlet.jsp.*;
import javax.servlet.jsp.tagext.*;

public class RSSChannelTag extends BodyTagSupport {
    private static final String NAME_ATTR = "channelName";
    private static final String LINK_ATTR = "channelLink";

    private String url;
    private RSSSubscriber rssSubs;

    public RSSChannelTag( ) {
```

Example 5-2. The RSSChannelTag class (continued)

```
        rssSubs = RSSSubscriber.getInstance( );
    }

    public void setURL(String url) {
        this.url = url;
    }

    // get the latest RSSInfo object from the subscriber
    // this method is called by the RSSItems tag as well
    protected RSSInfo getRSSInfo( ) {
        try {
            return rssSubs.getInfo(url);
        } catch(Exception ex) {
            ex.printStackTrace( );
        }

        return null;
    }

    // use the updated RSSInfo object
    public int doStartTag( ) throws JspException {
        try {
            RSSInfo rssInfo = getRSSInfo( );
            pageContext.setAttribute(NAME_ATTR,
                                rssInfo.getChannelTitle( ));
            pageContext.setAttribute(LINK_ATTR,
                                rssInfo.getChannelLink( ));
        } catch (Exception ex) {
            throw new JspException("Unable to parse " + url, ex);
        }
        return Tag.EVAL_BODY_INCLUDE;
    }
}
```

Although the RSS reading example is simple, it shows one of the many opportunities for asynchronous communication in a request-driven environment. The opportunity, of course, depends on how the data is accessed. Imagine accepting, parsing, and storing a quote for every stock on the NYSE, and only getting one or two requests for quotes before it is all updated again. The time and memory expended receiving these values asynchronously would be wasted. Of course, in some applications it's not acceptable to have any out-of-date data—like when you're transferring money at an ATM. In evaluating asynchronous methods, it is important to take into account the costs in terms of data staleness, network use, and memory use, as balanced against the benefits of speed and scalability.

Dynamic Content Caching

There is another class of dynamic data that is amenable to caching. Imagine an online car dealership where users go through a few pages selecting various options and then view the resulting car's price. The price computation could be a lengthy process, possibly accessing an external system that's also used by dealers, or even one that keeps track of dealer stock.

Certain cars and options—the sport package, a sunroof—are far more common than others. Since the same set of options always yields the same price, it's inefficient to recalculate it every time. Even worse for the efficiency of the site is all the overhead of generating the page dynamically: querying prices in the database and assembling multiple views into a composite. We would like to cache the page with the price calculated and the HTML generated.

In a perfect world, the application itself would not have to worry about caching at all. HTTP 1.1 allows caching dynamic GET requests, as long as we set the correct HTTP header fields.* Once these fields are set, the client, an intermediate cache, or even the HTTP server can do the caching. In practice, however, we frequently have to do it ourselves.

The Caching Filter Pattern

The *Caching Filter pattern* uses a servlet filter to cache dynamically generated pages. We talked a fair bit about filters, including their capabilities and implementation, when we talked about the Decorator pattern in Chapter 3. The caching filter is a specific implementation of a decorator. When applied to the front controller, it caches fully generated dynamic pages. The classes in the Caching Filter pattern are shown in Figure 5-4.

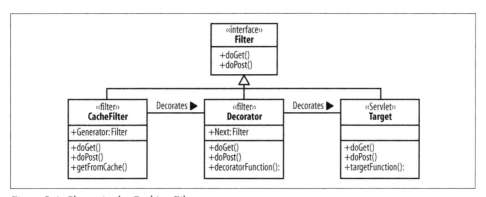

Figure 5-4. Classes in the Caching Filter pattern

The CacheFilter itself works just like any other filter: it presents the API of its one child. It also provides extra methods to read pages from the cache as well as to add the results of executing a particular request to the cache. When a request comes in,

---

* For more information on the variety of caching options available in HTTP 1.1, see section 13 of RFC 2616, available from: *http://www.w3.org/Protocols/rfc2616/rfc2616-sec13.html#sec13.*

the cached page is simply returned if it exists. If the page is not cached, the rest of the chain must be executed and the result stored in the cache. The process of handling a request is shown in Figure 5-5.

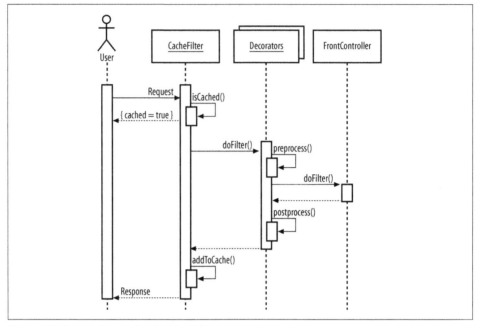

Figure 5-5. Interactions in the Caching Filter pattern

It is important to think about where caching filters are positioned in the filter chain. In principle, a caching filter can be added anywhere in the chain, caching the results from all the filters after it. There can even be multiple caches at different levels in the chain, perhaps caching part of the processing while still doing some of it dynamically.

 One frequent mistake is putting caches before security measures. This can lead to unauthorized clients reading cached copies of the data. If a filter is being used for security, it should come before the cache in the chain.

Implementing a Caching Filter

In order to cache the data, we need to change how data is communicated to the server. In many cases, the client simply requests the next page without passing all relevant parameters. The controller uses a combination of the requested page and parameters stored in the session to generate the final output. The client's request might look like:

```
GET /pages/finalPrice.jsp HTTP/1.1
```

To which the server would add its stored entries about the selected options. Unfortunately, the GET request looks exactly the same, regardless of the options selected. The fact that the user wants electric blue paint and alloy wheels is not reflected in the request at all. To find a cached page, the session variables would have to be read, sacrificing some of the speed gained by caching.

Instead, the URL should contain all the options in the query string. By including the options, our request might look like:

```
GET /pages/finalPrice.jsp?paint=Electric+Blue&Wheels=Alloy
```

We can implement the most efficient caching when the query string fully specifies the page (see the sidebar "GET, POST, and Idempotence").

GET, POST, and Idempotence

The HTTP 1.1 specification declares that GET requests are *idempotent*, which is Latin for "the same thing can be done." An idempotent action can be repeated as many times as necessary without any ill effects. Our car manufacturer example is an idempotent activity: you can request a final price on the car as many times as you want, without affecting the price.

Actually purchasing the car, however, is anything but idempotent. That's why HTTP provides the POST method to send information to a server. POSTs are not idempotent, which is why sometimes hitting the reload button in a browser brings up a message saying that a form must be resubmitted if the reload is to occur. POST requests have the side benefit of hiding the submitted information from the user (the query parameters don't appear on the browser's location display) and from anyone perusing the server's log files. Credit card information, for example, should only be transferred via a POST, even if you're also using SSL.

Because of idempotence, when implementing caching for dynamic content, we only do it for content generated via GET requests, and even then it's up to the developer to determine when caching is a safe approach.

To implement a caching filter, we will use the servlet's filter API. As we did in Chapter 3, we will decorate the response object we pass down the filter chain with one that stores the results of processing the rest of the chain. This wrapper is implemented in the CacheResponseWrapper class, shown in Example 5-3.

Example 5-3. The CacheResponseWrapper

```
public class CacheResponseWrapper extends HttpServletResponseWrapper {
  // the replacement OutputStream
  private CacheOutputStream replaceStream;
  // the replacement writer
  private PrintWriter replaceWriter;
```

Example 5-3. The CacheResponseWrapper (continued)

```java
// a simple implementation of ServletOutputStream
// that stores the data written to it
class CacheOutputStream extends ServletOutputStream {
  private ByteArrayOutputStream bos;

  CacheOutputStream( ) {
    bos = new ByteArrayOutputStream( );
  }

  public void write(int param) throws IOException {
    bos.write(param);
  }

  // read back the stored data
  protected byte[] getBytes( ) {
    return bos.toByteArray( );
  }
}

public CacheResponseWrapper(HttpServletResponse original) {
  super(original);
}

public ServletOutputStream getOutputStream( )
throws IOException {
  if (replaceStream != null)
    return replaceStream;

  // make sure we have only one OutputStream or Writer
  if (replaceWriter != null)
    throw new IOException("Writer already in use");

  replaceStream = new CacheOutputStream( );

  return replaceStream;
}

public PrintWriter getWriter( ) throws IOException {
  if (replaceWriter != null)
    return replaceWriter;

  // make sure we have only one OutputStream or Writer
  if (replaceStream != null)
    throw new IOException("OutputStream already in use");

  replaceWriter = new PrintWriter(
      new OutputStreamWriter(new CacheOutputStream( )));

  return replaceWriter;
}

// read back the stored data
```

Example 5-3. The CacheResponseWrapper (continued)

```
  protected byte[] getBytes( ) {
    if (replaceStream == null)
      return null;

    return replaceStream.getBytes( );
  }
}
```

By passing a CacheResponseWrapper to the next filter in the chain, we can store the output in a byte array, which can then be cached in memory or to disk.

The actual caching filter is fairly simple. When a request comes in, it determines if the page can be cached or not. If it can, the filter checks to see if it is in the cache and either returns the cached version or generates a new page and adds that to the cache. The filter code is shown in Example 5-4.

Example 5-4. The CacheFilter class

```
public class CacheFilter implements Filter {
  private FilterConfig filterConfig;

  // the data cache
  private HashMap cache;

  public void doFilter(ServletRequest request,
                       ServletResponse response,
                       FilterChain chain)
  throws IOException, ServletException
  {
    HttpServletRequest req = (HttpServletRequest)request;
    HttpServletResponse res = (HttpServletResponse)response;

    // the cache key is the URI + query string
    String key = req.getRequestURI() + "?" + req.getQueryString( );

    // only cache GET requests which contain cacheable data
    if (req.getMethod( ).equalsIgnoreCase("get") && isCacheable(key))
    {
      // try to retrieve the data from the cache
      byte[] data = (byte[]) cache.get(key);

      // on a cache miss, generate the result normally and
      // add it to the cache
      if (data == null) {
        CacheResponseWrapper crw = new CacheResponseWrapper(res);
        chain.doFilter(request, crw);
        data = crw.getBytes( );
        cache.put(key, data);
      }

      // if the data was found or added to the cache,
      // generate the result from the cached data
```

Example 5-4. The CacheFilter class (continued)

```
    if (data != null) {
      res.setContentType("text/html");
      res.setContentLength(data.length);

      try {
        OutputStream os = res.getOutputStream( );
        os.write(data);
        os.close( );
        return;
      } catch(Exception ex) {
        ...
      }
    }
  }

  // generate the data normally if it was not cacheable
  // or the cache failed for any reason
  chain.doFilter(request, response);
}

// determine if the data is cacheable
private boolean isCacheable(String key) {
  ...
}

// initialize the cache
public void init(FilterConfig filterConfig) {
  this.filterConfig = filterConfig;

  cache = new HashMap( );
}
}
```

Notice that we haven't made the cache variable static. According to the filter specification, only one filter instance will be created for each `filter` element in the deployment descriptor. We can therefore keep separate caches in each filter, allowing multiple caches at different points in the filter chain, without worrying about spreading the same data across multiple cache objects.

Our simple filter avoids two of the difficult parts of caching. The first is determining if a page can be cached at all. In most environments, there will be a mix of cacheable and uncachable pages. In our car dealership example, the various configurations of cars may be cacheable, but a user's credit card information certainly isn't! A typical solution is to provide a mapping, like a servlet or filter mapping in an XML file, to determine which pages can be cached.

The second difficulty this filter avoids is cache coherency. Our model assumes the generated page will never change. If the prices for certain options change, users will still see the old, cached copy of the page. Many coherency strategies are possible, depending on the nature of the generated pages; at the minimum, pages should expire from the cache

---

after some predefined period. If they don't, the cache grows without bounds, a situation discussed in Chapter 12, when we cover the Leak Collection antipattern.

Resource Pool

A *resource pool* is a collection of precreated objects that can be loaned out to save the expense of creating them many times. Examples of resource pools are everywhere in J2EE. When a connection comes in, a thread is retrieved from a thread pool to handle the request. If the processing requires an EJB, one may be allocated from a pool of EJBs. And if the EJB requires access to a database, the connection will come from—surprise!—a connection pool.

Pools are so prevalent because they solve two problems simultaneously: they improve scalability by sharing the cost of instantiating complex resources over multiple instances, and they allow precise tuning of parallelism and memory use.

To illustrate, let's discuss the classic use case for pools: database connections. The process of connecting to a database, especially a remote one, can be complex and costly. While it may only require a single method call, instantiating a database connection may involve any or all of the following steps:

1. Instantiate the database connection object.
2. Pass in the database address and user credentials.
3. Create a network connection to the database.
4. Perform a complex handshake to determine supported options.
5. Send user credentials to database.
6. Verify the user's credentials.

After all of these steps, the connection is finally ready to use. It's not just expensive in terms of time, either. The connection object must store many of the options it is passed, so each connection requires a fair bit of memory, too. If connections are not shared, the connections and costs grow with the number of requests. As the costs add up, the need to create and maintain database connections limits the number of clients that an application can support.

Obviously, sharing connections is a must for scalability, but sharing has costs, too. At the extreme, you could develop an entire application with a single database connection shared between all the clients. While this effectively removes the cost of creating the database connection, it limits parallelism since access to the database must be synchronized in some way. Sharing database connections also prevents individual components of the application from engaging in transactions (see Chapter 10).

A better solution is to create a number of connections that are shared in a common "pool" between clients. When a client needs access to a database, the client takes a connection from the pool and uses it. When the client is done, it returns the connection so another client can use it. Because the connections are shared, the startup and maintenance costs are amortized over many clients. The number of connections has an upward boundary, so the creation and maintenance costs don't spiral out of control.

Another major advantage of pools is that they create a single point for effective tuning. Putting more objects in the pool uses more memory and increases startup time, but usually means you can support more clients. Conversely, a smaller pool often improves scalability by preventing a single operation from hogging memory and CPU time. By changing the pool parameters at runtime, the memory and CPU usage can be tailored to each system the application runs on.

The Resource Pool Pattern

The *Resource Pool pattern* can be applied to many costly operations. Pools show the most benefits for objects like database connections and threads that have high startup costs. In these cases, the pattern amortizes the startup costs over multiple objects. But pools can also be adapted for operations—like parsing—that simply take a long time, allowing fine-grained control of memory and CPU usage. Figure 5-6 shows a generalization of a resource pool.

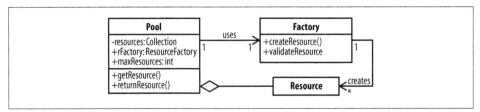

Figure 5-6. The Resource Pool pattern

The `Pool` object is responsible for creating, maintaining, and controlling access to the `Resource` objects. A client calls the `getResource()` method to get an instance of the resource. When it is finished, it uses the `returnResource()` method to add the resource back to the pool.

The pool uses a `Factory` object to create the actual resources. By using a factory, the same pool can work for many different kinds of objects. The factory's `createResource()` method is used to generate new instances of a resource. Before a resource is reused, the pool calls the factory's `validateResource()` method to reset the resource to its initial state. If, for example, the resource is a database connection that has been closed, the `validateResource()` method can simply return `false` to have a new connection added to the pool instead. For further efficiency, the factory may even try to repair the returned object—say, by reopening the database connection. This is sometimes called a *recycler method*.

There are really no limits on the `Resource` class itself. The contents and use of a resource must be coordinated between the creator of the pool and the various clients. Usually, pools only store one type of object, but this is not required. Advanced implementations of pools sometimes even allow a filter to be provided to the getResource( ) method in order to specify desired criteria of the resource.

Implementing a Resource Pool

Within a servlet engine, a pool of threads handles requests. Each request is handled by a single thread from this pool, which accesses shared instances of servlets to generate the result. In most application servers, the number of threads in the thread pool is configurable at runtime. The number of threads is a critical variable for tuning the scalability of your web application: if the pool is too small, clients will be rejected or delayed; if the pool is too large, the server can't to keep up and the application runs slowly.

Just because the servlet threads are already pooled does not mean we are done with pools. The servlet thread pool represents the most coarse-grained pool possible. Using a single pool assumes that the same thing limits all requests: for example, the speed of XML parsing or connecting to the database. In reality, different requests are usually limited by different operations. Having a separate pool for XML parsers and database connections could allow the total number of threads to be increased, with the limits placed at parsing or connection time, depending on the type of request.

As the pattern description suggests, implementing a resource pool in Java is quite simple. We would like our resource pool to be generic, so that we can easily create a pool of any object by writing an appropriate factory. Obviously, our pool needs to be thread-safe, as we assume that multiple threads will access it simultaneously (any pool used in a servlet environment will face this situation). Example 5-5 shows a simple pool implementation.

Example 5-5. ResourcePool.java

```java
import java.util.*;

public class ResourcePool {
    private ResourceFactory factory;
    private int maxObjects;
    private int curObjects;
    private boolean quit;

    // resources we have loaned out
    private Set outResources;

    // resources we have waiting
    private List inResources;

    public ResourcePool(ResourceFactory factory, int maxObjects) {
        this.factory = factory;
        this.maxObjects = maxObjects;

        curObjects = 0;

        outResources = new HashSet(maxObjects);
        inResources = new LinkedList();
    }
```

Example 5-5. ResourcePool.java (continued)

```java
    // retrieve a resource from the pool
    public synchronized Object getResource() throws Exception {
        while(!quit) {

            // first, try to find an existing resource
            if (!inResources.isEmpty()) {
                Object o = inResources.remove(0);

                // if the resource is invalid, create a replacement
                if(!factory.validateResource(o))
                    o = factory.createResource();

                outResources.add(o);
                return o;
            }

            // next, create a new resource if we haven't
            // reached the limit yet
            if(curObjects < maxObjects) {
                Object o = factory.createResource();
                outResources.add(o);
                curObjects++;

                return o;
            }

            // if no resources are available, wait until one
            // is returned
            try { wait(); } catch(Exception ex) {}
        }

        // pool is destroyed
        return null;
    }

    // return a resource to the pool
    public synchronized void returnResource(Object o) {

        // Something is wrong.  Just give up.
        if(!outResources.remove(o))
            throw new IllegalStateException("Returned item not in pool");

        inResources.add(o);
        notify();
    }

    public synchronized void destroy() {
        quit = true;
        notifyAll();
    }
}
```

Example 5-5 assumes the very simple factory interface we sketched earlier:

```
public interface ResourceFactory {
    public Object createResource();
    public boolean validateResource(Object o);
}
```

To see resource pools in action, let's look at an operation that is used frequently but rarely pooled: XML parsing. Like database connections, XML parsers can be expensive to create and maintain. By using a pool of parsers, we not only share the cost of creating them, we can control how many threads are performing expensive XML parsing operations at any given time. To create a pool of parsers, all we have to build is the XMLParserFactory shown in Example 5-6.

Example 5-6. XMLParserFactory

```
import javax.xml.parsers.*;

public class XMLParserFactory implements ResourceFactory {
    DocumentBuilderFactory dbf;

    public XMLParserFactory() {
        dbf = DocumentBuilderFactory.newInstance();
    }

    // create a new DocumentBuilder to add to the pool
    public Object createResource() {
        try {
            return dbf.newDocumentBuilder();
        } catch (ParserConfigurationException pce) {
            ...
            return null;
        }
    }

    // check that a returned DocumentBuilder is valid
    // and reset parameters to defaults
    public boolean validateResource(Object o) {
        if (!(o instanceof DocumentBuilder)) {
            return false;
        }

        DocumentBuilder db = (DocumentBuilder) o;
        db.setEntityResolver(null);
        db.setErrorHandler(null);

        return true;
    }
}
```

To use our pooled XML parsing mechanism, a simple client might look like:

```
public class XMLClient implements Runnable {
    private ResourcePool pool;
```

```
public XMLClient(int poolsize) {
    pool = new ResourcePool(new XMLParserFactory( ), poolsize);
    ...
    // start threads, etc.
    Thread t = new Thread(this);
    t.start( );
    ...
    // wait for threads
    t.join( );
    // cleanup
    pool.destroy( );
}

public void run( ) {
    try {
        // get parser from pool
        DocumentBuilder db = (DocumentBuilder)pool.getResource( );
    } catch(Exception ex) {
        return;
    }

    try {
        ...
        // do parsing
        ...
    } catch(Exception ex) {
        ...
    } finally {
        // make sure to always return resources we checkout
        pool.returnResource(db);
    }
}
}
```

Resource pools look good on paper, but do they actually help for XML parsing? And if we are going to use them, how do we choose the correct size? Let's take a minute to look at the real-world use and performance of pools.

An important step in using a pool is sizing it properly. For our test systems, we used a two-CPU server and a six-CPU server, both with plenty of memory; we expected to be able to handle a fair number of threads. Using a sample program similar to the one outlined above, we looked at how long it took to parse a 2,000-line XML file with various combinations of number of threads and pool size. Table 5-1 shows the optimal pool size for each thread count on each server. It's not surprising that for a CPU-limited task like XML parsing, the optimal pool size is generally pretty close to the number of CPUs in the system. For an I/O-limited task, like reading data from the network, we would expect very different results.

Table 5-1. Optimal pool sizes for various numbers of threads

Thread count	Optimal pool size 2 CPUs	Optimal pool size 6 CPUs
1	1	1
2	2	2
4	4	4
8	2	8
16	2	15
32	2	6
64	2	6
128	2	6
256	2	6
512	2	4
1024	2	6

Now that we have optimal pool sizes worked out, we can see the scalability improvements. We tried two variations of the sample program, one with the optimal pool size, and one with no pool, and compared the time required per thread. Figure 5-7 shows the results of our experiment.

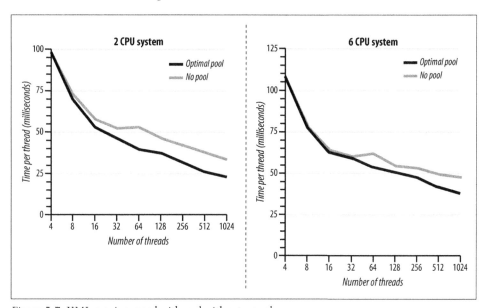

Figure 5-7. XML parsing speed with and without a pool

The pool gives a significant advantage, especially when more than 32 threads are active. These results fit into our theory that pools increase scalability for CPU-intensive tasks by limiting the overhead of switching between too many tasks at once. It should not be surprising that in addition to the speed gains we saw with pools, there was also much less variation between different trials with the same number of threads when pools were in use.

In this chapter, we looked at three patterns that increase the scalability of the presentation tier. The Asynchronous Page pattern shows how to cache data when it is read from external sources. The Caching Filter pattern describes how to cache entire pages as they are generated. The Resource Pool pattern creates a pool of expensive objects that can be loaned out. All these patterns also allow the developer to tune the application, balancing memory and CPU use for the entire system.

CHAPTER 6

The Business Tier

The word "enterprise" has a long and storied association with business. Adam Smith used the word in *The Wealth of Nations* back in 1776, and the antecedents go back another century. So, it's no wonder that when we talk about applications that support business processes we call them *enterprise applications*. The value of the application is bound up in the complexity of the business processes it represents, and in the amount of human effort the software removes from the equation. Virtually any large organization can benefit from properly deployed technology, from elementary schools to multinational corporations, and from volunteer groups to open source projects. In all of these situations, the value of the application depends on how well it supports the underlying business model.

This chapter introduces the business tier. We'll talk briefly about business models and business tier components, and draw some distinctions between them. The patterns in this chapter cover the domain model, which defines the entities that interact within your system, and the business logic, which defines the different actions that can be performed on the domain model. Our primary focus is on flexibility and extensibility: patterns that make it easier to balance the performance requirements of today with the inevitable change requests of tomorrow.

Business tiers are about complexity, memory, and scale. Business tiers are *complex* because they implement the rules the business must follow. The rules themselves can be simple ("mark each item shipped as removed from inventory," "when shipping to Massachusetts, add a 5% sales tax") but the interconnected system of rules can rapidly become more than any one person can easily handle. *Memory*, in the long-term recollection sense rather than the hardware sense, is important because businesses need to record every activity they participate in. Humans aren't well equipped to do this reliably, at least without tools and time. Finally, business tiers are about *scale*. Even if process and record-keeping activities are simple enough to be done by hand, repeating them several thousand times over the course of a day is costly, error-prone, and inflexible.*

---

* You can't run a query against a filing cabinet.

In the business tier, more than anywhere else, you have to keep an eye out for the unexpected. Creating domain models and business logic that meet the growth requirements of the environment presents a challenge to system architects. Even when the initial application requirements may not seem to impose much in terms of complexity, memory, and scale, change is inevitable. Business tiers require a substantial investment, so once created, they tend to be used and extended over the long haul. In fact, we rarely see successful enterprise applications enter an end-of-life stage. They're much more likely to be incorporated as a component of something else. Fifteen years from now there will be a vendor making a lot of money selling adapters to incorporate your old J2EE applications into whatever happens to be the new dominant environment. You'll often do the same thing yourself, integrating existing legacy systems into new J2EE frameworks.

A poorly implemented business tier imposes limitations on a system that fancy user interfaces can't overcome. On the other hand, a difficult user interface, or a middle tier that is slow or difficult to extend, prevents effective use of even the best-designed business and domain logic. A full J2EE application is an integrated whole, however compartmentalized it may be, that makes each tier more or less equally important. The art is in the interfaces that create the smoothly functioning whole. The business logic and domain model are the starting point that everything else grows out of.

Making the business tier a distinct, and somewhat isolated, section of the system helps us rope all these issues together. By implementing the business components separately from the presentation components, we can realize all the benefits we've been talking about over the last several chapters. The business tier presents interfaces to the presentation tier, exposing both business logic and possibly domain objects (we'll see in Chapter 7 why this isn't always necessary), but the business tier knows nothing of the presentation tier. It never generates HTML for web pages. In the same way, the object that represents a customer does not need to know how it is used; it only has to provide specific information on request.

While reading this chapter and those that follow, you may note that we harp quite a bit on the issue of network overhead. We do this not because we can't think of anything else to talk about, but because it's one of the most common performance killers in a distributed application, and J2EE applications are almost always distributed applications. Scale is very important. As we discussed in Chapters 1 and 5, any midsize application (a few thousand users) should be able to support at least twice its current maximum load without substantial hardware or software upgrades, and should be further scalable with relatively minor additional effort.

This chapter, and the three that follow, are about implementing the model for your application—the M in MVC. This chapter focuses on the business tier itself: the representation of the business processes underlying an application. In the next chapter, we'll look at some of the mechanisms for exchanging data between the business tier and the presentation tier. Chapter 8 returns to implementation and discusses database patterns for implementing the domain objects, and Chapter 9 wraps up with a discussion of business tier interfaces: the frontends the business tier delivers to the presentation tier.

The Business Tier

There are several ways to slice up a J2EE application. It's quite common to hear the phrases *domain logic*, *business logic*, *business object*, *business tier*, and other variants tossed around with wild abandon, resulting in more than a little confusion. What is the business tier? Is the application server part of the business tier, or does it enable the business tier? What about the database? The tables in the database? The servlet container?

All business tiers, as we use the term, have two functions in common. Business tiers:

- Provide a structured model for application data.
- Provide procedures for performing business-related activities.

Most also share the following characteristics. Business tiers:

- Are shared by multiple clients.
- Provide a framework for transactions, ensuring that the information in the domain model remains in a valid state.
- Provide a persistence mechanism for application data.

Most enterprise applications ultimately serve multiple clients, whether different types of clients (servlet applications versus Swing GUIs) or multiple instances of the same type (10,000 Swing GUIs, or an array of web servers). Most applications will use some transaction functionality at least once, but transaction implementations can be done via JTA, EJB, JDBC, or raw objects, depending on the needs and desires of the designer. Persistence is commonly associated with the transaction logic, often via JDBC and a database. Chapter 10 is devoted to transactions and concurrency management, so we'll skip lightly over it here.

The persistence mechanism, although we've listed it under the "most" heading, is essentially universal. Of course, the method by which different applications implement the persistence mechanism varies tremendously, from serialized objects to Enterprise JavaBeans, to database tables and JDBC. The business tier itself might be housed in a complex application server or as a humble application in a standalone JRE (or, quite frequently, in the same JRE as the presentation tier).

Business Tier Components

The standard J2EE application model defines a Server Side Business Logic layer, implemented via EJBs or other objects, which optionally accesses Enterprise Information Systems. We don't find that view quite as helpful, because it doesn't address what we actually put into the system: just how we'd implement it.

For the purposes of this chapter and those that follow, we subdivide the business tier into three parts: the *visible business tier*, the *resource layer*, and the *enterprise layer*. The visible business tier is what's exposed to the presentation tier, while the resource and enterprise layers provide the services that allow the visible portion of the business tier to do its job.

Although the business tier can be subdivided, it isn't the same kind of subdivision that we get with the tiers themselves. The coupling between the various components that make up the business tier generally has to be quite tight: you can't create a new set of domain objects and expect all the business logic to work properly. However, with proper compartmentalization, you retain some flexibility. In most applications, the business logic isn't tightly coupled to a particular database, and as a result we can potentially change the underlying database without having to rewrite the business process code.

Figure 6-1 shows a view of the business tier. Not every business tier will look like this, of course. Components higher on the chart access components that are lower on the chart, either directly or through intermediaries. Process logic, for instance, accesses domain objects and the enterprise layer.

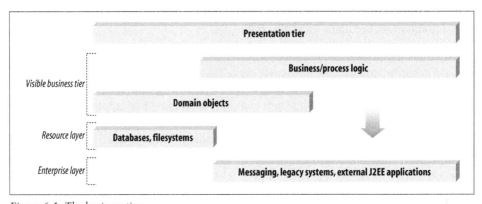

Figure 6-1. The business tier

Business tier components

Domain objects represent the "nouns" of the application. They're the concrete things that map to real or virtual concepts within the application. Objects (or database tables) represent customers, orders, stock items, user accounts, outstanding invoices, clinical measurements, or anything else that could substitute for one of the blanks in "a ___ is related to a ___."

The *business logic* reflects the *business process*. A business process is the set of steps required to fulfill one of the system's use cases, and can be thought of as a "verb" or a system activity. Business processes don't have a life of their own except in the project management sense: once the process is complete, a record may be kept for analysis, but an instance of the process itself only exists while it works towards a particular goal. For example, when an order is shipped, the order process is complete. (The domain object containing the record of the order, however, is permanent.)

Put together, domain objects and business logic are sometimes known as the *domain model*. They represent the "domain" of an application, including both the physical entities and the processes.

Figure 6-1 subdivides the business logic layer into domain objects and *process logic* (the business processes). The process logic manipulates the domain objects. In some cases, the process logic is the only part of the application visible to any of the lower tiers. For example, a J2EE application might embed process logic in EJB session beans, or via a web services interface. The session beans or web service backend are responsible for interacting with the domain objects. This is good practice, but it doesn't make sense for every aspect of every possible application.

Both domain objects and business logic are subject to *business rules*. A business rule might state that a particular order is associated with one and only one customer, or that employees may only report to managers and not to programmers. The business rules for the domain apply regardless of the application. For example, an orders system and an inventory system that deal with the same domain (stock management) could theoretically use the same domain model. The business rules embedded in the model should apply equally to either application. These rules don't show up on the diagram in Figure 6-1, but instead constrain the actions of the various pieces of the business logic layer.

Supporting players

The *resource layer* in a J2EE application is typically a database, but it can include any persistent storage mechanisms, both locally (on disk) or remotely (in messaging, transaction management, and other support systems). Chapter 8 is devoted to the patterns that apply to the resource layer. The resource layer should be largely invisible to the presentation tier, which interacts only with the business logic objects.

Finally, the *enterprise layer* consists of connections to other systems, whether they're legacy systems, J2EE systems, or web services. Business processes often involve handoffs to external systems. Sometimes these exchanges are handled quickly in near real time (such as a credit card authorization for an online merchant) and sometimes asynchronously (such as a request to approve a mortgage application). Chapter 11 addresses intersystem integration in detail.

Literature on software architecture often mentions *business services*. In a well-designed application that is properly divided into components that have fully defined interfaces between them, a business service is simply another phrase for a business tier component.

Business Tier Services

A service is a software component that performs an action on behalf of another component. A typical action might involve retrieving a piece of information for a client, or performing a specific operation for that client, often on a remote resource.

Directories are probably the most common software service, and are a good illustration of a service because they provide access to both information and resources. A corporate LDAP directory is an example of a directory that accesses information. Normally, the directory maintains all sorts of information about employees, including simple items like names and phone numbers, as well as more complex relationships, such as whom individual employees work for. A UDDI directory, on the other hand, returns resources: rather than providing information directly, it points an application towards a web service that can help.

When a Java application accesses an LDAP directory, it doesn't manipulate an object representation of that directory. Instead, it issues a request for specific information through the generic Java Naming and Directory Interface (JNDI). The request must explicitly state exactly what information is required (either by providing a specific name or a set of criteria); in response to the request, JNDI returns an object containing the requested information. If the application needs to update the directory, and has permission to do so, it can pass the object back, again specifying exactly how the directory should store it.

In each case, the service interface acts as the medium of exchange. Other business services, including web services, work the same way, fielding requests for information or actions and returning responses.

The most important thing to remember is that web services in particular are not inherently stateful. Each service call contains all the information required to complete a request, whether the service call is requesting the name of an object, asking that an equation be solved, or providing a business transaction to post. Of course, stateful remote components do exist: they're just called distributed objects.

Domain Objects

The patterns in this chapter focus on important aspects of business tier development. We start with the *Domain Object Model,* which is at the heart of most large J2EE applications. The Domain Object Model defines an object-oriented representation of the underlying data of an application. The benefits of this approach should be familiar by now: the tiers integrating with the business tier become simpler and are decoupled from the implementation of the business tier, allowing changes to the resource layer level implementation without affecting the UI components. Business processes can be included in the domain object model via methods attached to the entity objects in the model or to specialized objects.

We'll also look at the *Composite Entity pattern*, which provides a guideline for building domain objects in an efficient way. The goal is to balance flexibility and efficiency by creating object representations that can be used in the most efficient way.

Domain Object Model

The domain model is the portion of the business tier that defines the actual data and processes managed and implemented by the system. The process for creating an effective domain model varies depending on the project, the information available, and the future requirements of the system.

The *Domain Object Model pattern* is central to most J2EE applications. The pattern is fundamentally simple: create a Java object model that represents the concepts in the underlying domain. This may seem obvious, and you may even question whether it should be considered a pattern at all. It's certainly intrinsic to EJB. On the other hand, it's possible to build applications with J2EE technology that don't use a formalized domain model at all, and it's possible to build a domain object model without using EJB.

Many web applications get along fine without a domain object model. They keep their domain model entirely in the database component, never building an object representation. In this case, the model is relational rather than object-oriented: two-dimensional tables full of data, linked to other tables via a set of shared keys. The application updates the model by executing SQL statements directly from servlets, and produces HTML pages the same way. In some cases, business process information is also held in the database, in the form of stored procedures, or it is embedded in the servlet tier.

In contrast, a domain object model represents the application's entities (which would otherwise be found in database tables) and processes (which would otherwise be scattered throughout the application). The ultimate repository may still be a relational database, and the objects that make up the model are responsible for persisting themselves to the database in an appropriate way. The presentation tier can access the Java objects instead of manipulating the database directly. In building a domain object model, we translate the business model into object terms.

Figure 6-2 shows a simple domain object model for a system that issues government IDs. We'll leave the potential civil liberties issues inherent in this system aside, and focus on the domain modeling issues instead. We have three classes, one for the federal government, one for the state governments, and one for citizens. The federal government can be associated with multiple state governments, which can have multiple citizens. We also have four classes that perform business activities. The Passport Issue class uses the federal government and the citizen classes to issue a passport. The State License Issue class is abstract, and is extended by two other classes that issue particular kinds of state ID cards.

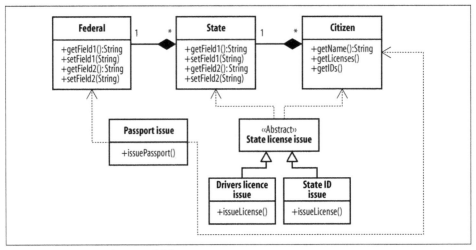

Figure 6-2. Domain Object Model for government IDs

This is a simple example, but it's amazing how many development projects get going without nailing these relationships down as much as possible at the start.

Next, we'll take a look at how we might get to this model.*

Building an Object Model

The analysis process for building an object model depends on the project, resources available, and processes within a particular organization. We find the following general approach to be both prevalent and useful.

Building an object model for the domain requires a solid understanding of the business foundations underlying the system. Often, developers aren't in a position to supply this information on their own, particularly when they're coming in as consultants or independent contractors. The information has to come from the business users. This process isn't always simple, since the users may be busy, unavailable, or in the case of a company developing a new product, nonexistent. Even when they can be tracked down, they don't always know what they want.†

Define the vision

The place to start is the business requirements for the software. Whole books have been written on the subject of gathering requirements effectively and presenting

---

* Of course, there are whole schools of thoughts that oppose "Big Design Up Front." But it's always safer to figure out the fundamentals in advance.

† Nothing in this chapter should, however, be taken as an excuse for engineers to run off and develop software without input from the end user community or some reasonable proxy thereof.

---

them as usable specifications. See, for example, *Software Requirements* by Karl Wiegers (Microsoft Press) and *Writing Effective Use Cases* by Alistair Cockburn (Addison-Wesley).

We find it helpful to start by creating a vision statement for the domain model. This statement, which can be exceedingly brief, should describe a high-level vision for the domain model, including its purpose and scope. An example might read: "An inventory, customer, and sales management system for use by all of the web-based applications and internal systems at XYZ Corporation." More than a paragraph is probably overkill. The vision statement should address current requirements and potential future needs, but it should take care not to overload the project with speculative features. Vision statements help to boost morale, too. Developers, like most corporate citizens, like to know that they're working on something that's been thought out in advance. A vision statement also helps keep change requests under control, since potential alterations can be evaluated in the context of the product vision.

Let's build towards the domain object model introduced in Figure 6-2. We're going about it a bit backward, since we've already shown you the model, but stick with us here. In our case, the vision statement might be, "The system will manage and issue official forms of identification for every citizen in the United States. It will support the major forms of identification issued by the federal and state governments."

Gather the user cases

The next step is to identify the use cases for the application or applications that will follow the domain model. In some situations, these use cases will be in the style introduced in Chapter 2. In other cases, you may need to work backward from a requirements specification. Working from requirements specifications can often be harder than working from pure use cases: the author of the specification may have unknowingly made some design decisions as he spelled out exactly what the system should do. Watch out for these implicit assumptions.

Our example National ID system might have several use cases, including "Issue Passport," "Verify Citizenship," and "Issue State License" (generalized from "Issue State ID" and "Issue Driver's License"). There are several actors involved, as well: the State Department, the local DMV, and citizens of the state and the country. The State Citizen actor generalizes to a Citizen, and the two use cases for issuing state IDs generalize to a parent use case for issuing state level licenses. Figure 6-3 shows a simple use case diagram for this application. Each use case, as we discussed in Chapter 2, needs to be specified with more than a name. For example, the Issue Passport use case might include the following steps:

1. Verify applicant's identity.
2. Verify applicant's citizenship.
3. Take and scan photograph.

4. Enter passport data into system.

5. Issue passport.

The Driver's License use case is similar, but involves verification that the applicant has passed her driving test, has a clean driving record, and is a citizen of the state in which she is applying for a license.

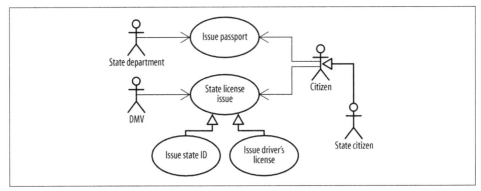

Figure 6-3. National ID system use cases

Find object candidates

The next step is to identify object candidates for each use case. In our example, we need to identify citizens for each use case, and we need to store information about who has been issued a particular ID; a Citizen object is an obvious choice. The State Department and the DMV could have their own objects, but we don't need access to any other aspects of the State Department or the DMV. We do need to know which states citizens are citizens of, so we have a State class, and a Federal class to hold the states.

Citizenship is constrained via a business rule within the domain model: a citizen is a citizen of any polity in whose object they are contained. So, all citizens are federal citizens, and each citizen is also a citizen of exactly one state. This is also an example of a domain boundary for the system: it only applies to the United States, or other countries that assign citizens to two hierarchical categories for purposes of licensing. Countries that devolve these responsibilities to, say, a city within a state would need to modify the model.

We define these relationships in the class diagram by making the associations between Federal, State, and Citizenship objects *composite associations*, rather than simple associations. Using this approach builds the business rule directly into the domain model, and also means that we've made a trade-off: supporting multiple citizenship or state citizens who are not federal citizens would be difficult in the future.

A composite association indicates that the contained object is not relevant outside of the container object. This doesn't mean that they can't be altered: a citizen can move from state to state, but he must be a citizen of at least one state if he is a federal citizen. This limitation raises an interesting point: people in military service aren't necessarily citizens of a particular state. How do we deal with this scenario? We can either ignore it (and assume the military has a different system), or treat the armed forces as the 51st state.

We now have the three domain objects in the system: the federal government, the state governments, and the individual citizens. These are our "nouns." We also define four classes, one of which is abstract, to represent the use cases we're implementing. In this case, we've kept things relatively simple and built a class to handle each activity. The two state-level activities share a superclass that contains methods common to both: for instance, a method to verify state citizenship.

We're now more or less done: the resulting class hierarchy is the one we introduced in Figure 6-2. In designing all of these classes, we've tried to keep one of the fundamental principles of object-oriented programming clearly in sight: the separation of responsibilities. Each class should be responsible for as little as possible, and should only be responsible for activities that bear on it directly.

For example, the `Citizen` class in the example above includes methods to retrieve the licenses and IDs created by the other classes, but doesn't include mechanisms for issuing passports and drivers' licenses. While these activities affect individual citizens, carrying them out is not the citizen's responsibility. However, the `Citizen` class might include a method, such as `verifyResidence( )`, which could be used in the license issue process.

Implementing a domain object model in J2EE

Traditionally, domain object models in J2EE are based on EJBs. However, just because EJBs exist doesn't mean that you need to use them. EJBs have two major advantages over Plain Old Java Objects (POJOs). First, they *can be accessed remotely*: the EJB server can be located on one system while the client is located on another. In design parlance, this means they are *remoteable*. Second, EJBs are *transactional*: a set of operations performed on one or more EJBs can be made contingent on the success of all the operations. We'll discuss transactions in much more depth in Chapter 10.

For enterprise applications with a Swing GUI interface, the ability to access objects hosted remotely is often vital: without this ability, the client will have to maintain its own connection with the resource tier, and changes to the business tier implementation will involve updating every single deployed client, creating an access control and scalability nightmare.

Domain Models and Iterative Development

One of the great things about Java is that it makes iterative development a lot easier than some earlier technologies. By delivering fast-paced releases that prioritize key functionality, developers can get a system out faster and incorporate user feedback and testing in more places during the development cycle. Java, and object-oriented languages in general, make it easier to build frameworks and fill in specific functionality as you go.

This approach raises some questions about domain model development, though. If, for example, the use cases that support customer account management won't be added to a system until the third or fourth iteration, should the components of the domain model that will be required by these use cases (and only these use cases) be incorporated into the initial design, or can they be incorporated later? To a certain extent, you can do both. Isolating individual tiers reduces the affect of changes made to the domain model later on: the presentation tier can remain ignorant of even substantial changes in the underlying database schema.

In general, we think it makes sense to consider all of the use cases when designing a domain model, even if you won't be implementing the user interfaces, presentation tiers, or business logic right away. Entity models, however well compartmentalized and designed, are always something of a pain in the neck to modify.

One technique that makes life easier is to put off finalizing the difficult-to-change aspects of the domain model, which are usually related to the persistence layer. Every aspect of the system is a use case, after all, even if it's not a "functional" use case. If persistence to a database table structure is a requirement, it can be postponed until later in the process, when the object model has had a chance to settle down. For development in the interim, you can serialize the object hierarchy to disk or use some of the approaches we'll discuss in Chapter 8. This method involves a bit more coding, but it can shorten the overall development cycle, since the domain model will be based more on feedback and less on sitting in a conference room trying to figure everything out with no practical data.

Designing domain models for the future involves a tricky balance of doing work now for a potential payoff later. A helpful approach when making any domain modeling decision is to consider what opportunities you might be closing off by adopting a particular approach.

EJBs often make sense when you need a coarse-grained entity model, remote access, and integral transaction support. Typical situations in which EJBs are appropriate include applications that are geared toward frequent and complex transactions, applications in which the domain model will be accessed by a number of systems at once, either via clustered web servers or a large number of Swing GUI clients, and applications that spread transactions across multiple services (databases, messaging servers, etc.). For more on when to use and not use EJBs, see the "Everything Is an EJB" antipattern in Chapter 12.

Plain Old Java Objects can be a little more work to code, but they are easier to deploy, since they don't require an EJB container. Because they don't provide a remote interface, they can be more efficient than EJBs when distributed capabilities aren't required. For the same reason, regular objects lend themselves to a more finely grained object model than EJBs do, since each regular object maps to a single object instance (EJBs require four or more). In many web applications, the same server can run the POJO model and the servlet container, keeping everything in the same JVM.

The tradeoff is that you need to support transactions on your own, rather than delegating to the EJB container (we'll look at strategies for dealing with this in Chapter 10). POJO models can also be difficult to cluster effectively, although the greater efficiency of this approach for many applications can reduce the need for clusters in the first place, at least for scalability purposes. Most modern databases, running on appropriate hardware, easily keep up with the load imposed by a high volume site, assuming the data model was designed properly. Since a POJO object model lives in the same JVM as the web tier, it's easy to cluster several web servers and point them to the same database, provided you have the right concurrency design.

The other nice thing about a POJO object model is that you're not stuck with it. If it turns out that you need an EJB interface after all, it's relatively easy to wrap BMP Entity and Session Beans around your existing objects and move them into an EJB server.

Some applications don't need to expose the entire data model (as found in the database) as Java objects. We'll look at strategies for interacting directly with relational databases in the next chapter.

Composite Entity/Entity Façade Pattern

One common mistake is mapping each table in the underlying database to a class, and each row in that table to an object instance. It's easy to fall into this trap when developing Enterprise JavaBeans using Container Managed Persistence, but it can happen just as readily with non-EJB technologies like Java Data Objects, O/R mapping tools, or coding from scratch. A good data model can actually make this temptation worse.

In the EJB world, a profusion of entity beans has severe performance consequences. Each bean requires not one but several objects to support it, and the server must do more to maintain the integrity of each bean and manage resources effectively. Since clients need to access a large number of distinct entity beans in order to accomplish any given task, communication overhead causes performance degradation proportional to the number of objects involved (see the Round-Tripping anti-pattern in Chapter 12).

These issues can be ameliorated using the *Composite Entity pattern*, which is also known as the *Entity Façade pattern*.* We'll see a few more façade patterns over the

---

* This pattern is referred to as Entity Façade in Oracle's BC4J application framework.

next couple of chapters, all based on the GoF *Façade pattern*. The Façade pattern provides a simple interface to a complex system: one object fronting for several objects or several database tables.

Composite entities are simply coarse-grained domain objects. When implementing a system using EJB, rather than mapping one bean class to each table and one bean instance to each row, a Composite Entity will collect information from multiple tables and multiple rows into a single entity bean. The entire domain model may still be represented, but not as a direct mapping to the underlying persistence structure.

Composite entities aren't the exclusive province of Enterprise JavaBeans. Any object representation of a domain model entity can use this approach to make itself more efficient and easier to use. Clients accessing composite entity objects have an easier time manipulating the domain model, since they have to manage fewer EJB instances at once. This is particularly the case when the database design has already been defined and can't be changed, either due to legacy system considerations or conflicting requirements.

On the implementation side, using a composite entity allows you to improve performance in at least two ways. First, the smaller number of entity beans reduces the amount of network activity required between the client and the server, as well as between the various beans within the server. With fewer objects in memory, a given quantity of computing resources can handle that many more connections. Second, mapping multiple tables to a single bean allows you to take advantage of the capabilities of the underlying database to merge information at the SQL level rather than the object level.

A composite entity schema

Let's look at a simple composite entity schema, which we'll use in the next few chapters. The example is the core of a data structure for managing patient visits at a small hospital. We will track patients, patient addresses, patient visits, notes recorded at each visit, staff members involved in a visit, and notes on the procedures that were performed.

There's no central table in this example. Instead, the tables queried depend on the needs of the application. The database structure is *normalized*: any time an entity within the database, such as a patient, visit, address, or staff member is referenced in more than one place, it is pulled out into a new table with a separate primary key (we'll talk more about primary keys in Chapter 8). Similarly, data with uncertain cardinality* is also pulled into separate tables, with a reference back to the primary key of its logical parent. For example, a patient may have multiple addresses: Home, Office, Billing, Insurance, and so forth. Rather than add fields to the Patient table for

---

* In other words, data that may appear once, more than once, or never, depending on the needs of the user.

---

each of these, we create a new table, PATIENT_ADDRESS, linked to the Patient table via a primary key. This allows us to add all the addresses we want. We do the same thing with visit notes, which are stored in the VISIT_NOTES table and linked to the VISIT table and the STAFF table (since there can be multiple visit notes per visit, and each visit note could be created by a different staff member, such as a radiologist or nurse). Figure 6-4 shows an illustration.

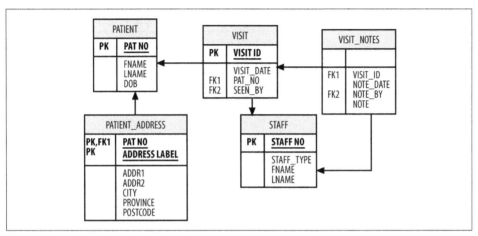

Figure 6-4. Patient and visit database schema

The simplest way of mapping this schema to an EJB object structure is to create a new EJB entity bean type for each table. This process allows us to easily use Container Managed Persistence, and allows simple remote updates to each type of data. On the other hand, it results in a profusion of entity beans. A healthy patient probably averages one or two visits a year, and sick patients will generally visit much more often. So the average number of yearly visits may be closer to four or five. Each visit might have 10 or more visit notes associated with it, depending on what procedures were performed. That means each patient could produce 40 or 50 new entities a year. These add up fast, since a single hospital might serve 10,000 or more patients (most of them just pop in for 20 minutes a year). Of course, a well designed EJB container will manage to avoid keeping most of this material in memory at all times, but it's still an awful lot of objects. That's the problem at the macro scale.

The An-Entity-Bean-for-Everything approach also causes problems at the micro scale. Remember that each time you access a remote EJB, you incur a network performance penalty that can be measured in milliseconds. A web page that requires accessing 40 different EJBs will take much longer to generate than one that requires 4, with a corresponding impact on your budget for application servers.

Figure 6-5 shows the hospital visit object model using a set of composite entities. There are still two classes of entity bean: the Patient bean and the HospitalVisit bean. The HospitalVisit bean contains objects representing the visit date, the attending physician, and all of the procedures performed during the visit. The Patient entity bean contains an Address object, and has a one-to-many relationship with a set of HospitalVisit entity beans.

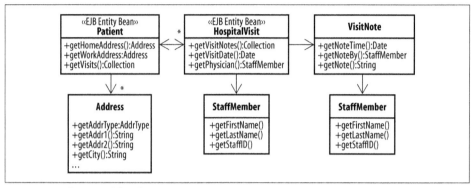

Figure 6-5. Object model with composite entities

When the EJB container instantiates the HospitalVisit bean, the bean loads all of the associated visit notes, as well as the staff information for both the attending physician and for each visit note. This process may take two or three queries, but it can be optimized for performance. For example, the visit note information and visit note staff information can be retrieved with one SQL statement. Here's a simple approach to building out the objects (we'll see much more of this in Chapter 8).

```
// Assume visit_id variable containing the visit primary key

Connection con = getConnection( );
Statement stmt = con.createStatement( );
ResultSet rs = stmt.executeQuery("select VISIT_DATE, FNAME, LNAME from " +
    "VISIT, STAFF WHERE VISIT.VISIT_ID = "+visit_id+" AND STAFF_NO = SEEN_BY");

if(rs.next( )) {
    // ... Read visit information
}

rs.close( );

rs = stmt.executeQuery("select NOTE_DATE, NOTE, FNAME, LNAME from " +
    "VISIT_NOTES, STAFF where VISIT_ID = " +visit_id+" AND STAFF_NO = NOTE_BY");

while(rs.next( )) {
    // load visit notes
}
// etc.
```

We leave the Patient and HospitalVisit objects as entity beans because they might need to be associated with a variety of other objects (such as bills or HMOs). We also need something that external components can access. The individual procedures and addresses, on the other hand, are not necessary outside the context of the entity beans that control them.

The StaffMember class is shown twice on the diagram to indicate that a particular instance of the object isn't shared between visits and notes. Like the VisitNote and Address objects, a StaffMember object is created at need by the parent object.

In EJB applications, composite entities are more difficult to implement using Container Managed Persistence, although it's certainly possible. For easier portability, it often makes more sense to use Bean Managed Persistence. In the next chapter, we'll look at some database-related patterns that make it easier to build both BMP and POJO entity objects, and in Chapter 9 we'll see some patterns designed to further reduce network traffic and to improve the separation of the entity model and the business logic.

CHAPTER 7

Tier Communications

The business tier is a critical part of any enterprise application. But it doesn't exist in a vacuum: the business tier requires an interface (often several interfaces) to the outside world. Of course, since we spent most of Chapters 3, 4, and 5 discussing the presentation tier, this should not be much of a surprise. But we glossed over something in those chapters: glueing the tiers together. Before we discuss the low-level business tier, we need to talk about integration; specifically, how data is exchanged between the tiers.

This chapter focuses on managing the communications between tiers using data transfer patterns. Our goal is to provide a basic vocabulary for talking about exchanging data between different components of the business tier and between the business tier and the presentation tier. Ultimately, we want to be able to do this in a well-structured, efficient, and flexible way.

Data Transfer Patterns

In an ideal world, every time we send data from one place to another, we would include all the information required for the current activity, with no waste and no need for the recipient to come back with questions. Anyone who has worked technical support is familiar with the situation: it's much easier to have the user explain the entire problem at once, with all the relevant detail, rather than have to ask a series of questions to determine whether the computer is on, if an error message was displayed, if the software was actually installed, and so forth. A single support person can handle more problems with fewer headaches.*

In Java terms, this ideal could involve transferring a single object containing a complete bug report, rather than transmitting several individual objects for each aspect of the report. Of course, we still have to deal with the trade-off between performance

---

* Readers of this book with less computer-literate family members are probably also familiar with this effect.

and flexibility. When objects interact with each other in a local JVM, the overhead of a method call is generally fairly small, while the overhead of additional objects, both in terms of developer time and runtime resources, can be fairly high. When dealing with a class representing a person, it may make more sense to include a set of address fields in the Person class itself, rather than creating a separate Address class to hold address information. The cost in code complexity of the additional fields may be balanced by the need to manage fewer objects at runtime.*

Once remote resources enter the picture, however, the rules change quickly. Just as with our technical support analogy, communications overhead becomes the chief bottleneck. Calling 5 methods on a remote EJB entity bean to retrieve a single address will rapidly turn a 200-millisecond operation into a 1-second operation. There are real benefits if we can keep the number of calls down, even if it means we aren't as purely object-oriented as we could be.

Network overhead isn't the only bottleneck. In an EJB environment the server might have to instantiate the bean from storage multiple times, either by passivating and activating or by calling ejbLoad( ) again. This process creates another whole layer of activity that must be finished before any data can be sent back over the network. While most servers will optimize against this possibility, excessive bean creation can degrade performance even over local interfaces. Web services face the same problem: the overhead of parsing each XML request can be pretty dramatic.

What's the moral of the story? The more complex and distributed an application is, the more opportunities there are for performance to degrade. That's the problem we try to solve in this chapter. The data transfer patterns in the next sections focus on improving performance by reducing the number of interactions between remote objects and their clients.

Data Transfer Objects

The *Data Transfer Object* (DTO) *pattern* is simple: rather than make multiple calls to retrieve a set of related data, we make a single call, retrieving a custom object that includes everything we need for the current transaction. When the presentation tier wants to update the business tier, it can pass the updated object back. The DTO becomes the charged interface between the presentation and business tiers, and between the various components of the business tier. We return to this concept in Chapters 8 and 9.

DTOs are primarily used to improve performance, but they have organizational advantages as well. Code that retrieves a single object presenting, say, a customer

---

* This is a trivial example. When dealing with things like addresses, the code flexibility provided by the additional object more than makes up for the overhead.

DTOs and Value Objects

Data transfer objects are sometimes referred to as *Value Objects*. It's an unfortunate accident of fate. The original Gang of Four described the Value Object pattern as a single object containing an unchangeable value.

There are several examples of value objects in the J2SE API: `String`, `Integer`, `Long`, `Boolean`, and the rest of the objects representing primitives. When you create an instance of one of these objects, its value is assigned immediately and never changes. Methods like the `substring()` method of `String` return a new object containing the new value, rather than acting on the current object. This behavior ensures the code can rely on the fact that once it obtains a particular instance of an object, the value won't change behind the scenes.

Data transfer objects are not immutable. They generally consist of a large number of properties that can be manipulated both before sending and after receipt—if nothing else, there's no way to get all the data in most DTOs into the constructor!

So why the confusion? The original version of Sun's J2EE Patterns referred to what we describe as the *DTO pattern* as the *Value Object pattern*. As a result, we lost one of the benefits of patterns: clarity of communication. The literature, including Sun's, has responded by adopting the DTO name for this pattern, leaving Value Object for the original pattern. No harm, no foul.

---

record, is easier to understand and maintain than code that makes dozens of extraneous getter and setter calls to retrieve names, addresses, order history, and so forth.

Figure 7-1 shows a potential class diagram for a DTO. The business and presentation tiers can create and manipulate DTOs, and share them with each other. In the class diagram, we've formatted the DTO as a JavaBean, but this isn't a requirement.

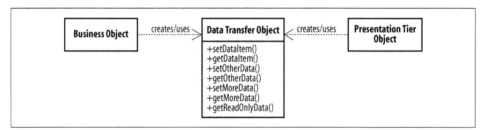

Figure 7-1. The DTO pattern

Data objects as DTOs

The simplest data transfer objects are simply the data objects used within the business object itself. Let's start by taking a look at a simple EJB that represents a `Patient` and associated data. The interface for the `Patient` bean is listed in Example 7-1. For the examples in this chapter, we're using the same database schema we introduced in

---

Chapter 6. In this case, we include information from the PATIENT and PATIENT_ ADDRESS tables.

Example 7-1. Patient.java

```
import javax.ejb.EJBObject;
import java.rmi.RemoteException;

public interface Patient extends EJBObject  {

  public String getFirstName( ) throws RemoteException;
  public void setFirstName(String firstName) throws RemoteException;

  public String getLastName( ) throws RemoteException;
  public void setLastName(String lastName) throws RemoteException;

  public Address getHomeAddress( ) throws RemoteException;
  public void setHomeAddress(Address addr) throws RemoteException;

  public Address getWorkAddress( ) throws RemoteException;
  public void setWorkAddress(Address addr) throws RemoteException;
}
```

We also make an assumption that the data model doesn't implicitly show: we're interested in home and work addresses, specifically. In the database, we'll identify these via the ADDRESS_LABEL field, which can contain "Home" or "Work" (our bean simply ignores any other values). The Address class itself is listed in Example 7-2. We've kept it simple, just using a single serializable object as a holder for a set of public fields.

Example 7-2. Address.java

```
import java.io.*;

public class Address implements Serializable  {
  public String addressType = null;
  public String address1 = null;
  public String address2 = null;
  public String city = null;
  public String province = null;
  public String postcode = null;
}
```

We could also implement the Address object as a JavaBean, particularly if we need to perform checks before setting values. However, the approach of creating a set of public fields makes it easier to remember that this is merely a transient data object rather than something capable of performing business operations or keeping track of object state. Instead, we store changes to the address by passing a new Address object to the setHomeAddress( ) and setWorkAddress( ) methods.

Since we have the Address object, we're going to use it internally, as well. There's no sense reinventing the wheel, and leveraging the object in both places means that if we add another address field, it will automatically be included in both the main bean and the DTO. Sometimes, of course, the requirements of the DTO and the business object differ; in those cases, you should never try to shoehorn the DTO object into the business object's internals, or vice versa.

Example 7-3 contains a partial listing of the PersonBean object that uses the Address data object, internally as well as for interacting with the outside world.

Example 7-3. PersonBean.java (partial)

```
import javax.ejb.*;
import javax.naming.*;
import java.sql.*;
import javax.sql.*;

public class PatientBean implements EntityBean  {
  private EntityContext context;

  private Long pat_no = null;
  private String fname = null;
  private String lname = null;

  private Address workAddress = new Address();
  private Address homeAddress = new Address();

  public Long ejbCreate(Long newId) {
    pat_no = newId;
     homeAddress.addressType = "Home";
    workAddress.addressType = "Work";
    return newId;
  }

  public void ejbPostCreate(Long newId) {
  }

  public Address getHomeAddress() {
    return homeAddress;
  }

  public void setHomeAddress(Address addr) {
     setAddress(homeAddress, addr);
  }

  public Address getWorkAddress() {
    return workAddress;
  }

  public void setWorkAddress(Address addr) {
    setAddress(workAddress, addr);
  }
```

Example 7-3. PersonBean.java (partial) (continued)

```java
  private void setAddress(Address target, Address source) {
    target.address1 = source.address1;
    target.address2 = source.address2;
    target.city = source.city;
    target.province = source.province;
    target.postcode = source.postcode;
  }

  public Long ejbFindByPrimaryKey(Long primaryKey) throws FinderException {

    Connection con = null;
    PreparedStatement ps = null;
    ResultSet rs = null;
    try {
      con = getConnection(); // local method for JNDI Lookup
      ps = con.prepareStatement("select pat_no from patient where pat_no = ?");
      ps.setLong(1, primaryKey.longValue());
      rs = ps.executeQuery();
      if(!rs.next())
        throw (new ObjectNotFoundException("Patient does not exist"));
    } catch (SQLException e) {
      throw new EJBException(e);
    } finally {
      try {
        if(rs != null) rs.close();
        if(ps != null) ps.close();
        if(con != null) con.close();
      } catch (SQLException e) {}
    }
    // We found it, so return it
    return primaryKey;
  }

  public void ejbLoad() {

    Long load_pat_no = (Long)context.getPrimaryKey();

    Connection con = null;
    PreparedStatement ps = null;
    ResultSet rs = null;
    try {
      con = getConnection(); // local method for JNDI Lookup
      ps = con.prepareStatement("select * from patient where pat_no = ?");
      ps.setLong(1, load_pat_no.longValue());
      rs = ps.executeQuery();

      if(!rs.next())
        throw (new EJBException("Unable to load patient information"));

      pat_no = new Long(rs.getLong("pat_no"));
      fname = rs.getString("fname");
      lname= rs.getString("lname");
```

Example 7-3. PersonBean.java (partial) (continued)

```
      ps.close( );
      rs.close( );

      ps = con.prepareStatement(
        "select * from patient_address where pat_no = ? and address_label in " +
        "('Home', 'Work')");

      ps.setLong(1, load_pat_no.longValue( ));
      rs = ps.executeQuery( );
      // Load any work or home
      while(rs.next( )) {
        String addrType = rs.getString("ADDRESS_LABEL");
        if("Home".equals(addrType)) {
          homeAddress.address1 = rs.getString("addr1");
          homeAddress.address2 = rs.getString("addr2");
          homeAddress.city = rs.getString("city");
          homeAddress.province = rs.getString("province");
          homeAddress.postcode = rs.getString("postcode");
        } else if ("Work".equals(addrType)) {
          workAddress.address1 = rs.getString("addr1");
          workAddress.address2 = rs.getString("addr2");
          workAddress.city = rs.getString("city");
          workAddress.province = rs.getString("province");
          workAddress.postcode = rs.getString("postcode");
        }
      }


    } catch (SQLException e) {
      throw new EJBException(e);
    } finally {
      try {
        if(rs != null) rs.close( );
        if(ps != null) ps.close( );
        if(con != null) con.close( );
      } catch (SQLException e) {}
    }
  }

// Remaining EJB methods go here
...
}
```

The setWorkAddress( ) and setHomeAddress( ) methods explicitly update the currently stored addresses rather than simply storing the addresses passed in as parameters. This prevents any possibility of crossed-over references when dealing with EJB local instances, and also gives us a compile-time alert if the DTO data structure changes dramatically, which would affect the persistence code as well.

Dedicated data transfer objects

In addition to using data objects as DTOs, we can create more complex DTO objects that effectively act as façades for the entity they're associated with. Example 7-4 shows the PatientDTO object, which can contain a complete set of information regarding a patient, including their unique identifier (the primary key for the EJB entity bean).

Example 7-4. PatientDTO

```
import java.util.ArrayList;
import java.io.*;

public class PatientDTO implements Serializable {

  public long pat_no = -1;
  public String fname = null;
  public String lname = null;

  public ArrayList addresses = new ArrayList();

}
```

Since this is a dedicated data transfer object, we've named it PatientDTO. We didn't use this convention with the Address object, since that was used for both exchanging data and managing it internally within the EJB. Of course, we could rewrite the EJB to use the PatientDTO object internally; but if we don't, we achieve some decoupling that allows us to extend the PatientBean later on while maintaining compatibility with presentation tier components that use the original PatientDTO. When adding new features to the Patient object, we might create an ExtendedPatientDTO object, or use the Data Transfer Hash pattern (discussed below).

Adding support for the full DTO is simple, requiring the following method for the PatientBean object, and the corresponding signature in the bean interface definition:

```
    public PatientDTO getPatientDTO() {
      PatientDTO pat = new PatientDTO();
      pat.pat_no = pat_no.longValue();
      pat.fname = fname;
      pat.lname = lname;
      pat.addresses.add(homeAddress);
      pat.addresses.add(workAddress);
      return pat;
    }
```

Data Transfer Hash Pattern

Sometimes the data transferred between tiers isn't known ahead of time, and as a result, it can't be stored in a JavaBean, since we need to define the JavaBean ahead of time. Sometimes the server half of a client/server application is upgraded, adding support for new data items, but some of the clients aren't. And sometimes an application changes frequently in the course of development. In these situations, it's helpful to have a DTO approach that doesn't tie the client and the server into using the same version of a DTO class, and doesn't requiring changing class definitions to send more (or less) data.

The *Data Transfer Hash pattern* defines a special type of DTO that addresses these issues. Rather than defining a specific object to hold summary information for a particular entity or action, a data transfer hash uses a Hashtable or HashMap object (generally the latter, to avoid unnecessary thread synchronization overhead) to exchange data with the client tier. This is accomplished by defining a known set of keys to identify each piece of data in the hash. Good practice here is to use a consistent, hierarchical naming scheme. For the Patient object, we might have *patient.address.home.addr1*, *patient.address.work.addr1*, *patient.firstname*, *patient.lastname*, and so forth.

Using hash maps for transferring data makes it very easy to change data formats, since in some cases you might not even have to recompile (for example, if your hash map generation code builds the map based on dynamic examination of a JDBC result set). It also makes it easier to soft-upgrade an application, adding more data, which can then be safely ignored by clients that don't support it.

On the other hand, a data transfer hash makes it difficult to identify what kind of data you're dealing with. It also makes compile-time type checking impossible, since a HashMap stores undifferentiated objects. This can get messy with nonstring data. And since data structures can't be verified at compile time, there must be close communication between developers working on the business and presentation tiers.

We can get around the first drawback by encapsulating a HashMap in a container object, rather than using it directly. This step allows us to identify a hash table instance as a data transfer hash, and also lets us tack on some helpful identifying information about the information we're exchanging. Example 7-5 shows a simple version, which allows us to specify an arbitrary map type along with the data. We call this a *named* HashMap.

Example 7-5. HashMapDTO

```java
import java.util.HashMap;

public class HashMapDTO extends HashMap  {
  private String mapDesc = null;

  public HashMapDTO(String desc) {
    mapDesc = desc;
  }

  public String getMapDescription() {
    return mapDesc;
  }
}
```

Row Set DTOs

The DTO types we've looked at up to this point have focused on single objects, or single objects with a set of dependent objects. However, many applications frequently need to transfer large sets of relatively simple data. This data may not warrant a specific object wrapper, or the exact data structure may not be known ahead of time. And sometimes it's simpler to work with a set of rows and columns than with an object, particularly when the task at hand involves presenting the data in rows and columns, anyway—a frequent activity on the Web.

The data for this kind of row-centric activity generally comes out of a database, and the native format of the database is row-column based. In these situations, we can build a DTO directly out of a JDBC result set without paying much attention to the data content itself. The DTO can then be sent to the ultimate consumer.

One approach to building a Row Set DTO is to use an object implementing the JDBC 2.0 RowSet interface. Since row sets in this context need to be disconnected from their original source, this approach means using a RowSet implementation that completely encapsulates all the rows in the result set. Obviously, if there are several thousand rows in the set, this approach can get very expensive.

There are two advantages to building a Row Set DTO using a RowSet interface. First, an implementation (WebRowSet) is readily available from Sun, although it isn't part of the standard JDBC distribution. Second, there are a lot of presentation tier components, such as grid controls, written to work with RowSets, so if your presentation tier (or one of your presentation tiers) is a rich client, you can plug the results right in.

The problem with the RowSet interface is that it can get a bit heavy. It supports full updating and navigation, as well as field-by-field accessor methods. As a result, the implementation is fairly complicated and resource-intensive. If you don't need the full capabilities of RowSet, a more lightweight implementation makes sense. Example 7-6 shows a lightweight version of RowSet that preserves the data-independent nature of the original.

Example 7-6. LightRowSet.java

```java
import java.sql.*;
import java.util.*;

/**
 * Provide a lightweight wrapper for a set of rows. Preserve types as best
 * as possible.
 */
public class LightRowSet implements java.io.Serializable {
    ArrayList rows = null;
    int rowCount = 0;
    int colCount = 0;
    String[] colNames = null;

    public LightRowSet(ResultSet rs) throws SQLException {
        rows = new ArrayList();
```

Example 7-6. LightRowSet.java (continued)

```
        if (rs == null) {
            throw new SQLException("No ResultSet Provided");
        }

        ResultSetMetaData rsmd = rs.getMetaData();
        colCount = rsmd.getColumnCount();
        colNames = new String[colCount];

        for (int i = 0; i < colCount; i++) {
            colNames[i] = rsmd.getColumnName(i + 1);
        }

        while (rs.next()) {
            Object[] row = new Object[colCount];

            for (int i = 0; i < colCount; i++)
                row[i] = rs.getObject(i + 1);

            rows.add(row);
        }

        rs.close();
    }

    /** Return the column names in this row set, in indexed order */
    public String[] getColumnNames() {
        return colNames;
    }

    /**
     * Return an iterator containing all of the rows
     */
    public Iterator getRows() {
        return rows.iterator();
    }

    /**
     * Return a particular row, indexed from 1..n. Return null if the row
     * isn't found.
     */
    public Object[] getRow(int index) {
      try {
        return (Object[]) rows.get(index - 1);
      } catch (ArrayIndexOutOfBoundsException aioobe) {
        return null;
      }
    }

    public int getRowCount() {
        return rows.size();
    }
}
```

The implementation of LightRowSet is very simple: it accepts a JDBC ResultSet from an external source and unpacks the data into a set of arrays. It uses the ResultSetMetaData interface to retrieve the column count and column names, and makes the header information, as well as the data, available via a set of getter methods. We conform to the SQL style of referring to rows and indexes based on a 1 to n (rather than Java's 0 to n-1) indexing scheme.

In practice, using the LightRowSet is easy. Here's the signature of an EJB session bean that uses it to return staff directory information:

```
import javax.ejb.EJBObject;
import java.rmi.RemoteException;
import com.oreilly.j2eepatterns.chapter7.LightRowSet;

public interface StaffDirectory extends EJBObject {
  LightRowSet getDirectory(String department) throws RemoteException;
}
```

And here's a simple implementation of getDirectory( ):

```
public LightRowSet getDirectory(String department) {
  try {
    Connection con = getConnection( );
    Statement stmt = con.createStatement( );
    ResultSet rs = stmt.executeQuery(
        "SELECT * FROM STAFF WHERE DEPT = '" +department + "'");
    LightRowSet lrs = new LightRowSet(rs);
    rs.close( );
    stmt.close( );
    return lrs;
  } catch (SQLException e) {
    e.printStackTrace( );
  } finally {
    try { con.close( ); } catch (SQLException ignored) {}
  }
  return null;
}
```

One drawback to the RowSet approach is that it exposes the underlying names of the columns in the table. Database columns aren't always appropriate for exposure to the outside world; they tend to be cryptic at best, and downright misleading at worst. A simple way around this problem is to assign meaningful column aliases to each column in the query. Rather then selecting everything from the staff table, we might prefer to do this instead:

```
SELECT FNAME as FIRSTNAME, LNAME as LASTNAME, REZPRIADDR AS ADDRESS,
TRIM(CITY) AS CITY
FROM STAFF WHERE DEPT = 'Oncology'
```

Writing SQL like this ensures that we have meaningful names for each column in the set. It also assigns a reasonable name to a result field that was generated by a database-side operation. If we didn't do this, the database would have to generate its own name for the trimmed CITY column.

CHAPTER 8
Database and Data Patterns

Storage is the one constant in enterprise development. Enterprise systems are, essentially, information management systems. To the user, the value of these applications comes from the centralization of information resources, which allows broader access and more flexible interaction. Of course, you can maintain an entire information model in memory, but that's not the best method: if someone trips over the cord, your business is back to square one. So production applications implement *persistence*, storing information to reliable media.

This chapter focuses on patterns for implementing and optimizing persistent storage in the business tier. The first section introduces some basic patterns for accessing persistent resources: the *Data Access Object* (DAO) *pattern* and the *Procedure Access Object* (PAO) *pattern*.

The rest of the chapter focuses on solving recurring problems in database-backed applications. Since Java object graphs generally store relations between objects directly, we need to translate Java's direct object-to-object relationships into something that we can store in a database. The solution is a *primary key*: a unique identifier associated with each logical entity in the database, which can be used to represent the relationships between objects. Since unique primary keys are so important to the database side of an application, we discuss patterns for generating and managing them.

As the primary key issue implies, there's no single, standard way to translate the data in an object model to a set of database tables (or to get the data from the database back into objects). So we'll finish the chapter with a look at a few database-object modeling approaches.

Data Access Patterns

The most common J2EE persistence mechanism is a relational database management system, or RDBMS. Therefore, we focus primarily on patterns that apply to relational databases.

Java, both in and out of J2EE, is chock full of database technologies. Enterprise Java-Beans were designed with the database backend in mind, and the JDBC API, which is part of the J2SE package but heavily used in J2EE environments, provides a powerful, low-level approach for connecting any Java object to an external database. Other technologies, such as Java Data Objects, provide a higher-level abstraction of the persistent data, handling much of the mapping between database tables and Java objects.

Of course, databases are not the only persistence mechanism available. Simpler applications can persist data to files on disk in text or binary formats, or to XML. Java objects themselves can be serialized directly to disk and reloaded later, although this approach makes it difficult for human beings to access and manipulate the data independently from the program that created it. Collectively, these persistence mechanisms are referred to as *data sources*.

Whatever data source we use, there are problems when we embed persistence logic directly into business components. When the business object is responsible for persistence, it means we've given two responsibilities to a single class. Doing so isn't intrinsically evil, but it can be problematic in several ways. First, the full persistence layer has to be implemented before the business object can be fully tested. Second, the business object becomes locked in to a particular persistence scheme. Finally, the business object code becomes more complex and difficult to understand, particularly when there is a separation between the programmers who understand the business logic and those who understand the persistence mechanism.

Data Access Object Pattern

We need to separate the business logic and the resource tier. The *Data Access Object pattern* separates the code that accesses the database from the code that works with the data. Other components of the application delegate responsibility for database access to a DAO object, which communicates with the rest of the system by passing around data transfer objects.

A DAO is responsible for reading data from an external data source and providing an object encapsulation for use by business components. Unlike an EJB entity bean, a DAO is not a remote object and should not contain any business methods beyond getters and setters for the data it provides access to. The applications' business process logic should be located elsewhere, where it can be tested independently and reused in the event that the persistence layer changes. DAOs are simply the access path to the persistence layer.

If you're not using EJBs, a set of DAOs can be used as the data model for simple applications that don't include much business logic beyond the control tier. Business process logic can be embedded in Business Delegate objects instead—we'll talk about those in more detail in Chapter 9. Figure 8-1 shows how a DAO object interacts with the rest of the system. A presentation tier object, such as a servlet or a Struts action, uses a business object to retrieve a data object. The business object uses a DAO to access the persistence mechanism, and receives a data object that it can manipulate, pass back to the presentation tier, or both.

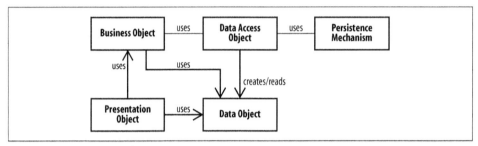

Figure 8-1. Data Access Object

Example 8-1 shows an interface for a DAO object that manages patient data in our simple model. Rather than provide individual fields, it uses the PatientDTO object (described in Chapter 7), which keeps the external interface of the DAO itself as simple as possible.

Example 8-1. PatientDAO.java

```
public interface PatientDAO {
  // Retrieve a patient's record from the database
  public PatientDTO findPatient(long pat_no);
  // Save a patient DTO back to the database
  public void savePatient(PatientDTO patient);
  // create a new patient, based on data in the PatientDTO,
  // and return a PatientDTO updated with the primary key for the new patient
  public PatientDTO createPatient(PatientDTO patient);
}
```

We might add other methods for other database-related actions, such as determining whether a patient record with a particular ID exists without having to actually load all the data (like the findPatient( ) method does).

Example 8-2 shows an implementation of the PatientDAO interface. Some of the code is similar to the ejbLoad( ) method in Example 7-3, although it is simplified, since the

PatientDTO uses a different approach to storing address information (an arbitrarily long list of Address objects, rather than fixed home and work addresses).

Example 8-2. PatientDatabaseDAO.java

```java
import java.util.*;
import java.sql.*;
import javax.sql.*;
import javax.naming.*;

public class PatientDatabaseDAO implements PatientDAO  {

  public PatientDTO findPatient(long pat_no)  {

    Connection con = null;
    PreparedStatement ps = null;
    ResultSet rs = null;
    PatientDTO patient = null;

    try {
      con = getConnection( ); // local method for JNDI Lookup
      ps = con.prepareStatement("select * from patient where pat_no = ?");
      ps.setLong(1, pat_no);
      rs = ps.executeQuery( );

      if(!rs.next( ))
       return null;

      patient = new PatientDTO( );
      patient.pat_no = pat_no;
      patient.fname = rs.getString("fname");
      patient.lname= rs.getString("lname");
      ps.close( );
      rs.close( );

      ps = con.prepareStatement(
        "select * from patient_address where pat_no = ? and address_label in " +
        "('Home', 'Work')");

      ps.setLong(1, pat_no);
      rs = ps.executeQuery( );
      // Load any work or home
      while(rs.next( )) {
        String addrType = rs.getString("ADDRESS_LABEL");
        Address addr = new Address( );
        addr.addressType = addrType;
        addr.address1 = rs.getString("addr1");
        addr.address2 = rs.getString("addr2");
        addr.city = rs.getString("city");
        addr.province = rs.getString("province");
        addr.postcode = rs.getString("postcode");
        patient.addresses.add(addr);
      }
    } catch (SQLException e) {
      e.printStackTrace( );
```

Example 8-2. PatientDatabaseDAO.java (continued)

```
    } finally {
      try {
        if(rs != null) rs.close( );
        if(ps != null) ps.close( );
        if(con != null) con.close( );
      } catch (SQLException e) {}
    }

    return patient;
  }

  public void savePatient(PatientDTO patient) {
    // Persistence code goes here
  }

  public PatientDTO createPatient(PatientDTO patient) {
    // Creation code goes here
  }

  private Connection getConnection( ) throws SQLException {
    try {
      Context jndiContext = new InitialContext( );
      DataSource ds = (DataSource)jndiContext.lookup("java:comp/env/jdbc/DataChapterDS");
      return ds.getConnection( );
    } catch (NamingException ne) {
        throw new SQLException (ne.getMessage( ));
    }
  }
}
```

Now that we have a DAO object, we can rewrite our ejbFindByPrimaryKey( ) and ejbLoad( ) methods in PatientBean to be much simpler. We can also use this code in presentation tier code when EJBs aren't involved at all.

```
    public Long ejbFindByPrimaryKey(Long primaryKey) throws FinderException {

      // mildly inefficient; we should have a simpler method for this
      PatientDatabaseDAO pdd = new PatientDatabaseDAO( );
      if(pdd.findPatient(primaryKey.longValue( )) != null)
       return primaryKey;

      return null;
    }


    public void ejbLoad( ) {
      Long load_pat_no = (Long)context.getPrimaryKey( );

      PatientDatabaseDAO pdd = new PatientDatabaseDAO( );
      PatientDTO pat = pdd.findPatient(load_pat_no.longValue( ));
      fname = pat.fname;
      lname = pat.lname;
```

```
    Iterator addresses = pat.addresses.iterator( );
    // Load any work or home addresses
    while(addresses.hasNext( )) {
      Address addr = (Address)addresses.next( );
      if("Home".equalsIgnoreCase(addr.addressType)) {
        homeAddress = addr;
      } else if ("Work".equalsIgnoreCase(addr.addressType)) {
          workAddress = addr;
      }
    }
  }
}
```

DAO Factory Pattern

DAOs offer applications a degree of independence from persistence implementations, but the application still needs to be able to instantiate the appropriate DAO and (usually) provide it with connection information to whatever data store is being used: server addresses, passwords, and so forth.

In applications that use a large number of DAOs, inheritance provides a simple solution for shared functionality: an abstract parent DAO class can implement methods for retrieving database connections and other resources, and each DAO implementation can extend the parent class and use the common functionality. But things get more complicated when one application needs to support multiple different databases (which may require very different DAO implementations).

The *DAO Factory pattern* allows us to abstract the process of finding an appropriate persistence mechanism away from the business/presentation components. Applications interact with a single class, which produces particular DAOs on demand. Each DAO implements a specific interface, making it trivial to switch persistence mechanisms without affecting the application as a whole.

Figure 8-2 shows why we implemented PatientDAO in the previous section as an interface and an implementing class, rather than just writing the database code directly into PatientDAO. We can write a series of DAOs implementing the interface, one for each unique persistence approach. We can then write a DAO factory object that knows how to instantiate each of these according to whatever criteria are appropriate. Alternately, we can go one step further and offload the creation of particular DAO types to type-specific factories. The core DAO factory, which is used by the business or presentation components, is then responsible only for selecting the appropriate factory.

Example 8-3 shows a simple DAO factory that creates specific DAO objects. We dispense with the layer of intermediate factories, since we've embedded the logic for locating data sources directly within our DAO objects. At some point, we must decide what form of persistence mechanism is required. In this case, we specify the persistence strategy as a system property.

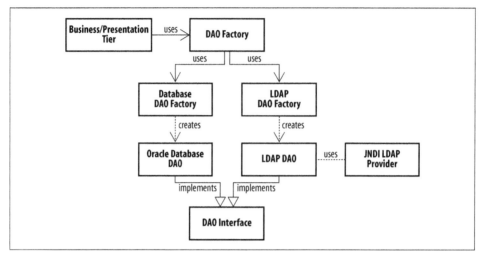

Figure 8-2. DAO factory with two DAO types

An alternative would be to develop a naming convention for the JNDI directory itself and have the DAO factory check for known data source types until it finds the one it needs. For example, the factory could attempt to retrieve a data source named "jdbc/oracle", and if it didn't find one could check for "jdbc/db2", and so on.

Example 8-3. PatientDAOFactory.java

```java
public class PatientDAOFactory  {

  private static final int DAO_ORACLE = 1;
  private static final int DAO_DB2 = 2;
  private static final int DAO_SYBASE = 3;
  private static final int DAO_LDAP = 4;
  private static final int DAO_NONE = -1;

  private int mode = DAO_NONE;

  public PatientDAOFactory( ) {
   String dataSource = System.getProperty("app.datasource");
   if ("oracle".equalsIgnoreCase(dataSource))
    mode = DAO_ORACLE;
   else if ("db2".equalsIgnoreCase(dataSource))
    mode = DAO_DB2;
   else if ("sybase".equalsIgnoreCase(dataSource))
    mode = DAO_SYBASE;
   else if ("ldap".equalsIgnoreCase(dataSource))
    mode = DAO_LDAP;
  }

  public PatientDAO getPatientDAO( ) {
    switch(mode) {
      case DAO_ORACLE:
        return new PatientDatabaseDAO( ); // Generic, works with Oracle
```

Example 8-3. PatientDAOFactory.java (continued)

```
    case DAO_DB2:
      return new PatientDatabaseDAO( ); // also works with DB2
    case DAO_SYBASE:
      return new PatientSybaseDAO( ); // But Sybase needs special treatment
    case DAO_LDAP:
      return new PatientLDAPDAO( ); // Or we can just hit the directory
    default:
      throw new DAOCreationException("No Data Access Mechanism Configured");
    }
  }
}
```

The getPatientDAO( ) method throws a DAOCreationException if no DAO type is configured at the application level. We've defined this as a runtime exception rather than a regular exception, since configuration issues of this kind will generally only occur when an application is first being configured, and we don't want to force explicit exception-handling every time the factory gives out a DAO. Different applications will handle error conditions differently.

You may have noticed we didn't do much to configure the DAO objects themselves. This is because most DAOs, whether used in a J2EE container or elsewhere, can manage their data sources via JNDI. This ability abstracts most of the configuration away from the application itself: database server addresses, login credentials, and so forth are all specified at the application server level.

Lazy Load

Accessing a DAO generally involves accessing data that lives outside the Java runtime environment, and calls outside the native Java environment are expensive. At the bare minimum, the system has to switch application contexts, and there are usually network connections and disk accesses involved. DAOs and DTOs partially address this problem, since they help assure that information isn't loaded too frequently. But loading a DAO for a complex data structure can still be an expensive operation.

The *Lazy Load pattern* speeds up DAOs and other persistence-dependent objects by postponing data retrieval until the data is specifically requested. When using lazy loads, individual methods like the findPatient( ) method of our PatientDAO will only retrieve the data required for immediate use. Objects implementing this pattern should break up the available data into as many discrete, logical pieces as possible.

Figure 8-3 shows the sequence in which an application might implement the Lazy Load pattern. Our DAO example in the previous section gathers all of the data it provides in a single activity, even though it involves querying multiple tables. If the application only needs patient names and not addresses, resources will be wasted as the DAO retrieves information that is destined to be ignored.

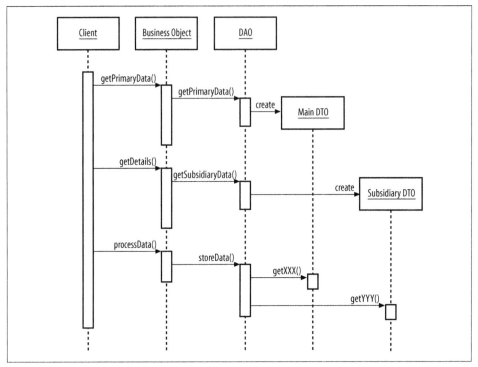

Figure 8-3. Lazy load sequence diagram

Using the Lazy Load pattern does not mean throwing out everything we said in Chapter 7 about the benefits of grouping information into objects for transfer between parts of the system! It just means that it's possible to go overboard: a mammoth object that retrieves every possible piece of data about a particular entity is going to waste time. An application retrieving customer information almost always wants a name and address, but it rarely needs detailed information on every order placed over the last 10 years. Finding the right balance depends on the design of your application. As a general rule of thumb, prefetching data that doesn't have a lot of extra cost (for example, additional columns in a table you're querying anyway) can be helpful, while queries to additional tables can be postponed.

The Lazy Load pattern can also be applied when building objects that access the database on behalf of the presentation tier. A frequent strategy for building quick and easy data models is to write a JavaBean that acts as a frontend for the database. This bean can then be passed to a JSP page or to a templating system like Jakarta's Velocity. The Lazy Load pattern can be helpful in this situation, since it allows development of a single component that can be used on a number of different pages, while only loading the data that each page needs.

The IsDirty Pattern

Reading and writing from the database are both expensive operations. Efficient data-handling code is particularly necessary in EJB environments, where you don't have control over when a bean's state is and isn't being written to the database. But all database access is expensive: you can count on adding 50 to a 100 milliseconds to any procedure just to cover overhead for each SQL statement that is executed. And that's exclusive of any additional time taken to execute the statement.*

Composite Entity Beans, DTOs, and DAOs provide opportunities to decrease reads from the database. The *IsDirty pattern* is used to decrease writes to the database. It's really the inverse of Lazy Load: only data that has changed in the bean is written back. Data that has been read directly from the database and not modified is considered clean; data that has been altered is considered "dirty."

This pattern can speed up composite entity beans dramatically. A well-written EJB container won't persist unless there's been some call to a business method on an entity bean, but once a BMP bean has been changed (at all), the container has no choice but to call the ejbStore( ) method. If the change affects one table and the total scope of the bean covers five, writing to just the changed table provides a dramatic efficiency gain.

Performance gains in non-EJB database components can be even more noticeable. Using the IsDirty pattern, your application might not know whether an object was modified and will therefore have to call its persistence methods at points where no data has actually changed. Implementing IsDirty puts the responsibility for persisting on the data object rather than the application.

In an EJB, we implement the IsDirty pattern in the setter methods of an entity bean, and in the ejbStore( ) method. In the Patient bean, we could implement the pattern by changing the setHomeAddress( ) method like this:

```
public void setHomeAddress(Address addr) {
  if(!homeAddress.equals(addr)) {
    homeAddrChanged = true; // mark changed

    homeAddress.address1 = addr.address1;
    homeAddress.address2 = addr.address2;
    homeAddress.city = addr.city;
    homeAddress.province = addr.province;
    homeAddress.postcode = addr.postcode;
  }
}
```

---

* The actual performance hit varies, and it's hard to measure accurately. These numbers come from some benchmarks done against a Java application using JDBC and an Oracle 9i database running on a separate server, connected via a 100 megabit local area network.

We now do a check to see if the data has changed; if so, we record the fact via a homeAddrChanged boolean in the bean class itself. This value is called a *hint*. We can use this variable in the ejbStore( ) method to determine whether we need to write the patient's home address back to the PATIENT_ADDRESS table.

Since a DAO object doesn't maintain the state of the data it reads, the IsDirty pattern can't be implemented in a DAO directly. However, if the DAO objects were written according to the general guidelines we discussed earlier, you should have enough granularity to use this pattern effectively.

Finally, there are situations in which you want to make absolutely sure that the data in the database matches the data in memory. This is generally the case if there's a possibility that the data in the RDBMS changed due to an external process after the Java object was created. When dealing with POJO data objects, you can implement a forcePersistence( ) method (or add a force parameter to the persistence method) that ignores dirty write hints.

Procedure Access Object

Previous generations of enterprise development tools have left millions of lines of legacy code lying around the average large company. Much of this code implements complex business processes and has already been tested, debugged, and adopted. In two-tier "thick client" applications, the business logic is often stored in the database itself in the form of stored procedures.

Stored procedures are often used to provide external integration interfaces for applications based on a database platform. Rather than providing external applications with direct access to the underlying tables, a system will provide a set of stored procedures that can be called by other systems at the database level. This set of procedures allows the main application to ensure that all contact with its database takes place through an approved path, complete with error-checking. It also, of course, provides external applications with a defined interface, allowing the developers to change the underlying table structures without having to perform all of the integration activities again.

Whatever the source, we can leverage those legacy stored procedures in a new J2EE system using the *Procedure Access Object pattern*. A PAO is simply a Java object that sits in between the business tier and the database; however, instead of accessing tables directly, it accesses stored procedures. The PAO is responsible for mapping the stored procedure to a Java object that can be used transparently by the rest of an application. Essentially, a PAO is a cross between a DAO and the command object defined by the GoF (Chapter 3 gives a brief introduction).

Figure 8-4 shows the structure of a sample PAO that handles new customer registration for an e-commerce system. The PAO accesses a stored procedure that creates a new customer record (accepting arguments via the IN parameters) and provides a new `CustomerID` (the OUT parameter). The PAO also does a little translation, combining the address and city/state/Zip properties into a single address field for use by the stored procedure (thus hiding a limitation of the legacy business logic from the main application).

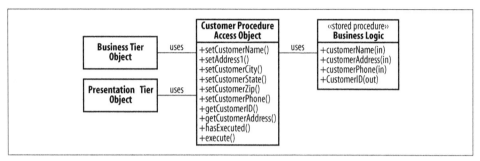

Figure 8-4. Customer management PAO

Using stored procedures in a J2EE application comes at a cost. Stored procedure programming languages are usually database-vendor-specific; Oracle's PL/SQL is the most prevalent. Although many vendors, including Oracle, are moving towards using Java as an internal stored procedure language, the mechanics of implementation still vary from vendor to vendor, and performance is usually somewhat less than the "native" language offers. Using stored procedures immediately locks your application to a single backend database (although a PAO abstraction can make it easier to develop stored procedure support for multiple databases in parallel).

Moving business logic out of the Java layer can complicate development, since you're now effectively maintaining two separate code trees for a single application: database code for database-centric business logic, and Java code for everything else. This complicates deployment, too, particularly when stored procedures and Java objects that depend on them must be kept synchronized: you can't just stuff everything into a JAR file anymore.

In exchange for the complexity, you get to reuse existing components, and can often extract a substantial performance benefit as well. Stored procedures can perform multiple SQL statements in sequence, and support the same data handling and flow of execution control as any procedural language. Since stored procedures execute in a database, they have a real performance edge in activities that execute multiple insert or update statements, or that process a large number of rows and perform some database operation on each one.

For example, a stored procedure that performs an expensive join across several tables, iterates through the results, and uses the information to update other tables will run much faster than a Java component that has to retrieve all of the information through the network, process it within the JVM, and then ship it back to the database (if more than one table is updated, the data may end up making several round trips).

Stored procedures also improve efficiency when dealing with data spread across multiple databases. Databases like Oracle support direct links between remote databases, which can be much faster than a JDBC link. When a performance-sensitive activity involves multiple databases, creating a link natively and handling the logic via a stored procedure will almost always provide a dramatic performance boost.[*]

Encapsulating your stored procedures in a procedure access object provides the same set of benefits that the DAO pattern does. You don't get portability, but you at least get plugability: you can swap PAOs the same way you swap DAOs, and easily replace them with complete Java implementations when appropriate.

 Procedure access objects are a specialized form of DAO objects; the primary distinction between them is that while a DAO has a limited scope of responsibilities (updating, inserting, and deleting data), a PAO can tackle virtually any business task.

Primary Key Patterns

Primary keys are the unique identifiers that allow one row in a database to be referenced by other rows in other tables. In the example we've been using throughout the chapter, there are primary keys on the PATIENT, STAFF, and VISIT tables identifying unique patients, staff members, and office visits. The primary keys allow us to reference a specific entity. Staff members and patients can be associated with multiple visits, and multiple visit notes can be associated with a single visit by referencing the appropriate primary key.

Primary keys are at the heart of relational database design: any J2EE application that directly inserts new records into a relational data structure has to be able to generate primary keys. Schemes for primary key generation vary widely. Many databases have field types that increment with each row, making it easy to generate new keys as needed. Since this kind of field isn't standard SQL-92, other database types require alternate approaches, and auto-increment fields aren't always the best approach anyway, particularly when you need to know the new key before writing anything to the database.

The patterns in this section describe approaches for creating primary keys within J2EE applications.

---

[*] As an added bonus, stored procedures are generally simpler to write than equivalent Java/JDBC code because they're entirely focused on handling database tasks. This specialization makes testing and validation easier.

PK Block Generator Pattern

Most Java-based primary key generation mechanisms rely on an object that hands out IDs upon request. These objects are generally shared by an entire application to prevent duplicate assignments. Objects requiring a new primary key request one from this core object as needed. The challenge is to assure that no key is ever given out twice.

The *PK Block Generator pattern* works by generating a block of unique numerical IDs based on a value retrieved from a database sequence. Sequences, which produce a unique number on request, are available in one form or another in most database packages (those that don't generally include the concept of an auto-incrementing field—in these cases, the implementation can either be adapted or the *Stored Procedures for Primary Keys pattern* can be used instead). The PK Block Generator approach ensures uniqueness and scalability, although it does not (like most approaches) guarantee that the generated keys will be contiguous or even in perfect order.*

The simplest sequence-based primary key scheme is to retrieve a new value from the sequence for every request. This process can get expensive, particularly when large numbers of keys are required. The PK Block Generator pattern modifies that approach by retrieving a base number from the sequence and multiplying it by a block size. The singleton object can then hand out keys from that block until the block runs out, at which point it retrieves a new base number and generates a new block. Since each base number produces a unique block, and the database will give out a single value from the sequence at most once, this approach works even in a networked environment where multiple JVMs share access to the same database.

Proper sizing of the block depends on the frequency with which new primary keys must be generated. The smaller the block, the more frequently a new one must be retrieved from the database, but the less likely you are to "waste" keys, since the remains of a block are discarded on VM restart.

If the PK Block Generator, as implemented in Example 8-4, is called from within an EJB, it's possible that it will get caught up in the bean's transaction. If that transaction is rolled back, the generator could theoretically end up handing out duplicate sets of IDs. The implementation in Example 8-4 deals with this problem by taking advantage of a quirk of Oracle's sequence implementation: sequence value requests aren't included in transactions. So even if the transaction that retrieves a sequence value is rolled back, the blocks won't be duplicated.

---

* In most applications, this works just fine. Primary keys should serve as unique identifiers and nothing else; assigning them additional significance based on order or other attributes simply overloads the field and makes the application more difficult to maintain. The same applies to primary keys with real-world significance: using name, city, and state as a unique identifier may work for a while, but eventually there will be two John Smiths in New York City.

A better way of dealing with this in a pure EJB environment is to front the block generator with a stateless session bean, configured with the TX_REQUIRES_NEW attribute. Other beans can call the session bean when they need a new primary key, with the assurance that any SQL calls will be included in a new transaction.

Example 8-4. SequenceBlock.java

```java
import java.sql.*;
import javax.sql.*;
import javax.naming.*;

public class SequenceBlock {

  private static int BLOCK_SIZE = 10;
  private static long current = -1;
  private static long getNextAt = -1;

  public static synchronized long getNextId() {
    if((current > -1) && (current < getNextAt))
      return current++;

    // We need to retrieve another block from the database
    Connection con = null;
    Statement stmt = null;
    ResultSet rs = null;
    try {
      con = getConnection();
      stmt = con.createStatement();
      // Oracle specific
      rs = stmt.executeQuery("SELECT SEQ_PK.NEXTVAL FROM DUAL");
      rs.next(); // Exception handler will kick in on failure
      long seqVal = rs.getLong(1);
      current = seqVal * BLOCK_SIZE;
      getNextAt = current + BLOCK_SIZE;
      return current++;
    } catch (SQLException e) {
      throw new IllegalStateException("Unable to access key store");
    } finally {
      if(rs != null) try { rs.close(); } catch (SQLException e) {}
      if(stmt != null) try { stmt.close(); } catch (SQLException e) {}
      if(con != null) try { con.close(); } catch (SQLException e) {}
    }
  }

  private static Connection getConnection() throws SQLException {
    try {
      Context jndiContext = new InitialContext();
      DataSource ds =
 (DataSource)jndiContext.lookup("java:comp/env/jdbc/DataChapterDS");
      return ds.getConnection();
    } catch (NamingException ne) {
      throw new SQLException (ne.getMessage());
    }
  }
}
```

This code generates blocks of primary keys by retrieving unique numbers from a database sequence. We then multiply this value by `BLOCK_SIZE` to get the initial key value for the block. We then give out keys from `seqVal * BLOCK_SIZE` through `(seqVal * BLOCK_SIZE) + BLOCK_SIZE - 1`. Once we've given out the full range of available keys, we get another sequence value and start again. If the system restarts, the code will retrieve a new sequence value and start over again: producing a gap in the order of the keys but never assigning the same key twice. Using the database sequence guarantees that every key will be unique.

It's also worth noting that while we've implemented this object as static, it probably isn't going to be static in real life. At the bare minimum, you'll need one instance of the `SequenceBlock` object per JVM, and if you have multiple class loaders (for different web applications, different EJB packages, and so on) you'll have one instance per loader. This is nice behavior, since it allows you to use the same object in different web applications on the same server, pointing to different databases and generating different sets of keys. But take heart—even multiple instances of the object pointing to the same database will produce unique primary keys by virtue of the database's role as an intermediary.

Stored Procedures for Primary Keys Pattern

Another approach to primary key generation is to use stored procedures to insert new records into the database via the Stored Procedures for Primary Keys pattern.[*] These procedures can take advantage of a variety of mechanisms to insert new records into the database with a unique primary key. Rather than running a SQL insert statement, your Java code calls a stored procedure within the database that is responsible for generating the new primary key and inserting the new record in the appropriate tables.

Broadly, implementation strategies for this pattern include:

- Database sequences
- Database auto-increment fields
- Computing a new key based on previous values

The first two approaches are the most common. The last method involves paying careful attention to transaction issues and providing redundant checks to ensure that no two entries have the same primary key; it should be avoided whenever possible (we mention it here because sometimes, when sequences and auto-increment fields are unavailable, it's the only possible approach). No matter which strategy you use, the key assignment algorithm is implemented in a stored procedure.

[*] We are considering running a contest for a better name.

Here's a simple example in Oracle PL/SQL. The procedure retrieves a new primary key from a sequence, uses it to create a new row, and returns the new patient identifier (the pat_no field) as an out parameter.

```
PROCEDURE INSERT_NEW_PATIENT
(
  fname_in  in  patient.fname%type,
  lname_in  in  patient.lname%type,
  pat_no    out patient.pat_no%type
) AS
new_pat_no  patient.pat_no%type;
BEGIN
  select seq_pk.nextval into new_pat_no from dual;

  insert into patient (pat_no, fname, lname)
    values (new_pat_no, fname_in, lname_in);

  pat_no := new_pat_no;
END;
```

We can run this procedure in Oracle's SQL*PLUS environment in order to insert a new row and then print the new key:

```
SQL> var new_pn number;
SQL> exec insert_new_patient('Wilbur', 'Porcino', :new_pn);

PL/SQL procedure successfully completed.

SQL> print new_pn;

       NP
----------
       10
```

It's obviously more useful to be able to do this in Java. We can use this procedure to add an ejbCreate( ) method to the Patient bean, allowing clients to create a new patient record by providing the first and last name of the patient. This is a logical place for a PAO or a stored-procedure-aware DAO, but in order to preserve our code, we'll keep it in the ejbCreate( ) method:

```
public Long ejbCreate(String firstname, String lastname)
  throws CreateException {
  Connection con = null;
  CallableStatement cstmt = null;

  fname = firstname; //Set EJB fields
  lname = lastname;

   try {
    con = getConnection();
    cstmt = con.prepareCall("{ call insert_new_patient(?,?,?) }");
    cstmt.setString(1, fname);
    cstmt.setString(2, lname);
    cstmt.registerOutParameter(3, Types.INTEGER);
```

```
      cstmt.execute( );
      pat_no = new Long(cstmt.getLong(3));

   } catch (SQLException e) {
      throw new CreateException(e.getMessage( ));
   } finally {
      if (cstmt != null) try { cstmt.close( ); } catch (SQLException se) {}
      if (con != null) try { con.close( ); } catch (SQLException se) {}
   }

   return pat_no;
}
```

The only complexity here is that we use a `CallableStatement` rather than a `PreparedStatement` to execute the stored procedure. Once the procedure is executed, we can retrieve the new patient number from the output parameter.

Object-Relational Mappings

So far in this chapter, we've assumed that the table structures for the business objects we're working with are known in advance. This is generally true when adapting legacy systems or coming into a project mid-way, but not when starting from scratch

When building new applications with a persistent backend (and that's pretty much always, whether a database is involved or not), you obviously need to design the persistence approach. Persistence models are much harder to change than other areas of an application, particularly when a version of a system has been moved into production use. Data must be either abandoned, an option that is generally not smiled upon by senior management, or converted, which is time-consuming and error-prone. Although modern database tools have made the process much easier and more flexible than in the past, there's still lots of pressure to get it right the first time.

Developers extending an existing application have it both easier and harder than those working on something new. In an existing application, the philosophical approach to persistence has usually already been chosen, so developers adding new features don't have to reinvent that particular wheel. On the other hand, adding a substantial amount of new persistence functionality to an existing system can involve stretching existing tables and methodologies beyond their original design intent, and it always involves migration hassles. Attempts to minimize migration efforts often require the creation of entirely separate table structures alongside the existing ones, which leads to data structures that are difficult to maintain, query against, or even understand.

The rest of this chapter looks at three approaches for mapping objects into the persistence layer. Again, this generally means the database, although two of the approaches can be applied to disk-based approaches (with varying degrees of success), or even to more esoteric persistence layers like JavaSpaces implementations.

Complex Class Relations

Before diving into table inheritance, it's worth spending a little bit of additional time discussing how entities are related to one another in the database. Since direct relationships between tables are handled by storing primary and foreign keys, the number of columns available for storing foreign keys limits the relationships between rows in any two tables. For example, Figure 8-5 shows a simple approach to associating a main table with a subtable.

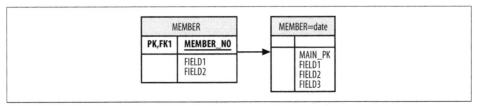

Figure 8-5. Two directly related tables

In the tables in Figure 8-6, it's impossible for one member to have more than one membership. If this is an acceptable limitation for the system, we don't have any problem. But what if want to keep track of people's older memberships, or allow someone to have multiple kinds of memberships (such as to the museum itself and to the Arty Films Club that meets every third Thursday)? One option is to have a row in the MEMBER table for each membership, but unless we know for sure that we're never going to have to add additional kinds of memberships in the future, that approach doesn't really accomplish what we want. What we want is to associate a single member with multiple memberships. To accomplish this goal, modify the table structure to include a "linking table" that stores multiple key relationships.

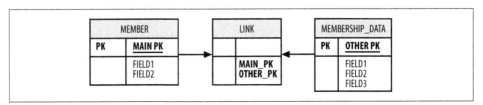

Figure 8-6. Two tables connected by a link table

This approach gives us the most completely normalized view of the data possible: no data is duplicated, queries are as simple as possible, and we have the flexibility to associate a member with multiple memberships.

Table Inheritance Pattern

In an ideal world, we want a database structure that reflects the object model while taking the greatest possible advantage of the underlying database. The *Table*

Inheritance pattern involves creating database tables that reflect the class structures within the application. We'll look at two different strategies for implementing table inheritance.

Most applications use variations of the Table Inheritance pattern, although the degree to which the table structures match the class structures often depends on whether the data model predates the application, and on the designer's level of experience with RDBMS design. EJB CMP implementations, particularly when you allow your deployment tool to develop the database structures, often use variations on this approach.

Table inheritance allows you to make relatively full use of the underlying database to enforce integrity and allow external systems, such as report generators and EAI tools, to access your application's data. It has the disadvantage of tying your database structure to your class structure, imposing additional work whenever one or the other must change. When writing database access code, implementing table inheritance by hand can take longer than other approaches.

Concrete Table Inheritance strategy

The *Concrete Table Inheritance strategy* provides an object mapping to a relational database by defining a table for each concrete class in the object model, along with tables defining the relationships between objects. In the example below, we have a simple class structure used for issuing ID badges at a museum. Members get one type of badge, and employees get another. The object model includes an abstract Person class, which contains information common to employees and members, and concrete Member and Employee classes. Figure 8-7 illustrates the structure.

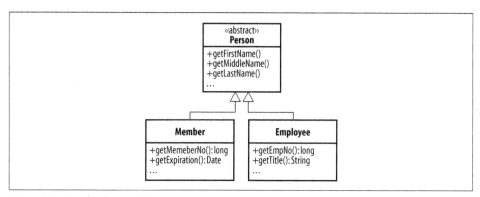

Figure 8-7. Simple abstract classes

Implementing concrete table inheritance for this structure gives us two tables, MEMBER and EMPLOYEE. Both tables contain the fields represented in the Person class, and also contain the additional fields present in the concrete implementing classes.

The advantage of concrete table inheritance is that it keeps the number of tables manageable, while still providing some separation, and the code is easy to understand.

Keeping all the data required to load a class instance in a single row of a single table also provides the best performance possible: in the world of databases, there is nothing more efficient than a single-row retrieval from a table based on a primary key.

Class Table Inheritance strategy

The major disadvantage of concrete table inheritance is that the database has no equivalent to the relationship between the abstract parent class and the concrete classes. While performing a query across members and employees is possible, it is difficult and convoluted. The *Class Table Inheritance strategy* supplies an alternative to the Concrete Table Inheritance strategy by providing a table for each class in the inheritance hierarchy, whether it's abstract or not. This makes it easier to run queries against common elements while ensuring that we unambiguously manage all the data associated with each entity.

With this approach, we address the Person-Member-Employee relationship by creating three tables, PERSON, MEMBER, and EMPLOYEE, each containing the fields specified by the equivalent class, and linked via a primary key on PERSON referenced as a foreign key by MEMBER and EMPLOYEE. Populating an instance of the Employee or Member classes requires reading from the PERSON table and the appropriate subtable. At the cost of increased complexity, this approach eliminates duplication, allows us to easily perform queries across all persons, and even allows a single person to be both an employee and a member, if necessary.*

 It's sometimes tempting to create a single large table containing every conceivable column, and use certain columns for certain types of records. This temptation should be resisted.

The Serialized Entity Pattern

Particularly in the early stages of development, sometimes we just need to build an easy-to-implement persistence system that incorporates the full richness of Java objects.

Many enterprise applications need to expose their underlying data to other systems: reporting and Enterprise Application Integration tools are two common examples. But not all applications do, either because an application is small, truly stand-alone, or because it provides its own interface to external systems, as is increasingly the case with web services. These applications don't need to worry about making their internal data externally intelligible.

---

* Of course, things can get confusing here on the Java side, since the Java object model doesn't support multiple inheritance. To support this kind of multiple relationship in your code, you would likely have to instantiate both an Employee and a Member object for the person. The advantage is that you can use the same database and the same record in the PERSON table.

The *Serialized Entity pattern* uses object serialization to store an object instance to persistent storage. In Java, this is done by implementing the Serializable interface, which allows an object and all of its fields to be written to a stream. The serialized object can be read back later and used to reconstruct the object in memory. Since serialization is stream-based, the objects can be stored directly on disk or within a database.

Serialized objects allow the object model to ensure data integrity across the application's complete data set via the usual Java programming practices. Since objects stored by reference in other objects are included in the serialization process, a complex object tree can be saved and restored in a single call, and changes to the data structure during development don't require any modifications to the persistence code.

The Serialized Entity pattern can be helpful during the development process. Implementing entity serialization is usually simple, particularly if it's done at a fairly high level in the object hierarchy. You can use serialization while your object develops, and switch over to implementing the Concrete Table Inheritance pattern or another approach once functional requirements have settled down. This strategy can be particularly effective in projects that use an iterative or test-driven design methodology, or in which requirements are in more flux than usual.

The pattern has two major disadvantages. Once stored in binary form, the objects are completely opaque to human inspection and to most if not all data analysis tools. Additionally, since the Java serialization method is based on the class itself, if the class signature changes, the serialized object becomes unusable. This means that when we're converting a production application, we must either write a conversion application that loads the old objects, converts them to the new object, and reserializes them, or develop a completely separate parallel transaction system that can be "played back" to rebuild the object model (see Chapter 10 for a little more discussion on transactions and auditing).

A serialized entity example

In this example, we'll serialize a DTO representing a museum member to the database and retrieve it. Here's the skeleton of the class we're persisting:

```
public class MemberDTO {
  public long getMemberNumber() {}
  public void setMemberNumber(long newMembernumber){}

  public String getFirstname() {}
  public void setFirstname(String newFirstname) {}
  public String getLastname() {}
  public void setLastname(String newLastname) {}
  public String getAddress1() {}
  public void setAddress1(String newAddress1) {}
  public String getAddress2() {}
  public void setAddress2(String newAddress2) {}
  public String getCity() {}
  public void setCity(String newCity) {}
  public String getState() {}
```

```
      public void setState(String newState) {}
      public String getZip() {}
      public void setZip(String newZip) {}
      public Long getFreePasses() {}
      public Long setFreePasses(Long passes) {}
   }
```

We'll leave out the concrete implementation for space (it can be downloaded with
the rest of the code examples for this book). The table structure looks like this:

```
SQL> desc members;
 Name                                Null?    Type
 ----------------------------------- -------- -------
 MEMBER_NO                           NOT NULL NUMBER
 OBJECT_DATA                                  BLOB
```

The DAO object that uses this table structure is shown in Example 8-5. We include
two methods: a finder to look up an object and a saver to persist it.

Example 8-5. MemberSerializedDAO.java

```java
import java.io.*;
import java.sql.*;
import javax.naming.*;

public class MemberSerializedDAO {

  public MemberSerializedDAO() {
  }


  public MemberDTO findMember(long member_no) {
    Connection con = null;
    PreparedStatement ps = null;
    ResultSet rs = null;
    MemberDTO member = null;

    try {
      con = getConnection();
      ps = con.prepareStatement(
        "select object_data from members where member_no = ?");
      ps.setLong(1, member_no);
      rs = ps.executeQuery();
      if(rs.next()) {
        ObjectInputStream ois = new ObjectInputStream(rs.getBinaryStream(1));
        member = (MemberDTO)ois.readObject();
        ois.close();
      }
      rs.close();
    } catch (ClassNotFoundException e) {
      e.printStackTrace();
    } catch (IOException e) {
      e.printStackTrace();
    } catch (SQLException e) {
      e.printStackTrace();
```

Example 8-5. MemberSerializedDAO.java (continued)

```java
  } finally {
    if (ps != null)
      try { ps.close( ); } catch (SQLException e) {}
    if (con != null)
      try { con.close( ); } catch (SQLException e) {}
  }

  return member;
}

public void saveMember(MemberDTO member)  {
  Connection con = null;
  PreparedStatement ps = null;
  ResultSet rs = null;

  long memberNo = member.getMemberNumber( );
  if(memberNo < 1)
    return;

  try {
    con = getConnection( );
    ps = con.prepareStatement("delete from members where member_no = ?");
    ps.setLong(1, memberNo);
    ps.executeUpdate( );
    ps.close( );

    ps = con.prepareStatement("insert into members " +
      "(member_no, object_data) values (?, ?)");
    ps.setLong(1, memberNo);
    ByteArrayOutputStream baos = new ByteArrayOutputStream( );
    ObjectOutputStream oos = new ObjectOutputStream(baos);
    oos.writeObject(member);
    ps.setBytes(2, baos.toByteArray( ));
    ps.executeUpdate( );

  } catch (IOException e) {
    e.printStackTrace( );
  } catch (SQLException e) {
    e.printStackTrace( );
  } finally {
    if(ps != null)
      try { ps.close( ); } catch (SQLException e) {}
    if(con != null)
      try { con.close( ); } catch (SQLException e) {}
  }
}

private Connection getConnection( ) throws SQLException {
  try {
    Context jndiContext = new InitialContext( );
    DataSource ds = (DataSource)
      jndiContext.lookup("java:comp/env/jdbc/DataChapterDS");
```

Example 8-5. MemberSerializedDAO.java (continued)

```
      return ds.getConnection( );
    } catch (NamingException ne) {
        throw new SQLException (ne.getMessage( ));
    }
  }
}
```

XML and serialized entities

The two major disadvantages of serialization can be overcome somewhat by using an XML-based serialization approach. There are a number of existing components that support XML serialization from Java objects, and if your implementation changes, it's easier to modify the existing data to load properly. XML creation and processing, though, are activities with high overhead.

Various technologies exist to make XML serialization easier, including the Java API for XML Binding (JAXB) and the Digester component available from the Jakarta project Commons library (*http://jakarta.apache.org*).

The Tuple Table Pattern

Serialized entities make it easy to change the structure of the objects in the application without having to adjust the persistence layer, but, as we mentioned, they have two major disadvantages: the persisted data is not human-readable, and existing data can be difficult to convert when the format changes. The *Tuple Table pattern* stores an object in the database in a highly flexible format that can be manipulated at the database level by normal human beings and can be easily extended without having to convert existing data.

Much of the data used in an enterprise application can be condensed into sets of fields. In simple applications, the fields can be stored as simple properties files, of the format:

```
name=value
othername=othervalue
```

And so forth. We can use this approach to persist objects to the database by assigning each object instance a primary key and then storing labeled values for each key (a *tuple*). Rather than storing an address in a table with an ADDRESS1 column, an ADDRESS2 column, a CITY column, and so on, we store it in a table with three columns: ADDRESS_KEY, FIELDNAME, and FIELDVALUE. An address might look like this in the database:

```
SQL> select address_key, fieldname, fieldvalue from addresses;

ADDRESS_KEY FIELDNAME    FIELDVALUE
----------- ----------   -------------------------------------------------
       9325 Address1     10 Main St
       9325 City         Upper Norfolk
       9325 State        NY
       9325 Zip          20123
```

In order to work with the result data, we can load it in a hashtable or map the values to fields in an object. If we want to add an Address2 field, all we have to do is start adding that row to the database and update our code accordingly. If we write things properly, the database will be seamlessly upward- and backward-compatible.

The primary advantage of this approach is extreme flexibility. By storing object fields as name and value pairs, we can modify the application to include new fields without changing the underlying database structure. Existing data can be preserved without requiring complicated migration scripts. And unlike serialized entities, the data can be viewed, edited, and analyzed from within the database environment itself, even though the SQL used in the analysis process might be a bit more complex than with a more rigidly defined data model.

The Tuple Table pattern can also make it easier to customize applications to different environments. Many enterprise applications are deployed in more than one environment, and often the data managed will differ slightly between implementations. For example, a CRM system deployed to one customer might need to track five different types of data per customer. The same system, deployed at another customer, might need to track four of those five data points, plus two others (such as membership in a customer loyalty program or a willingness to receive additional sales calls). Storing the customer data in a tuple table means that even if the classes using the data need to be modified for each client, the underlying schema can remain the same.

The primary disadvantage of the Tuple Table pattern is in its integrity enforcement. Relational databases are very good at enforcing rules at the column level, but aren't so good at enforcing rules at the data level. It's easy to tell the database to ensure that the value of the IS_PREVIOUS_CUSTOMER column is "T" or "F", but much harder to tell it to ensure that the value of the VALUE column is "T" or "F" if and only if the NAME column is "PreviousCustomer".

Tuple tables also exact a performance penalty. When retrieving field data from a database table, retrieving a single row containing only the field data is much more efficient than retrieving several rows, each of which contains both a name and a value. In addition to the extra networking overhead between the object and the database, the object must also do more processing. As usual, the tradeoff is between scalability and flexibility.

There are space considerations as well: storing a label for each individual piece of data will result in a much larger database, although with modern disk arrays this is less of a concern than in years past.

A tuple table example

We can use Java reflection with a DAO object to retrieve an object from a tuple table or write it back to the table. By using reflection, we can retrieve the field names directly from the object we're persisting. Here's the structure of the table we'll use:

```
SQL> desc object_data;
 Name                                      Null?    Type
 ----------------------------------------- -------- -------------
 OBJ_PK                                    NOT NULL NUMBER
 FIELDNAME                                 NOT NULL VARCHAR2(20)
 NUMERICAL                                          NUMBER
 STRING                                             VARCHAR2(255)
```

The OBJECT_DATA table doesn't know about particular object types; it's counting on the application to ensure that no two objects share a primary key. The FIELDNAME field stores the name of the field. The value of the field is stored in the NUMERICAL or STRING fields, depending on type. If both are null, the field is assumed to be null. Having a value in both columns is considered to be an invalid state.

Just like in the previous example, Example 8-6 is going to load an object of MemberDTO, describing a museum member. The findMember( ) method creates a new MemberDTO object based on a provided primary key. The saveMember( ) method takes a MemberDTO and saves it to the database, using the brute-force approach of wiping out the rows in the table for that primary key and replacing them. Also, on the Java side, we've limited our property types to String and Long objects, although they can be extended easily. We've also included a main( ) method that you can use to see how the program works.

Example 8-6. MemberTupleDAO.java

```java
import java.util.*;
import java.lang.reflect.*;
import java.sql.*;
import javax.sql.*;
import javax.naming.*;

public class MemberTupleDAO  {

  public MemberDTO findMember(long member_no)  {
    Connection con = null;
    PreparedStatement ps = null;
    ResultSet rs = null;
    MemberDTO member = new MemberDTO( );
    member.setMemberNumber(member_no);

    try {
      con = getConnection( );
      ps = con.prepareStatement("select fieldname, numerical, string " +
        "from object_data where obj_pk = ?");
      ps.setLong(1, member_no);
      rs = ps.executeQuery( );
```

Example 8-6. MemberTupleDAO.java (continued)

```java
    while(rs.next()) {
      String fieldName = rs.getString(1);
      String strVal = rs.getString(3);

      if(strVal != null)
        setVal(fieldName, member, strVal);
      else {
        // We do this indirectly to make database typecasting more reliable
        long lngVal = rs.getLong(2);
        if(!rs.wasNull())
          setVal(fieldName, member, new Long(lngVal));
      }
    }

    rs.close();
    ps.close();
  } catch (SQLException e) {
    e.printStackTrace();
    return null;
  } finally {
    if(con != null)
      try { con.close(); } catch (SQLException e) {}
  }

  return member;
}


public void saveMember(MemberDTO member)  {
  Connection con = null;
  PreparedStatement ps = null;
  ResultSet rs = null;

  long memberNo = member.getMemberNumber();
  if(memberNo < 1)
    return;

  Class[] stringParam = new Class[] {String.class};
  Class[] longParam = new Class[] {Long.class};

  try {
    con = getConnection();
    ps = con.prepareStatement("delete from object_data where obj_pk = ?");
    ps.setLong(1, memberNo);
    ps.executeUpdate();
    ps.close();

    ps = con.prepareStatement("insert into object_data " +
      "(obj_pk, fieldname, numerical, string) values (?, ?, ?, ?)");
    ps.setLong(1, memberNo);
```

Example 8-6. MemberTupleDAO.java (continued)

```java
      Method[] methods = member.getClass().getMethods();
      for(int i=0; i < methods.length; i++) {
        String mName = methods[i].getName();
        if(mName.startsWith("get")) {
          try {
            if(methods[i].getReturnType() == String.class) {
              ps.setString(2, mName.substring(3));
              ps.setNull(3, Types.NUMERIC);
              ps.setString(4, (String)methods[i].invoke(member, new Object[] {}));
              ps.executeUpdate();
            } else if (methods[i].getReturnType() == Long.class) {
              ps.setString(2, mName.substring(3));
              ps.setObject(3, (Long)methods[i].invoke(member, new Object[] {}),
                Types.NUMERIC);
              ps.setNull(4, Types.VARCHAR);
              ps.executeUpdate();
            }
          } catch (IllegalAccessException e) {
            e.printStackTrace();
          }catch (InvocationTargetException e) {
            e.printStackTrace();
          }
        }
      }
      ps.close();

    } catch (SQLException e) {
      e.printStackTrace();
    } finally {
      if(ps != null)
        try { ps.close(); } catch (SQLException e) {}
      if(con != null)
        try { con.close(); } catch (SQLException e) {}
    }
  }

  /**
   * Set a value on the target object, by searching for a set<fieldName> method
   * which takes a parameter of the same type as the "param" parameter.
   */
  private void setVal(String fieldName, Object target, Object param) {

    try {
      Class targetClass = target.getClass();
      Method setter = targetClass.getMethod("set" + fieldName,
                                            new Class[] { param.getClass() });
      setter.invoke(target, new Object[] { param });
    } catch (NoSuchMethodException e) {
      // Ignore it - it must not be in the target
    } catch (InvocationTargetException e) {
    } catch (IllegalAccessException e) {
      e.printStackTrace();
```

Example 8-6. MemberTupleDAO.java (continued)

```
    }
  }

  private Connection getConnection() throws SQLException {
    try {
      Context jndiContext = new InitialContext();
      DataSource ds = (DataSource)
        jndiContext.lookup("java:comp/env/jdbc/DataChapterDS");
      return ds.getConnection();
    } catch (NamingException ne) {
        throw new SQLException (ne.getMessage());
    }
  }

  public static void main(String [] args) {

    MemberTupleDAO mtd = new MemberTupleDAO();
    MemberDTO member = mtd.findMember(1);
    System.out.println(member.getFirstname() + " " + member.getLastname());
    System.out.println(member.getFreePasses());
    System.out.println(member.getCity());
    System.out.println(member.getAddress1());

    member.setMemberNumber(4);
    member.setFirstname("Reginald");
    mtd.saveMember(member);

    member = mtd.findMember(4);
    // Will display "Reginald" and the last name from the original member
    System.out.println(member.getFirstname() + " " + member.getLastname());
  }
}
```

When using tuple tables and reflection, remember that if you change the structure of your objects, you'll have to update the database to include the new field names. This isn't much of a chore: converting data is generally just a simple SQL UPDATE statement, and after the development phase is over, your model shouldn't change much.

CHAPTER 9

Business Tier Interfaces

If you've been reading this book straight through, you've been subjected to discussions of the top and bottom of a Java enterprise application: the presentation tier and the domain model. However, we've mostly talked around the interface between the two. That's because it's hard to talk about interfaces without knowing what's being interfaced.

But here we are. *Business tier interfaces* connect the domain model with the client (in thick-client applications) or the server-side presentation layer (in web applications). They also implement some of the business logic for an application, controlling and limiting the actions that the presentation tier can perform on the domain model.

Integrating the client with the business logic for an application poses a few problems for the developer. The big one, of course, is organizational. If you've been doing use case-oriented design, you probably have a very good idea of the activities your users need to perform, and of the various business rules that will apply. But how do you represent these as Java objects? That's a hard question. It's equally difficult to decide where to put everything. EJBs? Client code? Database stored procedures? In Chapter 6, we introduced the ideas of process (or business) logic and domain logic. This split provides the basis for dividing logic between different components of the business tier: process logic for verbs (the transformations of the domain model), and domain logic for constraints on the nouns (the defined interrelations of the object model itself). In Chapter 8, we discussed methods for connecting the domain model and the database persistence layer, and for hiding the nature of the persistence layer from the implementation of the domain model.

Here's the wrinkle: even after several years of madly webizing every legacy application in sight, many enterprise development projects still aren't starting from scratch. Instead, many IT teams are still putting web interfaces on existing applications. Often these projects go a step further and try to create a Java-based path for future development. But this approach can be dangerous: attempting to fit a Java layer over domain models and business logic code designed for an earlier set of technologies risks warping the design into a hybrid monstrosity with one foot in each world.

In this situation, the business tier interface provides the gateway between the Java world and the legacy world. Constructing this gateway may mean the difference between evolving the Java component of the application for years, gradually upgrading or replacing the legacy components, and throwing the whole thing away when the legacy systems are phased out.

This chapter focuses on patterns for packaging and presenting the business logic of an application. The *Business Delegate pattern* and the *Session Façade pattern* address the organization of process logic and the division between the domain logic and the process logic. As an added bonus, both of these patterns provide performance enhancements in addition to their organizational benefits. We'll also discuss the *Business Delegate Factory pattern*, which allows us to build more effective non-EJB applications by creating our own versions of some of the services provided by a full application server.

We also cover two patterns for connecting to remote business services. The *Service Adapter pattern*, which is a variation on the original Gang of Four *Adapter* pattern, can be used to provide a useful Java-based interface to non-EJB business tier resources. The *Service Locator pattern* provides centralized management of connections to Enterprise JavaBeans and other remote resources.

Abstracting Business Logic

The last few chapters explored ways to keep the presentation tier and the business tier separate. We accomplished this by wrapping the domain logic for the system in both regular and Enterprise JavaBeans and introducing various controller patterns, including the MVC and Service to Worker patterns, in order to mediate the interaction between the tiers. This decoupling makes the overall system easier to understand and maintain. But without a good way to communicate between the tiers, the advantages can quickly be lost. The *Business Delegate* and *Business Delegate Factory* patterns provide client-side objects that flexibly connect the presentation and business tiers.

Business Delegate

In an MVC design, the controller still has to interact directly with the business tier (the model). The view will do so as well, although in a read-only fashion and mediated through the controller. This exposes the underlying implementation details of the business tier to the presentation tier. The application needs to know enough about the business tier to perform the operations requested by the client, and enough about the networking infrastructure between the presentation tier and the business tier to locate the business objects in the first place. The result is a tightly coupled application.

The *Business Delegate pattern* defines a client-side object that handles communications with the business objects. It fulfills the model role in an MVC framework. The business delegate doesn't necessarily contain any business logic itself, but encapsulates knowledge about how to locate, connect to, and interact with the business objects that make up the application. These objects might be in the same JVM, or they might be remote Enterprise JavaBeans, CORBA components, web services, or other resources. The business delegate is also responsible for returning enough data to the controller to allow the controller to instantiate an appropriate view.

The business delegate wraps access to a series of business objects and business services into a single, easy-to-implement application call. It can also incorporate all of the networking code required to access those resources, including any retries, caching, or exception handling that might be required. Networking or database access exceptions can be converted into application exceptions for consistent and user-friendly handling.

The UML diagram in Figure 9-1 shows a basic set of object relationships for an application using business delegates. The client interacts with the business delegate object, which in turn interacts with a set of *business services*. Some of these services are instantiated directly, and others are retrieved via a *service locator* class. The service locator provides a directory interface to locate the various business services used by the business delegate. In EJB environments, this is often a JNDI server. We cover service locators later in this chapter.

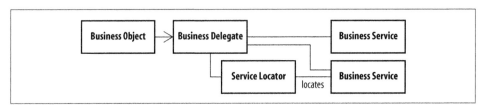

Figure 9-1. Business delegate

The major difference between our definition of Business Delegate and others is that we don't consider them to be pure EJB front ends. Rather, we consider them the client-side equivalent of an EJB session bean: an object that contains a front end to the process logic underlying an application. It doesn't matter whether the business delegate object implements that logic itself, parcels it out to other components, or does a little of both. The presentation tier delegates business process responsibilities to the business delegate, and that's more or less the end of that.

Our version varies from the version presented in Sun's J2EE Patterns collection.[*] For one thing, we make the Service Locator component optional. While Service Locators are often a good idea, we don't consider them vital to a business delegate implementation.

*http://java.sun.com/blueprints/patterns/

Organizing business logic into business delegates

If none of the external resources available to the business delegate are capable of incorporating all of the business logic, then the business delegate's own implementation should provide the missing elements. For example, consider a use case that involves retrieving stock information from a web service, computing a shipping charge, and submitting stock updates and shipping information to two additional web services. Because business delegates can be shared, we don't consider it bad practice to include the code for computing shipping charges in the business delegate implementation. Of course, it does make sense to consider ways to move that functionality into other areas that can be reused more easily, but that's almost always true. Incorporating the code directly into the presentation tier (having a servlet compute the charges before submitting the order), on the other hand, would easily prove problematic.

The quantity of business logic included in the business delegate depends on the application's persistence model. If the business tier consists exclusively of EJB entity beans that represent the data model, the business delegate will, of necessity, have to incorporate a substantial amount of domain knowledge. It must know which entity beans to create, remove, or update to perform a particular activity. A delegate for a legacy interface, on the other hand, may simply relay calls to an existing API that handles object management. In both cases, we consider the business delegate to be part of the business logic tier, even if the object itself is instantiated at the client tier.

We'll talk more about the division of business logic between business delegates and EJBs later in this chapter, when we discuss the Session Façade pattern.

Business delegate implementation

In an iterative or distributed environment, the business delegate can be stubbed out first, allowing development to proceed on the presentation tier while the ultimate business logic implementation is worked out. For applications that include complex relationships with external systems, this approach substantially accelerates development.

Example 9-1 shows a very simple business delegate. It performs a data validity check and then uses a DAO object to update the domain objects. In a real application, the business delegate doesn't need to be much more complex. It should be easy to see how we would convert this class to an EJB session bean.

Example 9-1. A business delegate

```
public class PatientManagementDelegate {

  public static PatientDTO createNewPatient(PatientDTO patient)
    throws InvalidPatientException{

    if(patient == null|| patient.getFirstName() == null
        || patient.getLastName() == null)
          throw new InvalidPatientException(
            "Patient Records Require Full Name");
```

Example 9-1. A business delegate (continued)

```
    PatientDAO pDAO = PatientDAOFactory.getPatientDAO( );
    PatientDTO newPatientRecord = pDAO.createPatient(patient);

    return newPatientRecord;
  }

}
```

The implementation of the business delegate can include other patterns as well, further hiding the business logic's complexity from the client. For example, a business delegate can use the Gang of Four Strategy pattern to retrieve data from different sources depending on runtime requirements or changing infrastructure (we touched on the Strategy pattern in Chapter 2).

In an EJB environment, business delegates usually work as a front end to a session bean (specifically, to a *session façade*, which we'll discuss later in this chapter). Implementing the presentation tier-to-EJB tier connection this way insulates the presentation tier programmers from the EJB environment, and simplifies error handling, since the various EJB exceptions can be caught, handled, and either resolved within the delegate or reported to the presentation layer in a consistent, simplified manner. A business delegate can throw exceptions related to the business process rather than exceptions related to the EJB environment.

Nesting business delegates

Since a business delegate is an access point to business logic and the domain model, there's no reason it can't use the resources of other business delegates. Business delegates can be nested arbitrarily deep, particularly when you're not in an EJB environment. This ability allows you to create separate business delegates for each use case and combine them as needed to implement the master use cases for your application.

For example, Figure 9-2 shows how a servlet, accessing a business delegate object to submit an order to a purchasing system, might actually invoke three different delegates, even though the servlet only sees one of them.

Nesting business delegates means that we have to keep track of the resources each delegate uses. For example, if each call to a business delegate retrieves a database connection and doesn't return it until all processing is completed (whether by instantiating DAO objects or retrieving the connection directly), a call stack containing five business delegate instances might hold onto five separate database connections. This means that a pool of 25 database connections can only support 5 concurrent users.

Using nested business delegates in an EJB application could result in inappropriate connections between different EJBs. If a session bean uses a business delegate to access another session bean, the business delegate may have to make a remote connection to the second bean, even if it's located in the same EJB server. If the session bean connected directly, it could easily use local interfaces instead. We'll address this issue later in this chapter with the Session Façade pattern.

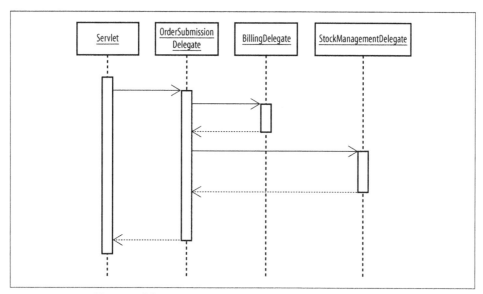

Figure 9-2. Nested business delegates

The other major issue raised by nested business delegates is transaction control. A presentation tier programmer will, absent indications to the contrary, expect that each call to a business delegate method takes part in one transaction. If each business delegate creates its own transaction, the nested delegates will handle their transactions separately from the parent delegate. At best, this process results in incomplete rollbacks when the parent delegate fails; at worst, it will result in database resource locks and the application slowing or grinding to a halt. Since this isn't a simple issue, we'll look at transaction issues in enterprise applications in much more detail in the next chapter, including a pattern, *Transactional Context*, which addresses the problem specifically.

Stateful business delegates

Business delegates can be stateful or stateless. To use a stateful business delegate, generate an instance of the business delegate class. To create a stateless business delegate, declare the business delegate methods as static, and call them accordingly. You can also make the business delegate class a singleton. Either way, all classes running in the same Java VM and class loader will share a stateless business delegate. For web applications, this means that all the code will share the delegate.

The tradeoffs between stateful and stateless business delegates are almost identical to the tradeoffs between stateful and stateless session beans in EJB. Stateful delegates require more resources and can be marginally slower, due to the overhead of creating the additional objects. On the other hand, they allow you to configure a particular instance to your needs, making the delegates themselves easier to reuse. Stateless delegates require less memory and present a simpler interface to the programmer.

Here's a rule of thumb: if a business delegate requires a resource that is both expensive to create and that must be created specifically for the current user (such as a JAAS security principal), and if that resource will be used multiple times within the same delegate by the same thread, use a stateful delegate. You should also use a stateful delegate if the delegate needs complex configuration specifically for the current invocation, rather than trying to pass in all configuration information with each method call. Otherwise, look for opportunities to use a stateless delegate.

Business Delegate Factory Pattern

Since the simplest business delegates are just objects with static methods, we don't need to worry about creating or configuring them. But once we start using stateful business delegates, things get more complicated—even with stateless delegates we can eventually accumulate so many of them that it becomes hard to keep track. Architectures using business delegates face the following problems:

- No standard for instantiating business delegates, making it difficult to exchange one delegate for another
- Instantiation code, which may include configuring the delegate to access runtime-specific resources, is spread across the application
- No centralized directory of available business logic

We can address these points with the *Business Delegate Factory pattern*. The Business Delegate Factory pattern is specialization of the Gang of Four *Factory pattern*, much as we saw in Chapter 8 with the DAO Factory pattern. A business delegate factory is a single object responsible for creating instances or one or more kinds of business delegates.

Depending on your application, the factory can produce a particular kind of business delegate (resulting in one factory per delegate class), or a set of delegates related by their configuration requirements or general functionality. Having a broad-spectrum factory makes it easier to find the various business delegates within an application, but also introduces additional compilation dependencies.

Like business delegates themselves, business delegate factories can be stateful or stateless. The same rules apply: if the factory needs to be configured for the current thread/user/block of code, or if creating a new delegate instance requires an expensive resource that cannot be shared between all users of the application, consider a stateful factory. Otherwise, consider a stateless factory.

Figure 9-3 shows the sequence diagram for a stateful factory creating a stateful business delegate. It's a simple process: the client application creates a new instance of the factory by calling a static newInstance( ) method. It then calls a setAttribute(...) method to configure the factory, and finally requests an instance of a particular business delegate type. The factory creates the delegate instance and returns it to the client. At the end of their useful lives, both the factory and delegate objects go out of scope and are garbage-collected.

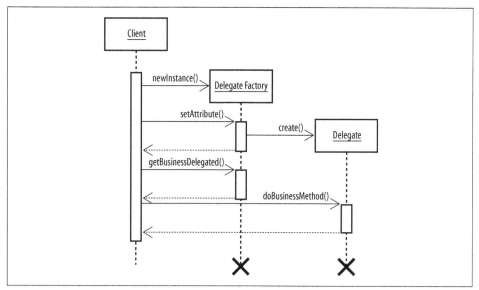

Figure 9-3. Stateful business delegate factory

A stateless business delegate factory would look similar but could include all of the code executed in the newInstance() and setAttribute() methods in static initialization blocks or in the getBusinessDelegate() method, which would now be a static method on the delegate factory class. If we implement the delegate as a singleton, the initialization can still take place at startup.

Modifying business delegate behavior

The Business Delegate Factory pattern lets you add functionality to your business delegates at runtime. As a simple example, consider logging. An application might need to support logging calls to business delegate methods but require different levels of detail, or different outputs, depending on the current status of the application. The simplest way of implementing this functionality (and the road most often taken) is to implement the logging functions in each business delegate object, perhaps tagging them with a "Loggable" interface, and toggling logging on or off via a centralized control class or at creation-time within the factory.

Other solutions take better advantage of the object-oriented nature of Java and create wrapper classes for each business delegate. The factory can wrap each delegate in the appropriate logging wrapper when logging is required, and skip the step when it isn't. The problem is that we need to maintain a separate logging wrapper for each business delegate class, and update them at the same time we update the delegate. It's a lot of work, and a lot of class profusion.

Obviously, we're leading up to something! The Java reflection API (which we've already seen in Chapter 8) includes a class called Proxy, which allows you to dynamically create an object that implements a given set of interfaces. An InvocationHandler object handles calls to methods on those interfaces, and the entire assemblage is referred to as a *proxy object*. Most uses of this class involve taking an existing object, extracting its interfaces, and creating a new object that implements those same interfaces while providing some additional functionality. The new object can delegate method calls to the original object or handle method invocations itself. Figure 9-4 shows how this can work in practice.

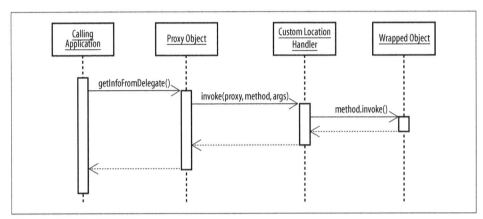

Figure 9-4. Wrapping an object with an InvocationHandler

The custom InvocationHandler includes a reference to the wrapped object. When the application calls methods on the proxy object, the invocation handler forwards the method on to the original object and returns the results to the application.

Example 9-2 shows how we can apply this technique to the logging problem. The DelegateLoggingWrapper class includes a single method, decorate( ), and an inner class defining a LoggingWrapperHandler, which implements the InvocationHandler interface. The invoke( ) method prints out the name of the method and the arguments passed into it, invokes the method on the original object, prints another message confirming success, and returns the result of the method call. In the next chapter, we'll use this approach to handle transaction management within and across business delegates.

Example 9-2. DelegateLoggingWrapper.java

```
import java.lang.reflect.InvocationHandler;
import java.lang.reflect.InvocationTargetException;
import java.lang.reflect.Method;
import java.lang.reflect.Proxy;

final class DelegateLoggingWrapper {
    /**
     * Decorates a business delegate object with a Logging Wrapper.
     * The object returned by this method will implement all of the
     * interfaces originally implemented by the target
```

Example 9-2. DelegateLoggingWrapper.java (continued)

```java
     * and loaded by the same class loader as that of the target.
     * @param delegate The Business Delegate to wrap
     * @return The business delegate wrapped in this wrapper
     */
    static Object decorate(Object delegate) {
        return Proxy.newProxyInstance(
            delegate.getClass().getClassLoader( ),
            delegate.getClass().getInterfaces( ),
            new LoggingWrapperHandler(delegate));
    }

    static final class LoggingWrapperHandler
                    implements InvocationHandler {
        private final Object delegate;

        LoggingWrapperHandler(Object delegate) {
            this.delegate = delegate;
        }

        /** Invoke the target method, but display logging
            information first. */
        public Object invoke(Object proxy, Method method,
                            Object[] args)
            throws Throwable {
            System.out.println("Invoked Business Delegate Method: " +
                method.getName( ));

            if (args != null) {
                for (int i = 0; i < args.length; i++) {
                    System.out.print(args[i]);
                    System.out.print(
                      (i < (args.length - 1)) ? "," : "\n");
                }
            }

            Object result = method.invoke(delegate, args);
            System.out.println("Completed Without Exception");

            return result;
        }
    }
}
```

Example 9-3 shows how to use invocation proxies in the business delegate factory itself. We've created a static factory object that produces runtime instances of each delegate object (to save space, we've included only one delegate type). The user can call static methods on the class in order to start or stop logging. If logging is enabled, the DelegateLoggingWrapper is used to add logging capability. Note that we've shifted the logging/no-logging decision all the way down to the wrap( ) method, rather than placing it in the delegate creation methods. While this adjustment is marginally slower, it reduces the amount of code we need to write in each delegate creation method, and makes it easier to add support for additional wrappers later.

Example 9-3. BusinessDelegateFactory with logging

```java
public class BusinessDelegateFactory {

  private static boolean useLogging = false;

  public static PatientManagementDelegate
              getPatientManagementDelegate( ) {
    PatientManagementDelegate delegate =
       new PatientManagementDelegateImpl( );
    return (PatientManagementDelegate)wrap(delegate);
  }

  private static Object wrap(Object o) {
    if(useLogging)
      return DelegateLoggingWrapper.decorate(o);
    return o;
  }

  public static void startLogging( ) {
    useLogging = true;
  }

  public static void stopLogging( ) {
    useLogging = false;
  }

  public static boolean getLogStatus( ) {
    return useLogging;
  }
}
```

You probably noticed that the proxy object requires interfaces, rather than concrete classes. Rather than maintain a single class for each business delegate we want to wrap, we now need to maintain an implementation class and an interface. This is simple enough to do (and still less work than maintaining separate wrapper classes for each delegate, since it's easy to update the interface at the same time a delegate changes: no additional code needs to be written). We assume you already know how to create an interface, but for completeness, Example 9-4 shows the interface for the patient management delegate.

Example 9-4. PatientManagementDelegate.java (interface)

```java
public interface PatientManagementDelegate
{
  public PatientDTO createNewPatient(PatientDTO patient)
    throws InvalidPatientException;
}
```

Example 9-4 expects a `PatientManagementDelegateImpl` object that implements this interface. The code for this class is exactly the same as in Example 9-1, but renamed and with an `implements` clause.

This approach to modifying behavior on the fly does have performance implications. Each request for a business delegate now carries the overhead of creating the proxy object, which increases the time required to create a new business delegate instance. Each method call also incurs additional overhead, both for the reflection activity itself and whatever activities the wrapper performs. In absolute terms, the difference due to reflection is measured in microseconds, and we don't consider it significant, particularly given that the business delegates and the wrapper objects are likely to be participating in much more resource intensive activities.

Since the Factory pattern itself is fundamental to good object-oriented programming (out of everything in the original Gang of Four book, it may well be the pattern most frequently encountered),[*] it's worth keeping the proxy approach in mind when implementing other areas of your system. We have already seen a number of different kinds of proxies, including the Decorators from Chapter 3.

Accessing Remote Services

Business delegates are great for providing local code with access to business resources, whether the resources themselves are local or not. For local resources the data lives on the same server—maybe even in the same JVM—as the business delegate. In these situations, connecting to the data is not a huge concern. J2EE, however, is designed to handle much more complicated scenarios. An enterprise J2EE deployment typically involves resources that are distributed between multiple servers. To fulfill requests, the servers hosting the presentation tier may need to communicate with application servers, messaging middleware servers, database servers, and legacy IS systems. Finding all these servers and maintaining the various connections can quickly complicate otherwise simple business delegates.

Since the work of connecting is not central to the business delegate, it is often beneficial to build a separate object that the delegates can use to access remote services. The Service Adapter and Service Locator patterns describe ways to do this, the former for non-J2EE business services and the latter primarily for EJBs. Figure 9-5 shows how the service locator and service adapter act as intermediaries between the business delegates and business services.

---

[*] Not that we've actually done any research on that.

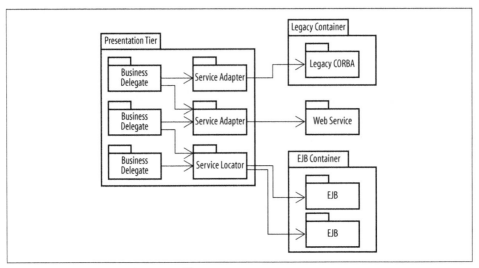

Figure 9-5. Using service adapters and locators

The Service Adapter Pattern

A business delegate might make use of several services to fulfill a particular use case. In order to keep the business logic code understandable and maintainable, we want to use the simplest interfaces possible. A service adapter encapsulates interactions with a remote service, hiding details of the implementation when they aren't central to fulfilling the business need.

The *Service Adapter pattern* is a variation on the Gang of Four Adapter pattern. The Adapter pattern wraps a class in a superclass that implements a standard interface. The Service Adapter pattern goes one step further by wrapping a remote service in a standard Java object that can be used without knowledge of the underlying access mechanism. The Java wrapper is responsible for:

- Locating the Remote Service.
- Translating Java method calls into a format that the remote service understands.
- Accessing remote functionality.
- Translating results into a pure Java representation.

The Service Adapter pattern is overkill for EJBs, which already map business methods to Java methods. The translation activities are not required, and the directory services abstracted by a service adapter can be better addressed in the EJB context with the Service Locator pattern, discussed later in this chapter.

However, if the native interface to the external service is not Java, a service adapter can bridge the gap. A good example is an application that needs to access a SOAP-based web service. The service might be delivered by SOAP over HTTP, SOAP over

SMTP, or via specialized, routed protocols like ebXML. The service adapter hides the complexities of creating a SOAP or ebXML message, allowing the developer to substitute different transport mechanisms as the needs of the application evolve. A SOAP-based service adapter in a prototype system can be replaced with a JMS-based adapter before going to production. Figure 9-6 shows a service adapter for a SOAP web service.

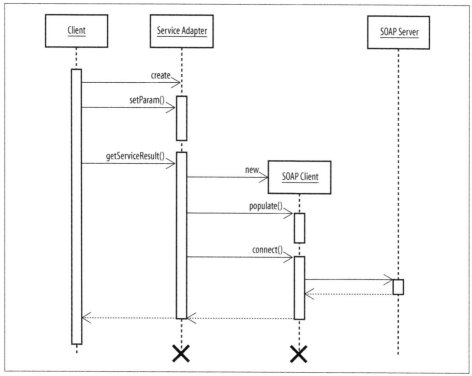

Figure 9-6. Service adapter for a SOAP web service

In J2EE 1.4 or earlier versions with the appropriate add-on modules, the JAX-RPC API and support tools can be used to build service adapters for web services. This largely eliminates the need to hand-code service adapters for web services.

The most recent Java IDEs support building service adapters directly from WSDL definition files. Some tools do this in a more platform-independent way than others, so it's worth watching for portability issues when using such tools. However, most of the generated code is either already reusable or can be easily modified to be so. Let's look at how this might work with a simple web service. Sticking with our health care theme, imagine a web service that returns a patient's medical records. Since complex data is more useful than simple data (and because we don't want to have to execute a few dozen web service requests for each use case), we've written the service to return a number of pieces of data with each request, in the form of a complex XML type. (If you're new to web services programming, now would be a good time to go read *Java Web Services*, by Dave Chappell and Tyler Jewell, also published by O'Reilly.)

A call to a web service can return a simple data type (numbers, strings, etc.) or a complex type. Complex types are defined within the WSDL file that specifies the web service, in the form of embedded XML Schema documents. In this case, the schema for the patient record type looks like this:

```
<schema
        targetNamespace="http://chapter9/IMedicalRecordService.xsd"
        xmlns="http://www.w3.org/2001/XMLSchema"
        xmlns:SOAP-ENC="http://schemas.xmlsoap.org/soap/encoding/">
        <complexType name="chapter9_PatientRecord">
            <all>
                <element name="FirstName" type="string"/>
                <element name="LastName" type="string"/>
                <element name="MiddleName" type="string"/>
                <element name="Address1" type="string"/>
                <element name="Address2" type="string"/>
                <element name="City" type="string"/>
                <element name="State" type="string"/>
                <element name="Zip" type="string"/>
                <element name="Country" type="string"/>
                <element name="PatientID" type="long"/>
            </all>
        </complexType>
    </schema>
```

Within our application, we've defined a JavaBean, PatientRecord, which corresponds with this type. The JavaBean includes the same String and long properties, in traditional get/set form, and is otherwise indistinguishable from any other JavaBean.

Example 9-5 shows a class that uses the Apache SOAP toolset to identify a web service, calls its getMedicalRecord() method with a patient identifier as a parameter, and translates the return value from the XML defined in the WSDL file (shown above) into the JavaBean defined within our application. It then returns the JavaBean to the code that called it.

The code is pretty simple, and it gets even simpler once you realize that it's largely auto-generated: our IDE put most of the adapter code together based on the WSDL file and the JavaBean. All we did was clean it up and replace a vendor-provided SOAPHTTPConnection implementation with Apache's freely available version.

Example 9-5. MedicalRecordServiceAdapter.java

```
import org.apache.soap.transport.http.SOAPHTTPConnection;
import org.apache.soap.encoding.soapenc.BeanSerializer;
import org.apache.soap.encoding.SOAPMappingRegistry;
import org.apache.soap.util.xml.QName;
import org.apache.soap.*;
import org.apache.soap.rpc.*;

import java.net.URL;
```

Example 9-5. MedicalRecordServiceAdapter.java (continued)

```java
import java.util.*;

public class MedicalRecordServiceAdapter {

  public MedicalRecordServiceAdapter( ) {
    m_httpConnection = new SOAPHTTPConnection( );
    m_smr = new SOAPMappingRegistry( );

    BeanSerializer beanSer = new BeanSerializer( );
    m_smr.mapTypes(Constants.NS_URI_SOAP_ENC,
      new QName("http://chapter9/IMedicalRecordService.xsd",
        "chapter9_PatientRecord"), chapter9.PatientRecord.class,
        beanSer, beanSer);
  }

  public String endpoint =
    "http://service.hospital.org/records/MedicalRecordService";
  private SOAPHTTPConnection m_httpConnection = null;
  private SOAPMappingRegistry m_smr = null;

  public PatientRecord getMedicalRecord(Long patientID)
    throws Exception {
    PatientRecord returnVal = null;

    URL endpointURL = new URL(endpoint);
    Call call = new Call( );
    call.setSOAPTransport(m_httpConnection);
    call.setTargetObjectURI("chapter9.MedicalRecordService");
    call.setMethodName("getMedicalRecord");
    call.setEncodingStyleURI(Constants.NS_URI_SOAP_ENC);

    Vector params = new Vector( );
    params.addElement(new Parameter("patientID",
      java.lang.Long.class, patientID, null));
    call.setParams(params);

    call.setSOAPMappingRegistry(m_smr);

    Response response = call.invoke(endpointURL, "");

    if (!response.generatedFault( )) {
      Parameter result = response.getReturnValue( );
      returnVal = (PatientRecord)result.getValue( );
    }
    else {
      Fault fault = response.getFault( );
      throw new SOAPException(fault.getFaultCode( ), fault.getFaultString( ));
    }

    return returnVal;
  }

}
```

Using this service adapter in a regular application is easy. To print out a patient's first name, all you would need to do is:

```
try {
    MedicalRecordServiceAdapter adapter =
        new MedicalRecordServiceAdapter();
    System.out.println(adapter.getMedicalRecord(new Long(4)).getFirstName());
}
catch(Exception ex) {
    ex.printStackTrace();
}
```

Session Façade

Enterprise JavaBeans take much of the complexity of building a distributed system out of the hands of the developer. They do not, however, eliminate that complexity: they hide it under an easy-to-use implementation (or at least easier). Just because you, the programmer, don't have to write the code for transporting data across a TCP/IP connection, doesn't mean that the data doesn't have to get transported.

Performance can be a challenge in EJB architectures, particularly when you don't have a lot of computing muscle to put behind your application. If a client application needs to access multiple entity beans in order to perform a transaction, it must make a network call each time it retrieves a new entity bean or calls an EJB method. The performance consequences are potentially huge, since a single network invocation can take several hundred milliseconds or more, depending on the amount of work that has to be done on the other side and the state of the intervening network.

The *Composite Entity Bean pattern* reduces the number of entity beans in a system and makes them easier to manipulate but does not address the broader performance problem. To make matters worse, even the best entity bean designs usually involve more than one bean per use case. A client wishing to modify more than one entity bean in the course of a transaction must handle transaction control itself, via the JTA API or another mechanism. Alternately, the business logic for the specific use case can be built into one entity bean, but this approach results in a massively overcomplicated entity bean design, in which domain objects have far too much knowledge of the context in which they are used.

EJB entity beans also don't provide much help when it comes to structuring business logic. The Business Delegate pattern helps organize an application's business logic in a convenient, easy-to-use manner, but doesn't control the number of network calls or simplify transaction management (although the burden can be shifted to the Business Delegate from the client application itself, which can be of some advantage to the programmers involved).

The *Session Façade pattern* addresses these issues by grouping sets of activities into a session bean that can be invoked by a client to complete an entire use case at once. The façade is a business-tier object that hides the session beans, entity beans, and other business services from the presentation tier. Figure 9-7 shows how the components fit together.

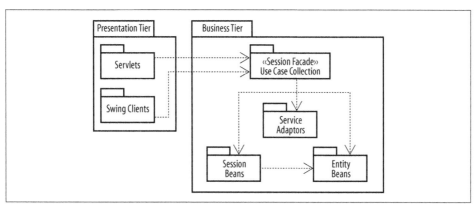

Figure 9-7. Package diagram for a session façade

Using the session façade simplifies transaction management. Since transaction control is implemented at the first point of entry into a method on the EJB, a business method attached to a session façade can manipulate all of the entity and session beans required to fulfill the current use case within a single transaction.

Figure 9-8 shows a potential class diagram for an EJB session façade that provides two business methods and makes use of generic business objects, EJB session beans, and EJB entity beans (in one case directly, in another indirectly via the session bean). The session façade can also use service adapters to access non-EJB resources.

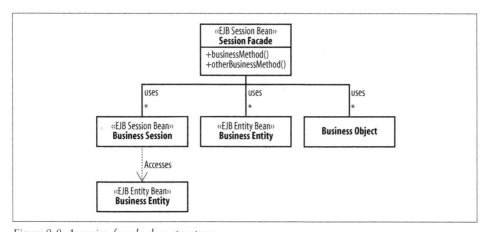

Figure 9-8. A session façade class structure

Session façades provide a performance boost because interactions between EJBs within a server are much more efficient than interactions between EJBs and remote clients: with EJB 2.0, local beans can use local interfaces to communicate with one another, cutting out the networking layer. All of the activities shown in Figure 9-9 can take place on the server. The client needs to call only one of the façade's business methods.

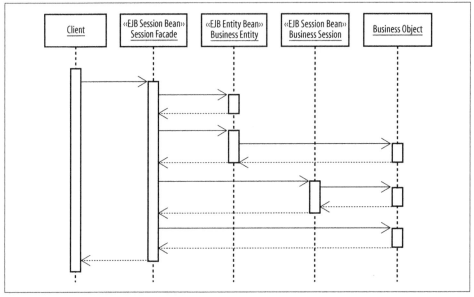

Figure 9-9. Sequence diagram for a session façade

Not all session beans are session façades! Business rules usually should not be implemented within the façade itself. A mathematical formula assessing a customer's credit rating, for example, belongs either in the entity bean representing the customer or in a separate, "utility" session bean, depending on how tightly coupled it is to the entity and whether the rule needs to be reused in other contexts. Conversely, remote applications shouldn't access any EJBs except for session façades. That same credit rating assessment *should* be included in (or at least accessible via) a session façade when the use case reports a credit assessment back to the presentation tier.

Use cases can be divided between a set of façades, although splitting use cases between session façades can be as much an art as a science. Creating a separate session façade for each use case can rapidly lead to a profusion of session façades. At the same time, avoid creating a single session façade for the entire application, unless the application is extremely small. All-encompassing session façades are sometimes known as "God Façades" or "God Objects." A God façade inevitably becomes difficult to maintain as the number of included use cases increases.

When organizing logic into a session façade, try to locate groups of related use cases. An e-commerce system, for example, might use a single session façade for all activities related to processing sales: checking inventory, setting shipping, arranging handling, and billing customers. Another façade might support catalog activities, and a third could handle account management for individual customers.

It's helpful to organize your use cases in an outline format, using the highest-level items as your top-level session façades. This technique usually leads to a nice balance between class complexity and class profusion.

Implementing a session façade

The EJB 2.0 specification introduced local EJBs, which can boost the performance of session beans by avoiding excessive round trips to the same server (see the Round-Tripping antipattern in Chapter 12). By restricting local EJBs to the same JVM, much of the overhead associated with translating data to and from network formats can be avoided. Example 9-6 shows a simple session façade, which uses the local interfaces of a number of EJBs to process a sale.

Example 9-6. A session façade EJB

```
import javax.ejb.*;
import java.util.*;
import javax.naming.*;

public class SaleFacadeBean implements SessionBean {
    private SessionContext context;
    private LocalCustomerHome customerHome;
     private LocalItemHome itemHome;
     private LocalSalesRecordHome recordHome;

    public void setSessionContext(SessionContext aContext) {
        context=aContext;
    }

    public void ejbActivate( ) {}
    public void ejbPassivate( ) {}

    public void ejbRemove( ) {
        customerHome = null;
        itemHome = null;
        recordHome = null;
    }

    public void ejbCreate( ) {
        try {
            InitialContext ic = new InitialContext( );
            customerHome =
                (LocalCustomerHome)
                ic.lookup("java:comp/env/ejb/local/Customer");
            itemHome =
                (LocalItemHome)
                ic.lookup("java:comp/env/ejb/local/Item");
            recordHome =
                (LocalSalesRecordHome)
```

Example 9-6. A session façade EJB (continued)

```
            ic.lookup("java:comp/env/ejb/local/Record");
      } catch(Exception ex) {
          throw new EJBException(
          "Error looking up home object: " + ex, ex);
      }
  }

  public ReceiptDTO doSale(int itemNumbers[], int customerId) {
      try {
          LocalCustomer cust =
          customerHome.findByPrimaryKey(customerId);

          LocalItem items[] = new LocalItem[itemNumbers.length];
        for (int i = 0; i < itemNumbers.length; i++) {
              items[i] = itemHome.findByPrimaryKey(itemNumbers[i]);
          }

          LocalSalesRecord record =
          recordHome.createRecord(items, cust);

          return (new ReceiptDTO(record));
      } catch(Exception ex) {
      throw new
          EJBException("Error processing sale: " + ex, ex);
      }
  }
}
```

Web services session façades

The primary benefits of a session façade, including a reduction of network overhead and a centralization of business process logic, apply to any business service. Web services in particular benefit from the session façade approach, especially when they've been wrapped in a service adapter. Since SOAP connections are even less efficient than CORBA or JRMP (EJB) connections, the overhead involved in accessing a web service is much greater than the overhead associated with EJB connections. The same calculus that applies to session façades also applies in this circumstance.

A web services session façade consists of adding an additional method to the web service, rather than creating an entirely new object, as with EJBs. The new method factors the business logic that makes multiple calls to the web service out to the web service side rather than the client side. The simplest implementations just make the same sets of SOAP connections (to itself) as the client would, taking advantage of the fact that all of the processing is local rather than networked. Assuming that the web service itself takes advantage of properly compartmentalized design (separating the business objects from details of the web services interface), the new method could even access the business objects directly, effectively refactoring the web service down to a simpler model.

Session façade and business delegate

Session façades and business delegates are often used together. This symbiosis generally involves simplifying the business delegate implementation, by moving all of the business logic implementation to the session façade. The business delegate is responsible for EJB or web services lookups and handling networking exceptions. Business method invocations are simply passed on to the session façade. Since this conversion often doesn't affect the rest of the client code, using business delegates can pave the way for extending your architecture to EJBs in the future.

Finding Resources

A presentation tier is only as good as the data it has to present. In some applications, finding data is as simple as instantiating the appropriate business delegate and calling a method. But life gets complicated when an application grows to encompass a range of resources that are spread across a number of services. To help manage distributed components, J2EE specifies that they should be connected via the Java's directory API, JNDI. JNDI is a simple, standard API that allows communication with a variety of directories such as LDAP and NDS. Using a directory server, clients are somewhat shielded from the complexities of distributed environments. The canonical J2EE picture is shown in Figure 9-10.

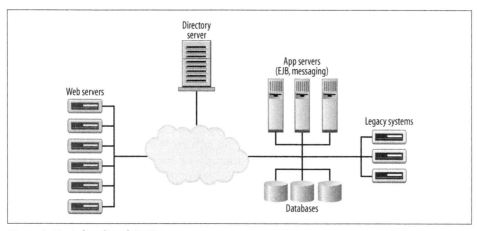

Figure 9-10. A distributed J2EE environment

The nice thing about a directory is that a client can get a reference to a resource anywhere on the network, remote or local, with a single lookup. This decouples the client from a particular server implementation. Of course, there is no such thing as a free lunch, and anyone who has actually built a distributed J2EE environment knows that all we have done is shift a development headache to a deployment headache.

Finding resources on the network has performance implications. Connecting to a remote EJB might first require querying the directory server for the EJB's location. While the cost may not seem substantial, we effectively double the number of connections required for a given operation. When we add the costs for connecting to databases, message queues, legacy applications, and web services, connecting to the directory server becomes a bottleneck.

The Service Locator Pattern

The *Service Locator pattern* simplifies connecting to remote services, while minimizing the costs associated with these connections. A ServiceLocator object acts as an intelligent connection from the presentation tier to the various remote services. The service locator is the application's central point of access for directory services. A more advanced locator may use pools and caches to improve efficiency. Figure 9-11 shows the classes involved in the Service Locator pattern.

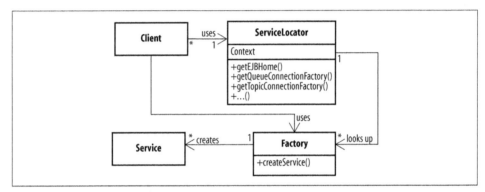

Figure 9-11. Service locator classes

The service locator's client may be a presentation-tier object, such as a servlet that needs access to business data, or a business tier object. When a client needs access to some object in the directory, it calls the appropriate method on the service locator for that service. The locator then uses the directory or an internal cache to find the service's factory and return it to the client. The client can use this factory to create an instance of the service.

Factory objects are responsible for creating instances of services. For EJBs, the factories are the home interfaces for each bean. For JMS queues, they are the TopicConnectionFactory and QueueConnnectionFactory objects associated with each topic or queue. DataSource objects produce database connections.

A locator might seem like a roundabout way to access services, but it has distinct advantages. In a complicated environment, connecting to a directory server can be an involved process, requiring connection parameters and credentials. Scattering lookups throughout the application makes switching directories a real headache. Having

---

a single, central service locator means there's a single piece of code to modify when the underlying directory changes.

The biggest advantage, however, is in efficiency. As we keep mentioning, the ServiceLocator is an ideal location for a cache. By caching mappings between directory names and objects, the locator can prevent many queries to the directory. This speeds up the client and allows more clients to access a single directory.

Service Locator Variations

The connection between the presentation tier and the underlying business tiers is a critical one. In most systems, the vast majority of requests that comes in to the presentation tier require some connection to the business tier. Anything that reduces the cost of this connection will provide an overall gain in scalability. Because it abstracts access to the business tier, the service locator is the logical place to tune connections to the backend. Here are a few variations on the basic service locator that help it handle certain situations:

Constant services locator

> A typical ServiceLocator takes a JNDI directory name from the client and performs the requested lookup. This creates a coupling between *all* the various client calls to the locator and the directory structure—and when the directory structure changes, the client must be updated in many places. One variation of the ServiceLocator defines a constant set of services and lets clients access those services with a locator-specific name. This decouples the clients from the actual directory structure, allowing access to the new directory with only a single change to the locator.

Caching service locator

> We've seen that the ServiceLocator is a good place for a cache. Most implementations simply cache factory objects, leaving it up to the client to create the actual services. A more advanced locator might do more caching: for example, caching actual service objects. For services without cache-coherency issues, such as stateless session EJBs, caching the service saves the overhead of creating or locating them from the factory object.

> One of the main problems with caching in a ServiceLocator is keeping the cache up-to-date. When a service is moved or goes away, the clients are stuck getting invalid objects from the locator's cache. To fix this problem, the locator must validate the objects in its cache. Validating objects as they are returned to clients might seem logical, but requiring remote requests removes the efficiency gained by using caching. Instead, the locator is usually designed to validate cached objects with a low priority thread that runs in the background. This precautionary step won't catch every bad object, but it will catch most of them, and the client can always request a new one if a bad object slips through the cracks; the incidence is low enough that you still realize major gains.

Locator pool

The ServiceLocator object is usually implemented as a singleton, sharing a single instance of the JNDI context. Unfortunately, the InitialContext object is not thread-safe, so lookups can become a bottleneck. Instead of a singleton ServiceLocator, some people choose to use pools of locators. These pools can save lookup time while reducing thread contention.

The task of maintaining connections to services on a network can be a difficult one. In a complicated environment, services can come and go, and move from server to server. Keeping up with dynamic services using static methods such as those presented here can be nearly impossible. While it is outside the scope of J2EE, Jini technology centers around an elegant architecture for connecting network services. Jini can greatly simplify the deployment and maintenance challenges presented by a dynamic, distributed system.

Implementing a Service Locator

The most common implementation of service locators is for EJBs. In this case, the ServiceLocator contains a method called getEJBHome( ), which, given a JNDI directory name and a class name, returns an EJBHome object. When a servlet needs access to an EJB, it calls the service locator instead of making its own call to JNDI to locate the EJB's home object. The locator returns the EJBHome, and the client uses it to create, update, or delete EJB. These interactions are shown in Figure 9-12.

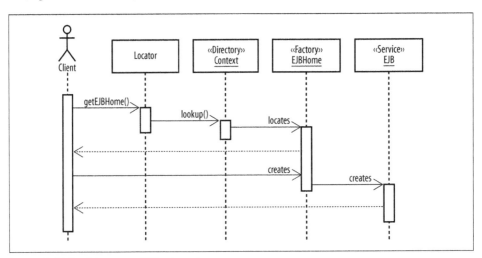

Figure 9-12. Looking up an EJB using a locator

Implementing the simple ServiceLocator is quite easy. Example 9-7 shows a ServiceLocator that looks up EJBs in a JNDI directory based on the name and class

---

passed in. While it does cache the lookup results, it does no validation of the initial input and no maintenance of the cached objects.

Example 9-7. The ServiceLocator class

```
public class ServiceLocator {

 private static ServiceLocator instance;
 private HashMap cache;
 private Context context;

 // return the singelton service locator
 public static ServiceLocator getInstance()
 throws ServiceLocatorException {
  if (instance == null)
   instance = new ServiceLocator();

  return instance;
 }

 // Creates a new instance of ServiceLocator
 private ServiceLocator() throws ServiceLocatorException {
  cache = new HashMap();

  // initialize the shared context object
  try {
   context = new InitialContext();
  } catch(NamingException ne) {
   throw new ServiceLocatorException("Unable to create " + "initial context", ne);
  }
 }

 // get an EJB from the cache or directory service
 public EJBHome getRemoteEJB(String name, Class type)
 throws ServiceLocatorException {
  // see if it's in the cache
  if (cache.containsKey(name)) {
   // cache HomeHandle objects since they are maintained
   // by the container
   HomeHandle hh = (HomeHandle)cache.get(name);

   try {
    return hh.getEJBHome();
   } catch(RemoteException re) {
    // some kind of problem -- fall through to relookup below
   }
  }

  // access to the shared context as well as modifications
  // to the HashMap must be synchronized.  Hopefully the
  // majority of cases are handled above
  synchronized(this) {
   try {
```

Example 9-7. The ServiceLocator class (continued)

```
    Object rRef = context.lookup(name);
    EJBHome eh = (EJBHome)PortableRemoteObject.narrow(rRef, type);

    cache.put(name, eh.getHomeHandle( ));
    return eh;
  } catch(Exception ex) {
    throw new ServiceLocatorException("Unable to find EJB",ex);
  }
 }
 }
}
```

Creating a client to use this locator is equally simple. For an EJB for patient records in a hospital, we might use:

```
ServiceLocator sl = ServiceLocator.getInstance( );

PatientHome ph = (PatientHome)sl.getRemoteEJB("Patient",
 PatientHome.class);

Patient p = ph.create( );
 ...
```

We do not cache EJBHome objects at all, but rather instances of the derived HomeHandle class. The HomeHandle is a container-specific object that can be used to get an EJBHome object in a persistent way. When the HomeHandle's getEJBHome( ) method is called, it is up to the container to find the latest version of the EJBHome object. Home handles can even be serialized and stored on disk. As with any container-implemented field, your mileage will vary depending on your vendor. Most containers are pretty good about maintaining home handles, although they are not to be trusted when resources move from server to server.

Also, note the use of fine-grained synchronization. From the documentation, we learn that the InitialContext object is not thread-safe at all, while the HashMap object is safe to read from multiple threads, but not to write. This means that the first block—reading the map and returning a cached object—does not require any synchronization. By synchronizing only what we need instead of the whole method, we allow the majority of cases to be fulfilled from the cache even while a lookup is in progress.

In this implementation, we chose to only cache EJB Home objects, not EJBs themselves. Obviously, some EJBs are easier to cache then others. Session EJBs are usually only relevant for the life of a single session, so it doesn't often make sense to cache them. It's more logical to cache entity EJBs, but the cache must be kept up-to-date when they are accessed by multiple sources.

CHAPTER 10

Enterprise Concurrency

The most dramatic difference between an enterprise system and a "regular" application is the number of users it must serve. As a result, enterprise applications face problems that don't often occur on the desktop. A word processor, for example, doesn't have to handle two users making changes to one paragraph at the same time—at the most, it might have to notify the second user that the document is already in use.

Of course, all data-centric applications, whether they serve one user or 10,000, need to concern themselves with the validity of their data. An action that seems simple to the user ("Order a book") may require complex, choreographed activities within the application ("Check inventory, reserve stock, charge credit cards, arrange shipping, etc."). The more operations an application performs, the more likely one of those activities will fail—and when it does, the system must be able to carry on. Providing for this capability is easy in standalone applications: just don't save your changes if the mail merge fails. But if other users have been modifying the same databases at the same time, the brute-force approach to data integrity won't pan out.

A lot of ink has been spilled on these issues. Since we're always eager to help, we've coined a new term for an old concept: *enterprise concurrency*. Enterprise concurrency has two elements: *transaction management* and *concurrency management*. Transaction management, abstracted to a high level, controls the implementation of the individual use cases within a system, ensuring that changes to underlying data are performed consistently and that the system is always in a valid state. Concurrency management controls how different users access a system.

The two concepts might not seem linked at first, but they are. Concurrency problems can often be stated in terms of *transaction boundaries*. A transaction boundary defines a set of actions that must be performed together and without interference. Concurrent applications face transaction management problems that differ from their single-user brethren's in degree more than in kind.

Transaction Management

Here's a common situation that arises in enterprise development: you need to perform a set of actions as if they were a single action.[*] In real life, the simplest transactions take place within one resource, such as a database, and within a very short period of time. A bank transaction implemented by changing values for a particular field in two different rows of a table, via two update statements executed one after the other, is a simple transaction. You don't want to record the value of one update without the other. Even if the chance of something interfering—money automatically being deducted to pay a bill between the two updates, for instance—is small, it's a chance that can't be taken. To make life even more exciting, the odds of something going wrong increase dramatically when you start coordinating the transaction across space (multiple databases, messaging systems, EJBs, etc.) and time (multiple user requests to a web application).

Complex activities call for complex transactions. Let's take the ubiquitous stock-trading system example: for a brokerage firm to execute a buy order, it must charge a user's account, execute the trade, and send various confirmation messages. The confirmation messages shouldn't be sent without the trade, the account shouldn't be charged without the trade, and the trade shouldn't be executed without confirmations being sent. Each activity in the chain might involve a different system or technology, yet the entire process needs to be treated as one concrete business activity. Each activity might also consist of a subtransaction; for example, charging an account involves checking for sufficient funds and then transferring funds to a different account.

About Transactions

A *transaction* is an activity that changes the state of a system in a particular way. The purpose of formalized transaction management is to make sure that a system is altered in a manner that ensures the underlying state of the system is always valid. A transaction, therefore, is made up of a series of operations that result in a valid change of a system's state.

The simplest use for transactions is for preventing incomplete operations. If an activity calls for two SQL statements to run, enclosing them in a transaction ensures that either both run, or neither; if the second statement fails, the entire transaction will be *rolled back*, undoing the effects of the first statement. If each SQL statement succeeds, the transaction will be *committed*, permanently updating the state of the systems.

---

[*] This may, in fact, be the ur-pattern of enterprise development, fundamentally underlying everything else. We'd speculate more on this front, but suspect that the discussion would be less a matter of engineering than of theology.

The other benefit of using a transaction is to ensure that the overall view of the system is always in a consistent state, even when multiple transactions are in process. Without proper transactions, even if every activity completes successfully, an application faces three subtle threats: dirty reads, nonrepeatable reads, and phantom reads. A *dirty read* occurs when two or more processes attempt to work on the same data at the same time. Imagine a transaction that reads two properties, A and B, from an object, performs a calculation, and updates a third property, C. If another transaction modifies A and B after the first transaction has read A but before it has read B, the computed value of C will not only be out-of-date, it may be entirely invalid! Figure 10-1 shows what can happen.

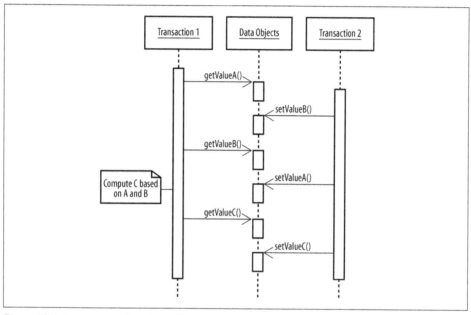

Figure 10-1. Two transactions in conflict

When the transactions are complete, the value of the C property on the data object has been computed based on the original A and the new value for B. This was *never* a valid value for C! The same problem can arise if you're using database tables rather than objects (and, in fact, that version of the problem happens more often; if nothing else, you can synchronize on an object).

A *nonrepeatable read* is similar to a dirty read, in that the problem comes from two transactions working with the same data at the same time. In this case, the first transaction might read a table that is subsequently modified by another transaction. If the first transaction reads the table again, it finds a new value. The original read, therefore, is nonrepeatable: the transaction can execute the same query multiple times and receive different answers.

The difference between a nonrepeatable read and a dirty read is that in a nonrepeatable read, the transaction that changes the data has completed. Systems can therefore allow nonrepeatable reads without also allowing dirty reads (in which the change becomes visible as soon as it is made within the transaction, rather than when the transaction is committed).

Phantom reads occur when one transaction is reading data while another transaction is modifying the same data. For example, imagine a program runs an SQL SELECT statement to retrieve a set of rows from the database, and then runs the same statement again a few seconds later. If another process has subsequently inserted rows into the table, the second query will return rows that weren't present in the first query. Conversely, if rows are deleted by the other transaction, they won't show up on the second query. This is sometimes acceptable, but not always: since the same query returns different results, the application doesn't have access to a consistent view of the database in order to do its work. Phantom reads differ from nonrepeatable reads in that they deal with the presence of data altogether rather than the contents of the data being read.

ACID Transaction Pattern

We've discussed two requirements of transaction management: performing multiple actions as one and ensuring the consistency of an underlying resource (generally a database). The *ACID Transaction pattern* defines four properties that can be used to implement a transaction. These four properties create a framework of operations that meets the needs we discussed in the previous section.*

A transaction that meets the ACID requirements is:

Atomic
Consistent
Isolated
Durable

Transactions must be *atomic* because we want every action within the transaction to succeed or fail as a unit. If a transaction reserves inventory, charges a credit card, and ships the inventory, we want to make sure the reserved inventory is still available if the credit card charge fails.

Transactions must be *consistent* because we need the state of the system to be correct after each activity. A system that has inventory reserved but no plans to ship it isn't in the correct state. The business rules within the domain model must be satisfied at the beginning and end of every transaction, regardless of whether the transaction succeeds.

---

* So, is this a pattern? If you've spent time doing transactional programming, you're probably familiar with the ACID properties as part of the infrastructure of an enterprise system. However, a surprising number of programmers haven't been formally exposed to them; since they're fundamental, we're promoting them to pattern level.

Saying a transaction is *isolated* means that the transaction in progress is invisible to other transactions until it has been committed. This property, in particular, ensures that the overall view of the database remains consistent. Each transaction is shielded from dirty, nonrepeatable, and phantom reads, ensuring that any data loaded from the underlying resources was valid at least at one point in time. Keep in mind that there's no guarantee that the data is still valid: if another transaction started and finished while the first transaction was still in effect, the first transaction may be working from an older, though possibly consistent, set of data. We'll look at strategies for dealing with this issue in the next section of this chapter.

Finally, the *durability* property ensures that after a transaction is completed it will persist in the system. Of course, there's no absolute guarantee—somebody could take a sledgehammer to the database server—but the result of the transaction will be visible to all subsequent transactions.

Transaction isolation

Perfect transaction isolation is expensive. By allowing dirty reads, nonrepeatable reads, phantom reads, or some combination of the three, applications can reap greatly improved performance. It's not difficult to see why: avoiding these problems requires either keeping track of multiple versions of data, or requiring the system to delay some transactions until others have finished, or some combination of both. Some applications require perfect transaction isolation, but many, possibly most, don't. For performance reasons, applications often want to break the perfect isolation that a pure ACID transaction would enjoy.

JDBC supports four transaction isolation modes (five if you count turning it off). They are, in order from least stringent to most stringent:

TRANSACTION_NONE
No transactions supported.

TRANSACTION_READ_UNCOMMITTED
Data is visible as soon as it is written to a table. This mode provides basic transaction support, but dirty reads, nonrepeatable reads, and phantom reads are all possible.

TRANSACTION_READ_COMMITTED
Data is visible after commit( ) is called. No dirty reads allowed, but nonrepeatable and phantom reads are possible.

TRANSACTION_REPEATABLE_READ
The state of each row in each affected table is kept for the duration of the transaction. Rows are locked as soon as they are read. Dirty and nonrepeatable reads are both prevented. Phantom reads can still occur.

TRANSACTION_SERIALIZABLE
Perfect isolation is maintained. Each transaction will effectively lock each table that it accesses.

Of course, not all databases support each level. Oracle, for example, does not support the READ_UNCOMMITTED or REPEATABLE_READ isolation levels. Since isolation levels are set on a per connection level, it's possible to use different isolation levels across an application. Read-only SQL can use TRANSACTION_NONE; applications doing multipart updates that aren't likely to affect other transactions can use READ_COMMITTED; and data analysis activities that demand a consistent view can use SERIALIZABLE.

System and business transactions

Virtually any interaction with the domain model underlying an application can be represented as a transaction. Complex operations can be treated as a single transaction or split into several smaller transactions. When we write about transactions in design documentation, we often split them into system transactions and business transactions: the former approach is for the implementation details, and the latter is for the business modeling activity.

Business transactions will be instantly recognizable to the end user: they include actions such as withdrawing money from an account, finalizing a purchase, or submitting an order. These transactions have fundamental constraints your application must abide by. Business transaction boundaries flow logically from your use cases and requirement specifications. Each business transaction is made up of one or more system transactions.

A *system transaction* is implemented by the underlying resource layer, whether it's a database, EJB, messaging system, or something else. The tools for handling system transactions are provided by the Java APIs that access the particular infrastructure. Most programmers who've worked with database backends have been exposed to JDBC's transaction management API, which implements database level transactions.

The following code shows how to use JDBC's transaction management support. This code fragment starts a transaction (by turning off automatic commits on the Connection), attempts to run two SQL statements, each of which modifies the database, and then commits the transaction after both statements have run. If either statement fails (as indicated by an SQLException), the transaction is rolled back. A finally block cleans up database objects and closes the connection, regardless of whether the transaction succeeded.

```
Connection con = null;
Statement stmt = null;
PreparedStatement pstmt = null;

try {
  con = dataSource.getConnection(); // retrieve from a javax.sql.DataSource
  con.setAutoCommit(false);

  stmt = con.createStatement();
  stmt.executeUpdate("INSERT INTO VALUABLE_DATE (NUMVAL) VALUES (42)");
```

```
      pstmt = con.prepareStatement("UPDATE VITAL_DATA SET DATA = ? WHERE ID=33");
      pstmt.setString(1, "This is really important"");
      pstmt.executeUpdate( );
      // commit the transaction
      con.commit( );

   } catch (SQLException e) {

      try {
        con.rollback( );
      } catch (SQLException se) {} // report this in severe cases
        e.printStackTrace( ); // handle it better

   } finally {

      if(stmt != null)
        try { stmt.close( ); } catch (SQLException ignored) {}
      if(pstmt != null)
        try { pstmt.close( ); } catch (SQLException ignored) {}
      if (con != null)
        try { con.close( ); } catch (SQLException e) {}

   }
```

The details of the system transactions may be opaque to the end users. This is because many complex applications make a set of changes to a variety of resources, including multiple databases, messaging systems, and proprietary tools, in the process of fulfilling one user request. A business transaction, which maps much closer to a use case, is more recognizable to the end user, and may consist of several system transactions linked in various ways.

One of the primary purposes of the EJB API was to blur the line between system and business transactions. EJBs make it easier to link system transactions involving multiple resources; in fact, the process is largely transparent to the programmer. A single call to a method on a session façade can start a system transaction that encompasses all of the activities within a business transaction, and includes multiple databases, messaging systems, and other resources.

If we aren't using an EJB environment, we'll need to build business transactions out of multiple system transactions. If we're using two databases, we'll need a system transaction for each one. We'll also need system transaction resources for anything else we want to include in the transaction. The JMS API, for instance, includes a transaction management idiom that's similar to the one in JDBC: the JMS Session interface, which is analogous to the JDBC Connection interface, provides a commit( ) method and a rollback( ) method.

A business delegate implementing a business transaction can start as many system transactions as it needs. If every transaction completes successfully, each system transaction is committed. If any transaction fails, your code can roll back all of them.

Transactions and Objects

Graphs of objects are not naturally amenable to transactions. Unless transaction capability is baked into an environment at a very low level, capturing the web of relations between the different objects is very difficult. Modifying an object in a meaningful way often involves creating or destroying references to a variety of other objects. A single business transaction often creates or modify customers, orders, line items, stock records, and so on. Transaction control across a single object, however, is relatively easy. When you don't have to worry about dynamically including external objects in a transaction, it's a (relatively!) simple matter to record changes to objects.

Databases don't face this problem because the relationships between tables are defined by key relationships (if you're not familiar with primary keys, turn back to Chapter 8). A transaction might include edits to five or six different tables in a database and those edits might affect the relations between entities, but as far as commits and rollbacks are concerned, the relationships don't matter.

In the end, the application is ultimately responsible for maintaining the consistency of the data. Consistency can be maintained by declaring "constraints" on the database that disallow updates and inserts that don't meet a particular set of conditions, or by enforcing the business rules at the application logic level by forbidding entry of invalid or inappropriate data.

The EJB specification provides transaction support at the object level by assigning a primary key to each entity bean. References between objects are handled not by direct Java references, but by the application server, using the keys. This method allows the application server to monitor each object for changes in internal state and changes in its relationship with other objects. Entity beans can be included in a running transaction as they are touched upon by application code.

For example, an EJB stateless session bean can be declared as TX_REQUIRED, which requires the EJB container to create a transaction (or join an existing transaction) whenever a method is invoked on the bean. Initially, the transaction will not encompass any objects on the server. As code execution goes forward, any entity beans requested by the session bean will be included in the transaction. If the session bean method executes successfully, all of the changes will be committed to the system. If the method fails, any changes made to any transaction-controlled objects will be rolled right back.

Transactional Context Pattern

In an EJB environment, transaction management is taken care of transparently. By setting transaction levels on session and entity beans and accessing database connections and other resources through the application server, you get most of your transaction support automatically. If a method on a session façade fails in mid-execution, all of the entity bean changes it made are undone—any JMS messages are unsent, and so on.

If you're not running in an environment that handles transactions for you, you need to build them yourself. Since 95% or more of enterprise transaction management code involves the database, the standard approach is to use the transaction functionality that is built into the JDBC API and the underlying databases. Transactions can then be handled at the DAO level: each DAO method starts a new transaction, updates the database, and commits the transaction.

Handling transactions at the DAO or PAO level, though, can be limiting. For one thing, the transaction boundary generally does not lie at the DAO level. Instead, transactions usually sit at the business delegate/session façade level. This level is, of course, the use case level. Since a business delegate might call several DAOs in the course of completing its activities, and might even call other business delegates, handling transactions at this level is not going to give us the degree of control we want: if the last DAO fails, the changes made by the first DAOs remain in the database, leaving the application in an inconsistent and incorrect state.

The *Transactional Context pattern* allows us to spread a transaction across multiple, otherwise unrelated objects. A transactional context is an environment that business logic and data access components execute inside. It controls access to transaction control resources such as database connections, and is responsible for starting, stopping, committing, and rolling back transactions. As we stated, the EJB environment itself provides a transactional context, but if you're not using an application server, it's possible to write your own.

For simple applications, the business delegate itself can serve as the transactional context for the DAO objects it uses. All the software really needs to do is decouple the DAO objects from the code to retrieve database connections from the application's connection pool. The business delegate can retrieve the connection itself, set up the transaction, and pass the same connection into a series of DAOs or other business delegates. As long as the DAOs don't call any transaction management code themselves (the JDBC setAutoCommit( ), commit( ), and rollback( ) methods), all activities against the database will be included in the same transaction. Failures at any point can be used to roll back the transaction for all the affected components.

This approach works fine for simple activities and within DAOs, but it breaks down for larger scale applications. For one thing, the business delegate object is now aware of transaction management in all its gory (well, not too gory) details. It's perfectly appropriate for the business delegate to be aware of the business constraints surrounding a transaction, but less appropriate for it to be responsible for implementing them. If nothing else, the ability to easily switch back and forth between local business delegates and remote EJB session façades vanishes: the EJB specification specifically disallows independent transaction control.

A more elegant implementation involves placing control of the transaction context with an outside object that is known to the business delegates, DAOs, and other components. Figure 10-2 shows how it works.

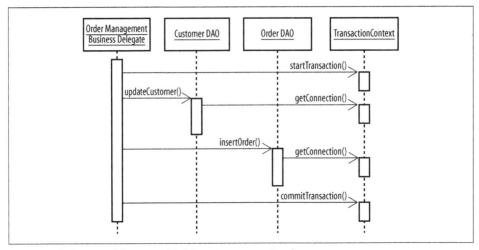

Figure 10-2. Business delegate and DAOs using transactional context

In this example, the business delegate informs the context control object that it wishes to start a transaction. The context object obtains a connection and starts the database transaction. It then passes the connection to any other object, such as the two DAOs, that have access to it. The DAOs use the connection, and their activities are included in the transaction. After calling all the DAOs it needs, the business delegate commits the transaction.

Implementing transactional context with business delegates

In Chapter 9, we discussed business delegates and business delegate factories, and promised that we'd provide a way to easily integrate transactions without requiring a full EJB environment. Many applications are small enough to run in a simple web container such as Jakarta Tomcat. In these cases, where business logic is embedded in business delegates and DAOs, we need to manage our own transactions within business delegates.

Our solution is to associate a database connection with a web application's request scope. When a request comes into the web server, we assign a single JDBC Connection object to support every database-related activity from the start of the request to the end of the request. This allows us to declare a transaction that spans multiple objects, which is similar to the behavior an EJB server would provide.

This approach requires one decision: which level of the application should have knowledge and control of the transaction boundary? Earlier we placed this responsibility at the DAO level when dealing with DAOs in non-EJB environments. In this case, we need to put the responsibility at the business delegate or even the business delegate factory level.

The first step is to provide an idiom for sharing a connection across multiple objects. This procedure might seem daunting, since it's easy to imagine having to pass connection references from object to object. In fact, it's pretty simple, at least in the servlet world. Since each servlet request takes place on its own thread, we can use Java's ThreadLocal class to build a static ConnectionManager object that can be associated with a particular request.[*] The connection manager provides part of our transactional context. Example 10-1 shows an implementation, which includes methods for setting and retrieving the current connection.

Example 10-1. ConnectionManager.java

```
import java.sql.Connection;

public final class ConnectionManager
{
    private static final ThreadLocal currentConnection = new ThreadLocal( );

    static Connection setConnection( Connection connection ) {
        Connection priorConnection = (Connection)currentConnection.get( );
        currentConnection.set( connection );
        // We return the prior connection, if any, to give the application
        // the opportunity to deal with it, if so desired. It's important
        // that all database connections be properly closed.
        return priorConnection;
    }

    public static Connection getConnection( ) {
        return (Connection)currentConnection.get( );
    }
}
```

Once the connection has been set up, using the connection manager is easy: just call the getConnection( ) method when you need a connection. Unlike a JNDI connection pool, you don't call the close( ) method when you're done with the connection; the system does it for you (Example 10-2), so closing it prematurely just makes trouble for the next block of code that needs to use it. Here's a simple example of correct usage:[†]

```
Connection con = ConnectionManager.getConnection( );
try {
  con.setAutoCommit(false);
  // Do SQL
  con.commit( );
  con.setAutoCommit(true);
```

---

[*] There's a caveat: while ThreadLocal has been around since JDK 1.2, the original implementation was sluggish at best. JDK 1.3 introduced some performance improvements, but it wasn't until JDK 1.4 that overhead became reasonable.

[†] We could write a wrapper class, which would allow us to safely ignore calls to close( ); when we're retrofitting existing code, this can sometimes save time and reduce the potential for unforeseen bugs.

```
    } catch (SQLException e) {
      // Report somehow
      // Rollback exception will be thrown by the invoke method
      con.rollback();
      con.setAutoCommit(true);
    }
```

The only rule is that you have to finish with the connection in the same scope you retrieved it: if you stash a reference to the connection in a place where it might be accessed by another thread, the other thread has no guarantee of the connection's transactional state or even validity. For example, if you retrieve the connection within a persistence method attached to a domain object, you can't cache that Connection object within the domain object for use later: if other methods need it, they must retrieve it from the ConnectionManager itself.

The safest possible version of this strategy would wrap the connection in a wrapper object that simply passed all of the methods in the Connection interface through to the actual connection object, with the exception of the close() method.

Now that we have the connection manager, we need to associate a connection with our thread. We do this via a servlet filter, shown in Example 10-2. The filter is responsible for interacting with a JNDI data source and opening and closing connections.

Example 10-2. ConnectionFilter.java

```java
import java.io.IOException;

import javax.servlet.*;
import java.sql.*;
import javax.sql.*;
import javax.naming.*;

public class ConnectionFilter implements Filter {

    private DataSource dataSource = null;

    /**
     * Create a datasource from a parameter defined in web.xml.
     */
    public void init(FilterConfig filterConfig) throws ServletException {
        try {
            InitialContext iCtx = new InitialContext();
            Context ctx = (Context) iCtx.lookup("java:comp/env");
            dataSource = (DataSource)
              ctx.lookup(filterConfig.getInitParameter("JNDI_datasource"));
        } catch (Exception e) {
            ServletException se = new ServletException();
            // Uncomment in JDK 1.4 for easier troubleshooting.
            // se.initCause(e);
            throw se;
        }
    }
}
```

Example 10-2. ConnectionFilter.java (continued)

```java
    public void destroy( ) {
    }

    /** Retrieve a connection, run the filter chain, and return the connection.
     * */
    public void doFilter(ServletRequest request, ServletResponse response,
        FilterChain chain) throws IOException, ServletException {

        Connection con = null;

        try {
          con = dataSource.getConnection( );

          // Set the connection, and retrieve the previous connection for
          // disposal
          Connection previousCon = ConnectionManager.setConnection(con);
          if(previousCon != null)
            try { previousCon.close( ); } catch (SQLException e) {}

          // Run the rest of the filter chain.
          chain.doFilter(request, response);

          // Make sure we disassociate the connection, just in case.
          ConnectionManager.setConnection(null);
        } catch (SQLException e) {
          ServletException se = new ServletException(e);
          throw se;
        } finally {
          if (con != null)
            try { con.close( ); } catch (SQLException e) {}
        }
    }
}
```

This approach has a side benefit, by the way: if your application needs a connection in several places during the course of a single request, using the ConnectionManager instead of repeated JNDI requests means less code and a slight performance boost.

We could stop now that we have a connection manager associated with our threads. Each business delegate that wants a transaction that spans multiple DAOs or transactionally ignorant subdelegates can retrieve the connection, set the transaction status, run its code, and commit or roll back as appropriate. However, we've placed a lot of responsibility for implementing transactions on the business delegates, which is probably not a good thing. Instead, we can push responsibility all the way up to the business delegate factory, using the proxy approach introduced in Chapter 9. The TransactionWrapper class shown in Example 10-3 decorates an object with an InvocationHandler that wraps each method call in a transaction (again, see Chapter 9 for an introduction). Coupled with the ConnectionManager, we now have a complete transactional context implementation: a way of sharing the transaction environment and a way of controlling the transaction status.

Example 10-3. TransactionWrapper.java

```java
import java.lang.reflect.InvocationHandler;
import java.lang.reflect.InvocationTargetException;
import java.lang.reflect.Method;
import java.lang.reflect.Proxy;

import java.sql.Connection;

final class TransactionWrapper {

    /**
     * Decorates a business delegate object with a wrapper. The
     * object returned by this method will implement all of the interfaces
     * originally implemented by the target.
     *
     * @param The Business Delegate to wrap
     * @return The business delegate wrapped in this wrapper
     */
    static Object decorate(Object delegate) {
        return Proxy.newProxyInstance(delegate.getClass().getClassLoader(),
            delegate.getClass().getInterfaces(),
            new XAWrapperHandler(delegate));
    }

    static final class XAWrapperHandler implements InvocationHandler {
        private final Object delegate;

        XAWrapperHandler(Object delegate) {
            // Cache the wrapped delegate, so we can pass method invocations
            // to it.
            this.delegate = delegate;
        }

        /** Invoke the method within a transaction. We retrieve a connection,
         * set auto commit to false (starting the transaction), run the original
         * method, commit the transaction, and return the result. If any
         * exceptions are thrown (SQLException or not) we roll the transaction
         * back.
         *
         * Note that we don't use a finally block to reset the connection to
         * autocommit mode. This approach gives us a better idea of the root
         * cause of any error. In JDK 1.4, we might modify the catch block
         * to attach the original Throwable as the root cause for any exception
         * thrown by the rollback() and setAutoCommit() methods. */
        public Object invoke(Object proxy, Method method, Object[] args)
                throws Throwable {
            Object result = null;
            Connection con = ConnectionManager.getConnection();
            try {
                con.setAutoCommit(false);
```

Example 10-3. TransactionWrapper.java (continued)

```
            result = method.invoke(delegate, args);
            con.commit( );
            con.setAutoCommit(true);
        } catch (Throwable t) {
            // Rollback exception will be thrown by the invoke method
            con.rollback( );
            con.setAutoCommit(true);
            throw t;
        }

        return result;
    }
  }
}
```

The final step is to modify our business delegate factory to wrap an object instance in a transaction wrapper, as we did in Chapter 9. If you've read the code closely, you'll see that we commit the database transaction after every method invocation. Proxy handlers wrap the object from the view of application, but not from within the object itself (unless you do some complicated passing of self-references, which is pretty hard to manage). So you don't need to worry about your methods spawning a new transaction for each internal method call. Figure 10-3 shows the chain of method invocations for a simple example: the application calls the getCustomer( ) method on the proxy object; the proxy object calls the invoke( ) method of our InvocationHandler, which in turn calls the original object. If the original object calls methods on itself, they won't be passed through the invocation handler.

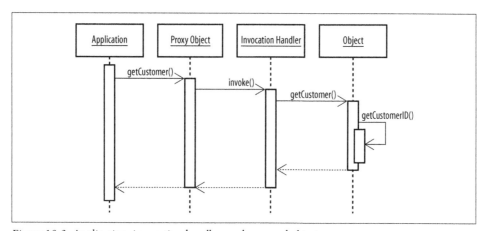

Figure 10-3. Application, invocation handler, and wrapped object

This behavior has two implications. First, we don't have to worry about the business delegate creating new transactions by calling its own methods, since those calls don't go through the proxy. Second, if we want to nest business delegates we must ensure that the nested delegates are not wrapped in the proxy when the parent delegate retrieves them. This may involve providing two different object creation methods on the business delegate factory: one to create a wrapped object that generates a new transaction with each method invocation, and one to create an unwrapped version that joins existing transactions.

Nesting business delegates only comes up sometimes, but many, if not most, business delegates will call multiple DAO methods in the course of a single business delegate method. That's why we wrap at the business delegate level rather than the DAO level.

General Concurrency Patterns

System transactions can solve half of our concurrency problems, but they only really help for activities that can be run all at once. In other words, a system transaction works well when we can run four SQL statements one after the other in a single call to a DAO or during the duration of a single HTTP request. But once we start working with longer-lived transactions, things get messy. While a system transaction is running, the ACID properties limit the access that the outside world has to the data the transaction is working with. If a transaction is over in 500 milliseconds, this limitation isn't always a problem. If a transaction lasts 10 minutes, though—particularly if it prevents any other processes from even reading the underlying tables—we've got a real problem. And what happens if the user gets up and walks away?

At first, none of this may seem like a big deal: how often do we spread transactions across multiple pages? The answer is: surprisingly often. Take that most common of use cases, the Edit Data screen. Even if all the data to be changed fits on a single page, how are you going to deal with the conflicts that occur if two users are editing simultaneously? If two users start editing a single record, the first to save her changes might have all her work transparently destroyed the moment the second user clicks the Save button.

If you can confine all of your concurrency worries to a single request, you're lucky. Skip ahead to the next chapter, which talks about enterprise messaging and shows you how to do some pretty cool stuff. But if you're like the rest of us, read on.

This section proposes two patterns for controlling concurrency across long-running transactions, particularly those that span multiple user interactions with the system. In the last section of the chapter, we'll look at a few patterns that can be used to implement either approach.

All of these patterns help solve the problem of offline concurrency: maintaining a transaction even when the user isn't actually doing anything. In a web application, the user is offline between each request to the web server, so this issue often comes up.

Locking Resources

Before we proceed, we need to go into a more detail about the mechanics of protecting data. The primary mechanism for preventing and resolving resource conflicts is called a *lock*. The term should be familiar to anyone who has worked with file I/O in multiuser or multithreaded systems, or to anyone who has used a document repository or version control system. A thread can place a lock on a resource, signaling to the rest of the system that it needs to perform some action and the rest of the system must wait for access until the lock is released. Databases, EJB servers, and other transaction managers use locks to enforce the ACID properties on transactions. For example, a transaction might lock a particular row within a database table.

There are three main kinds of locks: read-only locks, write locks, and exclusive locks. A *read-only lock* indicates that a resource is being accessed but not modified, and that the resource cannot be modified during the read process. An object can support multiple read-only locks, and will become writeable when the last lock is released. A *write lock* claims the privilege of writing to an object: only the lock holder can modify the resource until the lock is released. Any other threads attempting to change the resource have to wait. An *exclusive lock* (also known as a *read-write lock*) grabs exclusive access to a resource, preventing other threads, users, or resources from either reading or modifying it.

If you're using locks at all, you'll definitely use a write lock. This type of lock prevents the typical thread conflict situation, in which one thread reads from an object, another thread writes to it, the first thread writes to the object, and the second thread reads from it. In this case, the second thread doesn't experience the behavior it expects.

Read-only locks are only needed when a consistent view of the data is critical. Since a read-only lock can't be obtained when a write lock exists, an application can use them to prevent dirty reads, where an object is seen in mid-transaction state. Read-only locks are the primary mechanism for supporting atomicity in transactions.

The more oppressive the lock, the greater the performance penalty. Exclusive locks, which prevent any access to an object, are the most costly. The cost comes both from the overhead of managing the lock itself and the delays imposed upon the rest of the application when accessing an object.

Optimistic Concurrency Pattern

Many systems have large numbers of objects subject to transaction control, but relatively few transactions affecting the same objects at the same time. These applications require a high-performance solution that will maintain transactional integrity without penalizing performance. The *Optimistic Concurrency pattern* provides a solution.

An optimistic locking scheme assumes that the chance of collisions is low. The system runs under the basic assumption that if something does go wrong, it's OK for the end user to have to do a little more work to resolve the problem, such as rekeying a little data or coming back later and trying again. This approach doesn't excuse you from identifying and preventing the conflict: it just means that you don't have to do it preemptively. If one out of every thousand transactions has to be rekeyed, so be it—just make sure that you let people know when they have to do it.

The simplest strategy for optimistic concurrency is to implement a versioning scheme. Each entity under concurrency control is given a version identifier, which is changed every time the data is altered. When modifying an object, you note the version number, make your changes, and commit those changes if someone else hasn't changed the version number of the underlying object since you started making your changes. In an object-only environment, the process might look like this:

1. Clone the object.
2. Make changes to the clone.
3. Check the version number of the original object.
4. If the versions are the same, replace the original with the clone and update the version. Otherwise, give the user an error and have him repeat steps 1 through 3.

If you start this process while someone else is already on step 2, and he finishes before you get to steps 3 and 4, you'll get an error on step 4. (We'll look at the Version Number pattern in more detail later in this chapter.)

Pessimistic Concurrency Pattern

If an application includes a large number of users working with a relatively small set of data, collisions are more likely than under the optimistic concurrency scheme. Even if the likelihood of collision is low, the cost of resolving a concurrency conflict after the users have done their data entry might be very high: even the most reasonable users aren't going to be terribly excited at the prospect of rekeying five screens of data every third time they try to enter data into the system.

In these cases, we can use the *Pessimistic Concurrency pattern* to control access to resources. Pessimistic concurrency is simple: when a user wants to begin work on a resource, she obtains a lock on that resource. The lock is held until the entire update process is complete, and then released. For the duration of the lock, other users attempting to lock the resource are informed that the resource is unavailable. The lock-holder is assured that no underlying changes will occur during the edit process.

In web applications where data entry for a transaction might be spread across several pages and multiple requests (and, most important, across time), the pessimistic locking approach makes a lot of sense: multipage web-based edits can be particularly vulnerable to information being modified from several sources at once—imagine two users accessing an edit system that uses five separate pages to edit different elements of a composite entity (or see Chapter 6). You should be able to see at least two potential conflicts, regardless of whether the data to be edited is loaded at the start of the edit process or on a page-by-page basis.

Pessimistic locking requires much more care than optimistic locking, particularly in a web environment. It's very easy for a user to lock a resource (perhaps a highly contentious one) and then walk away and have lunch. Depending on the architecture you use, the lock might exist forever: if the session times out, the user will never get to the point in the flow where the lock is released. For this reason, locks used with pessimistic concurrency schemes have time limits attached; you must either re-request the lock within a set amount of time, or the lock is released and your work is not saved. This kind of lock is often referred to as a *lease*. Support for *leases* should be implemented within the locking framework rather than the application logic itself.

Implementing Concurrency

Now we have a basic framework for locking and concurrency management; let's look at three patterns for implementing locking and concurrency in various environments.

Lockable Object Pattern

Some small applications keep their entire domain model in memory. This ability makes business logic easier to program, since you only need to deal with objects in memory (persistence, in this sort of application, can involve anything from serializing the entire object graph to disk to periodically writing changes to a database). The *Lockable Object pattern* is a simple approach to implementing locking in a nondistributed system where a single instance of a single application handles all changes to the data.

You can implement a simple lockable object using the Java synchronized keyword. As long as all attempts to access the object are synchronized properly, you don't have to worry about lost updates, dirty reads, or other concurrency problems. Unfortunately, synchronization has a few problems. First, each thread accessing a synchronized object blocks until the object becomes available, potentially tying up large numbers of threads while waiting for time-consuming processing to complete. Second, synchronized doesn't help if a user needs to hold onto an object across multiple threads: for instance, a web-based update process spread across two or three requests for a servlet.

To create a solution that lasts across threads, we need to be user-aware. For a lockable object, we accomplish this by creating a Lockable interface, which can be implemented by all of the data objects that might be subject to locking. One such an interface is shown in Example 10-4.

Example 10-4. Lockable interface for the Lockable Object pattern

```
public interface Lockable {
    public boolean isLocked();
    public void lock(String username) throws LockingException;
    public void unlock(String username) throws LockingException;
}
```

When an application wants to use an object that implements the Lockable interface, it calls the lock( ) method with the username of the current user. If the object throws a LockingException, then no lock was obtained and the system should either wait and try again later or deliver a complaint to the user. Otherwise, it has a lock and can make whatever updates it needs. The application is responsible for calling unlock( ) when it's finished with the object.

Example 10-5 shows a simple object implementing the locking interface. You can, of course, develop a more sophisticated interface. One obvious extension would be to add a timeout to each lock. Depending on your application's needs, you can either implement the Lockable interface separately for each object, or implement it in a base class from which each of your data objects descends.

Example 10-5. Customer object with locking interface

```
public class Customer implements Lockable {

    private String lockingUser = null;
    private Object lockSynchronizer = new Object();

    public void lock(String username) throws LockingException {
        if (username == null) throw new LockingException("No User Provided.");
        synchronized(lockSynchronizer) {
            if(lockingUser == null)
                lockingUser = username;
            else if ((lockingUser != null) && (!lockingUser.equals(username)))
                throw new LockingException("Resource already locked");
        }
    }

    public void unlock(String username) throws LockingException {
        if((lockingUser != null) && (lockingUser.equals(username)))
            lockingUser = null;
        else if (lockingUser != null)
            throw new LockingException("You do not hold the lock.");
    }

    public boolean isLocked() {
        return (lockingUser != null);
    }

    // Customer getter/setter methods go here
}
```

One reviewer of this book rightly pointed out that the locking behavior in the example above belongs in a base class rather than in an interface implementation. The behavior of Example 10-5 is extremely generic, and there is, indeed, no reason why it shouldn't be provided in a base class. We chose to implement it as an interface for two reasons. First, locking logic might well change between different Lockable objects. Second, we might want to implement the same locking functionality on objects in a range of different object hierarchies, including some which already exist, or where we can't change the behavior of the base class. None of this changes the maxim that it always makes sense to implement functionality as high up the inheritance hierarchy as possible.

Lock Manager Pattern

Lockable objects themselves aren't always enough. Many DAO-based architectures don't maintain a particular object instance representing any particular bit of data within the system, especially when the application is spread across multiple servers. In these cases, we need a centralized registry of locks.

The *Lock Manager pattern* defines a central point for managing lock information by reference. Rather than assigning a lock based on a particular object instance, a lock manager controls locks based on an external object registry, which usually contains the primary keys associated with the objects under transaction control.

There are two common kinds of lock manager implementations: online and offline. Online lock management tracks everything within the JVM, and offline lock management uses an external resource, such as a database, to share locks across a number of applications. We'll look at both approaches next.

Online lock manager strategy

The simplest implementation approach for a lock manager is to handle everything in memory and in process. This is sometimes referred to as an *online lock manager*. Online lock managers are suitable for smaller applications contained in a single JVM.

Example 10-6 shows a lock manager implemented as a standalone Java object. The LockManager class provides methods for managing a set of managers—one for each type of resource you want to protect. Requesting a lock and releasing the lock are simple activities. This relatively simple implementation doesn't address some of the major production concerns: a more robust version would support releasing all locks for a user and setting an interval for the lock's expiration.

Even with synchronization code, this implementation is extremely fast: on a single-processor system with 10,000 active locks, the code can release and request several hundred thousand locks per second.

Example 10-6. LockManager.java

```
import java.util.*;

public class LockManager {
  private HashMap locks;

  private static HashMap managers = new HashMap( );
```

Example 10-6. LockManager.java (continued)

```java
/**
 * Get a named Lock Manager. The manager will be created if not found.
 */
public static synchronized LockManager getLockManager(String managerName) {
  LockManager manager = (LockManager)managers.get(managerName);
  if(manager == null) {
      manager = new LockManager();
      managers.put(managerName, manager);
  }
  return manager;
}

/**
 * Create a new LockManager instance.
 */
public LockManager() {
  locks = new HashMap();
}

/**
 * Request a lock from this LockManager instance.
 */
public boolean requestLock(String username, Object lockable) {
  if(username == null)
    return false; // or raise exception

  synchronized(locks) {
    if(!locks.containsKey(lockable)) {
      locks.put(lockable, username);
      return true;
    }
    // Return true if this user already has a lock
    return (username.equals(locks.get(lockable)));
  }
}

/**
 * Release a Lockable object.
 */
public Object releaseLock(Object lockable) {
  return locks.remove(lockable);
}
}
```

To see how this works, consider the following code fragment:

```java
CustomerBean obj1 = new CustomerBean(1);
CustomerBean obj2 = new CustomerBean(2);
CustomerBean obj3 = new CustomerBean(3);

LockManager lockManager = LockManager.getLockManager("CUSTOMER");
```

```
System.out.println("User 1, Obj1: " + lockManager.requestLock("user1", obj1));
System.out.println("User 2, Obj1: " + lockManager.requestLock("user2", obj1));
System.out.println("User 2, Obj2: " + lockManager.requestLock("user2", obj2));
System.out.println("User 1, Obj3: " + lockManager.requestLock("user1", obj3));
System.out.println("Release Obj1  " + lockManager.releaseLock(obj1));
System.out.println("User 2, Obj1: " + lockManager.requestLock("user2", obj1));
```

When run, this code produces the following output:

```
User 1, Obj1: true
User 2, Obj1: false
User 2, Obj2: true
User 1, Obj3: true
Release Obj1 user1
User 2, Obj1: true
```

When implementing this type of lock manager, it is important that you properly override the equals( ) and hashCode( ) methods on the objects you are locking. These methods are used by the HashMap object to keep track of different locks, and if you don't manage them properly, you may find yourself managing locks at a Java object level rather than at a data model object level. As a result, it often makes sense to handle locks based on a primary key object, rather than the actual object itself. In the example above, we could use java.lang.Long objects containing the customer's unique identifier, rather than the CustomerBean objects directly. It would eliminate uncertainty about where the CustomerBean came from, and make it easier to transition to an offline lock manager strategy as your application grows.

Offline lock manager strategy

An online lock manager is sufficient when the application runs on a single application server (whether that server is a simple servlet container or an expensive application server). It is insufficient, however, when application load is spread over multiple servers. Using an embedded lock manager prevents us from scaling the application horizontally by spreading users across multiple web servers accessing the same back end. Each server could give out a lock on the same resource with predictably disastrous consequences.

The solution is to shift lock management out of the servlet container and into the database. Doing this puts the locks closer to the shared resource, and allows us to put the same database behind as many web servers as we want without having to worry about two different servers giving different users simultaneous access to the same resources.

Example 10-7 provides a simple implementation of a database-backed lock manager. It uses a table named LOCK_TRACKING to keep track of locks. The LOCK_TRACKING table contains one row for each lock, and each row specifies the object type (allowing us to lock different kinds of objects with one lock manager), the object key (which we assume is a long), and the username of the user who did the locking. We also store the date the lock was obtained, and use it to create a method that releases all locks older than 15 minutes. Here's how the LOCK_TRACKING table is defined in Oracle:

```
create table lock_tracking (
  object_type   varchar2(30),
  object_key    number,
  username      varchar2(30) not null,
  obtained      date default sysdate,
  primary key (object_type, object_key);
);
```

We need to prevent multiple users from obtaining locks on the same type/key pair. We count on the fact that the JDBC driver will throw an SQLException if an insert operation fails. The primary key prevents the database from storing more than one row in the table for each type/key pair. We obtain a lock by inserting a row in the table, and delete the row to remove the lock, clearing the way for another user to obtain a lock.

Example 10-7. OfflineLockManager.java

```java
import locking.LockingException;

import javax.sql.DataSource;
import java.sql.Connection;
import java.sql.SQLException;
import java.sql.PreparedStatement;
import java.sql.ResultSet;

public class OfflineLockManager {
 private DataSource dataSource;
 private static final String LOCK_INSERT_STMT =
    "INSERT INTO LOCK_TRACKING "+
    "(OBJECT_TYPE, OBJECT_KEY, USERNAME) VALUES (?, ?, ?)";

 private static final String LOCK_SELECT_STMT =
    "SELECT OBJECT_TYPE, OBJECT_KEY, USERNAME, " +
    "OBTAINED FROM LOCK_TRACKING WHERE " +
    "OBJECT_TYPE = ? AND OBJECT_KEY = ?";

 private static final String RELEASE_LOCK_STMT =
    "DELETE FROM LOCK_TRACKING WHERE OBJECT_TYPE = ? "+
    "AND OBJECT_KEY = ? AND USERNAME = ?";

 private static final String RELEASE_USER_LOCKS_STMT =
    "DELETE FROM LOCK_TRACKING WHERE USERNAME = ?";

 // Oracle specific lock release statement;
 // release all locks over 15 minutes (1/96 of a day)
 private static final String RELEASE_AGED_LOCKS_STMT =
    "DELETE FROM LOCK_TRACKING WHERE OBTAINED < SYSDATE - (1/96)";

 public OfflineLockManager(DataSource ds) {
   dataSource = ds;
 }
```

Example 10-7. OfflineLockManager.java (continued)

```
public boolean getLock(String objectType, long key, String username)
        throws LockingException {

    Connection con = null;
    PreparedStatement pstmt = null;
    boolean gotLock = false;

    try {
      con = dataSource.getConnection();
      // use strict isolation
      con.setTransactionIsolation(Connection.TRANSACTION_SERIALIZABLE);
      con.setAutoCommit(false);
      pstmt = con.prepareStatement(LOCK_INSERT_STMT);
      pstmt.setString(1, objectType);
      pstmt.setLong(2, key);
      pstmt.setString(3, username);

      try {
         pstmt.executeUpdate();
         gotLock = true;
      } catch (SQLException ex) {
      } // a SQLException means a PK violation, which means an existing lock

      if (!gotLock) {
         // This means there was a Primary Key violation: somebody has a lock!
         String lockingUsername = getLockingUser(con, objectType, key);
         if ((lockingUsername != null) && (lockingUsername.equals(username)))
            gotLock = true; // We already have a lock!
      }

      con.commit(); // end the transaction
    } catch (SQLException e) {
      try {
        con.rollback();
      } catch (SQLException ignored) {}
      LockingException le = new LockingException(e.getMessage());
      le.initCause(e); // JDK 1.4; comment out for earlier JDK releases
      throw le;
    } finally {
       if (pstmt != null)
           try { pstmt.close(); } catch (SQLException ignored) {}
       if (con != null)
           try { con.close(); } catch (SQLException ignored) {}
    }

    return gotLock;
}

/**
 * Release a lock held by a given user on a particular type/key pair.
 */
```

Example 10-7. OfflineLockManager.java (continued)

```java
public boolean releaseLock(String objectType, long key, String username)
        throws LockingException {
  Connection con = null;
  PreparedStatement pstmt = null;
  try {
    con = dataSource.getConnection();
    pstmt = con.prepareStatement(RELEASE_LOCK_STMT);
    pstmt.setString(1, objectType);
    pstmt.setLong(2, key);
    pstmt.setString(3, username);
    int count = pstmt.executeUpdate();
    return (count > 0); // if we deleted anything, we released a lock.
  } catch (SQLException e) {
    LockingException le = new LockingException(e.getMessage());
    le.initCause(e); // JDK 1.4; comment out for earlier JDK releases
    throw le;
  } finally {
    if (pstmt != null)
        try { pstmt.close(); } catch (SQLException ignored) {}
    if (con != null)
        try { con.close(); } catch (SQLException ignored) {}
  }
}

/**
 * Release all locks held by a particular user.
 * Returns true if locks were release.
 */
public boolean releaseUserLocks(String username) throws LockingException {
  Connection con = null;
  PreparedStatement pstmt = null;
  try {
    con = dataSource.getConnection();
    pstmt = con.prepareStatement(RELEASE_USER_LOCKS_STMT);
    pstmt.setString(1, username);
    int count = pstmt.executeUpdate();
    return (count > 0); // if we deleted anything, we released locks.
  } catch (SQLException e) {
    LockingException le = new LockingException(e.getMessage());
    le.initCause(e); // JDK 1.4; comment out for earlier JDK releases
    throw le;
  } finally {
    if (pstmt != null)
        try { pstmt.close(); } catch (SQLException ignored) {}
    if (con != null)
        try { con.close(); } catch (SQLException ignored) {}
  }
}

/**
 * Release all locks over 15 minutes old.
 */
```

Example 10-7. OfflineLockManager.java (continued)

```java
public boolean releaseAgedLocks() throws LockingException {
  Connection con = null;
  PreparedStatement pstmt = null;

  try {
    con = dataSource.getConnection();
    pstmt = con.prepareStatement(RELEASE_AGED_LOCKS_STMT);
    int count = pstmt.executeUpdate();
    return (count > 0); // if we deleted anything, we released locks.
  } catch (SQLException e) {
    LockingException le = new LockingException(e.getMessage());
    le.initCause(e); // JDK 1.4; comment out for earlier JDK releases
    throw le;
  } finally {
    if (pstmt != null)
        try { pstmt.close(); } catch (SQLException ignored) {}
    if (con != null)
        try { con.close(); } catch (SQLException ignored) {}
  }
}


  /**
    * Returns the user currently hold a lock on this type/key pair,
    * or null if there is no lock.
    */
  private String getLockingUser(Connection con, String objectType,
                                long key) throws SQLException {
    PreparedStatement pstmt = null;
    try {
      pstmt = con.prepareStatement(LOCK_SELECT_STMT);
      pstmt.setString(1, objectType);
      pstmt.setLong(2, key);
      ResultSet rs = pstmt.executeQuery();
      String lockingUser = null;
      if (rs.next())
        lockingUser = rs.getString("USERNAME");
        rs.close();
        return lockingUser;
    } catch (SQLException e) {
      throw e;
    } finally {
      if (pstmt != null)
          try { pstmt.close(); } catch (SQLException ignored) {}
    }
  }
}
```

All of the locking examples in this chapter require the application to specify the user requesting the lock. This method works fairly well for simple applications, but it also creates a few problems. In particular, every piece of code needs to know the identifier associated with the current user or process. Passing this data around, particularly through multiple tiers and multiple levels of abstraction, can be pretty dicey—at best, it's one more parameter to include in every method call.

We can work around this problem somewhat by incorporating a username directly into the transaction context, much as we incorporated the database connection into the context. As a result, the current username is available for any code that needs it, without the intervening layers necessarily being aware of it. The JAAS security API uses a similar approach and can be productively integrated into a transaction and concurrency control scheme.

Version Number Pattern

Particularly in an optimistic concurrency scenario, resolving concurrency conflicts requires determining whether an object has changed—but we don't want to task the entire application with keeping track of changes. The *Version Number pattern* allows us to associate a simple record of state change with each data object by recording a version number that is incremented with each change to the underlying data. The version number can be used by DAOs and other objects to check for external changes and to report concurrency issues to the users. The version number can be persistent or transient, depending on the needs of your application. If transactions persist across crashes, server restarts, or acts of God, then we should include the version number as a field within the object, persisted along with the rest of the fields. We will implement a persistent version number if we're instantiating multiple copies of the object from persistent storage (for example, via a DAO).

If we create one object instance that remains in memory for the life of the system, we may not need a persistent version number.

Example 10-8 demonstrates a simple versioned object, with version information retrieved via the getVersion() method. We also provide an equality method, equalsVersion(), that does a content-based comparison, including the version number. Depending on the needs of your application, you might want to make the equals() method version-aware as well. The equalsVersion() method allows you to determine whether an object has been touched as well as whether it has been changed. This can be important when your persistence layer needs to record a last update date: if the object is fed its original values, the version will be incremented while the data remain unchanged. This might indicate a meaningful update, if only to say that all's well.

Example 10-8. VersionedSample.java

```
public class VersionedSample implements Versioned {
    private String name;
    private String address;
```

Example 10-8. VersionedSample.java (continued)

```
private String city;
private long pkey = -1;

private long version = 1;

public VersionedSample(long primaryKey) {
    pkey = primaryKey;
}

public long getVersion( ) {
    return version;
}

public String getName( ) {
    return name;
}

public void setName(String name) {
    this.name = name;
    version++;
}

public String getAddress( ) {
    return address;
}

public void setAddress(String address) {
    this.address = address;
    version++;
}

public String getCity( ) {
    return city;
}

public void setCity(String city) {
    this.city = city;
    version++;
}

public boolean equalsVersion(Object o) {
    if (this == o) return true;
    if (!(o instanceof VersionedSample)) return false;

    final VersionedSample versionedSample = (VersionedSample) o;
    if(o.pkey != this.pkey) return false;

    if (version != versionedSample.version) return false;
    if (address != null ? !address.equals(versionedSample.address) :
        versionedSample.address != null) return false;
```

Example 10-8. VersionedSample.java (continued)

```java
        if (city != null ? !city.equals(versionedSample.city) :
            versionedSample.city != null) return false;
        if (name != null ? !name.equals(versionedSample.name) :
            versionedSample.name != null) return false;

        return true;
    }
}
```

CHAPTER 11

Messaging

Your application is done. Time to sit back and relax, right? Well, generally, no. You see, there's this thing that people in business tend to do when confronted with new applications. "Wonderful," they say. "Now can we connect it with our other system?" And the dance of development begins again.

In fact, the future often arrives before the application is even finished. More and more, the usefulness of any given system depends on how well it can connect to other systems, sharing data and participating in ever more elaborate processes. Sometimes every system is shiny and modern, and all the interactions take place directly in Java. But usually many of the systems are old, incompatible, or both: they could include COBOL, thick Client/Server, and even Java and .NET applications created by other developers or spread across many organizations and isolated by heavy-duty firewalls. Each of these systems has different interfaces and different data formats. Some are always accessible, and some are available only transiently. Some interactions are vitally time sensitive, and some aren't. It's like a railway through a jungle—hard enough to navigate to begin with, but even worse when most of the tracks are a different gauge. The task of the enterprise integrator is to keep the traffic moving effectively.

In earlier chapters, we talked about remote procedure calls and web services as an approach for addressing integration issues. This chapter focuses on solving these problems by using *messaging* to create more flexible, less tightly-coupled systems.

Messaging is an important component in an increasingly service-oriented enterprise environment. In the past, providing the same service to multiple applications involved either rebuilding it each time or developing custom integration software. Messaging makes it easier to build or purchase specialized tools for particular applications, since a variety of applications can share a single expensive resource without each development team having to spend a lot of time developing interfaces.

Messaging provides great new opportunities to enterprise designers. Of course, there is a drawback: messages are by nature *asynchronous*. Messages sent by one application to another don't immediately arrive at the recipient, and the sender doesn't have any automatic confirmation of delivery. Of course, this situation can work to your advantage: you don't need 100% uptime for every system and network in your organization. And it's surprising how many applications don't require an immediate response, as long as the message is delivered.

On the integration front, centralized Extract, Transform, and Load (ETL)* applications have begun to incorporate messaging support to support multiple different applications sharing a single ETL server. The systems accept commands and input data from messages. In custom development, applications that require expensive or difficult-to-maintain software can be centralized as well: if 10 web applications need to send faxes, a centralized fax server can provide that service to all of them, rather than requiring a fax modem on each web server with all the attendant hardware and administration. The web applications, whether running on Solaris, Linux, or something else entirely, can communicate with the fax service via messaging.

The patterns in this chapter focus on two aspects of messaging. We start by discussing message distribution strategies, including different ways to use a message within an application. The second half of the chapter presents patterns for baking messaging into your applications; they cover retrieving messages from a message service and developing strategies for processing messages in the most flexible way possible.

Messaging in J2EE

Most discussions of messaging in the J2EE world focus on JMS, the Java Message Service API, which is a core component of the J2EE standard. JMS provides access to heavy-duty messaging software. A JMS-enabled application can take advantage of a range of services, such as delivery guarantees, quality of service contracts, and an easy-to-use Java interface.

The patterns in this chapter apply to JMS applications, but many of them can be used alongside another message transport mechanism: trusty old Internet email. Email has gotten relatively short shrift in most texts on enterprise software development, and we're hard pressed to see why; it's easy to use, and the infrastructure is nearly ubiquitous. There's even a handy J2EE API, JavaMail, designed for dealing with it. We look at most of the patterns in this chapter through the lenses of both JMS and JavaMail. Of course, JavaMail and JMS are hardly equivalent, and we'll point out some of the differences in the next few pages.

---

* ETL applications provide data translation and conversion for integration activities: synchronizing data between different schemas, translating from COBOL output files to relational databases, and so forth.

Asynchronous Messaging Versus Web Services

This chapter doesn't cover message-oriented web services, partially because messaging is such a broad subject. If you think about it, most of what an application does can be cast in terms of messaging: method calls, for instance, are messages from one class to another, with immediate receipt and confirmation of delivery.

For our purposes, there's one major difference between asynchronous messaging and web services: web services are synchronous. When you're remotely accessing an EJB session bean or other Remote Procedure Call interface, it's expected that the service you're looking for will be available and online, and a web service is the same way. Web services use XML messages that conform to the SOAP specification, but they deliver the message immediately or not at all. The SOAP protocol doesn't mandate a delivery mechanism, but web services do. (HTTP—that's where the "web" part comes from.) These messages, like method calls, are synchronous: they happen immediately, and both sides of the exchange must coordinate with each other.

In this chapter, we're focusing on asynchronous messaging: communication between multiple systems in something other than real time. In an asynchronous exchange, the sender dispatches the message and goes on with other work. The recipient may receive the message milliseconds, minutes, hours, or days later, depending on the transport mechanism, system design, network conditions, and so forth (sunspots have been known to play a role here).

Even though the core web services concept is synchronous, that doesn't mean web services can't be deployed in support of an asynchronous application: you just need to write a little more code. Once you've done that, the underlying principles and patterns start to look a lot like the ones in this chapter.

Messaging and Integration

Back around the dawn of computing, sending a message between systems was easy: you wrote the data onto a magnetic tape, took the tape out of the computer, and carried it over to the other computer. Assuming the two computers shared a common data format, you were all set. When networks were invented, programmers devised integration techniques based on direct network connections. An application opened a connection to another application, and if the network was running and the target application was responding, the two systems could interact with each other, as long as they shared a common format for data. The problems with this approach should be familiar: the system wouldn't work if one application was down, or if there were intermittent network failures, or if the systems had different data formats. Building direct linkages and custom protocols were also a time-intensive and nonstandard approach, which had to be revisited with each new application or new version. And did we mention the data formats?

There are other approaches; many systems communicate with each other by reading and writing shared files, or by accessing shared tables within a database. The former method works well when two applications are running on the same physical machine or connected by a reliable network that supports file sharing. The latter works well for multiple applications and applications spread across a variety of systems. Both approaches have the benefit of being asynchronous: you don't need to have all the applications running in order for any single system to read or write data. But programmers still need to agree on formats and create the infrastructure to share the data resources. Programmers also have to be particularly careful of concurrency issues (see Chapter 10 for more on concurrency).

The original Unix mail system used the shared-files approach, allowing users on the same system to run the `mail` program at different times to leave messages for others and to read messages left for them. But with the rise of the Internet, and particularly with the development of always-on TCP/IP networks, users started to send messages to people using different computers, and even at different locations. The result was first UUCP and then SMTP, both of which provide a mechanism for routing messages between systems without having to actually create a direct connection between the sender and the recipient.

SMTP, in particular, did two things. First, it provided a standard, allowing different vendors and different platforms to send email to each other. MS Exchange, Lotus Notes, and Unix mail all use vastly different internal formats, but the common SMTP message and address formats made it largely a non-issue. Second, SMTP allowed administrators to set up an SMTP server for their domains. SMTP servers received messages from users and routed them to other systems for distribution. If the destination system was unavailable, the SMTP server could hold on to the outgoing message for a few hours and try again, rather than ignominiously failing.

SMTP servers were the first widely deployed messaging middleware. They introduced most users to the idea of *asynchronous messaging,* in which a message is sent and received at different times. In the last few years, asynchronous messaging has become a big deal in the enterprise development area because it provides the same advantages SMTP provides for email: it develops a standard method of packaging information and an infrastructure that allows messages to be sent reliably.

Figure 11-1 shows a simple use case diagram, where every single interaction could be implemented via a messaging approach. The customer emails a form to the software implementing the Purchase Product use case, which in turn sends a message to the software implementing the order processing use case, which, in turn, interacts with the Purchasing Server system actor via another set of messages.

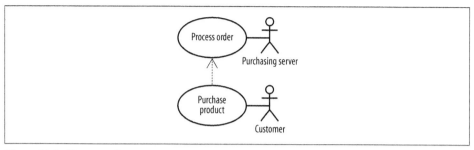

Figure 11-1. Use cases that can use messaging

Types of Messaging

Deciding to use asynchronous messaging in your application is a big step, but it's by no means the last. There are a number of ways to implement asynchronous messaging, each involving a different *Quality of Service* guarantee. The U.S. Postal Service, for instance, promises to deliver a first class letter within four days, and makes their best effort to deliver the letter intact. Most letters duly arrive in the expected time-frame and in reasonable condition. However, some letters get lost, and others are damaged. Because this isn't good enough for every snail-mail enabled application, the USPS provides a set of additional delivery services: return receipts, certified mail, Priority Mail, and Express Mail. An Express Mail letter is all but certain to arrive at its destination the following day, in good condition.

Messaging middleware is the same. Depending on the sophistication and configuration of your messaging platform, you can achieve a variety of different service levels. The higher levels involve more maintenance and are generally more expensive to configure. In this chapter, we're going to talk about two different kinds of messaging. The first is *guaranteed messaging*, which is implemented via middleware and provides high reliability and control. We use JMS to handle guaranteed messaging in Java. The second is *nonguaranteed messaging*, which lacks the reliability and security of guaranteed messaging, but can be implemented with much less programmer time and less cost for external middleware.

Guaranteed messaging

Guaranteed messaging uses middleware to ensure that a message is properly delivered to its destination, both ungarbled and in a reasonably timely fashion. The middleware implementing the messaging framework guarantees a message sent to a valid destination eventually arrives, even if the destination is temporarily unreachable.

Guaranteed delivery doesn't imply complete certainty. Specifying a nonexistent destination won't get your message delivered, regardless of how expensive your middleware is. And if a destination system is unavailable for a long period of time, the middleware will probably return the message to its sender rather than wait indefinitely. What is guaranteed, however, is the contract between the messaging client and the server governing how a message will be handled. Undeliverable messages won't vanish into the night but will be handled according to a specific and well-known set of rules.

Message Oriented Middleware systems implement guaranteed messaging. Senders and recipients work through a MOM server, which is responsible for tracking all elements of the message lifecycle. MOM servers often provide a range of options for the message content itself: XML, Java objects, raw binary data, and so on. J2EE clients interact with MOM servers using JMS, the Java Message Service. JMS, which is part of J2EE 1.3, provides a standard programmatic interface to the different MOM implementations, much as JDBC does for database servers. Sonic Software's SonicMQ and IBM's MQSeries products are two of the leading MOM products.*

Nonguaranteed messaging

Nonguaranteed messaging is like standard postal service. Your message will probably get there, but you don't know exactly when or in what condition. You also don't know if something goes wrong: there's no notification when your letter slips out of the bag and gets wedged in a corner of the Duluth post office.

Internet email, as defined by RFC 822, is the archetypical nonguaranteed messaging system. In fact, it's very consistent: messages sent to a valid address almost never get lost, and are delivered in a timely manner. In a controlled environment, receipt rates in the five-nines (99.999%) range aren't out of the question. Of course, delivery guarantees are only part of the issue. RFC 822 messaging provides no guarantee that a message will *only* be delivered and processed once, or that the message won't be changed in transport (corporate firewalls and virus detection packages frequently modify the format of a message). The application is responsible for verifying integrity and making sure that the order of processing is handled correctly. There are also no security guarantees; with SMTP, for instance, it is trivially easy to create a "spoof" message that appears to be from a particular source: receipt of a message provides no assurance that the message is genuine.

In return for a little extra work, you get the basic global infrastructure for free. Nonguaranteed messaging is often the only option when dealing with widely distributed sites, getting integrations up and running quickly with external partners, or when one actor in the messaging interaction is a human.

In J2EE, email integration is handled via the JavaMail API, which, out of the box, supports sending messages via SMTP and receiving them via POP3 or IMAP.†

---

* For more on JMS, see *Java Message Service* by Richard Monson-Haefel and David Chappell (O'Reilly).

† For more on JavaMail, see Chapter 12 of *Java Enterprise in a Nutshell*, Second Edition, by William Crawford, Jim Farley, and David Flanagan, and Chapter 10 of *Java Enterprise Best Practices* by the O'Reilly Java Authors (both published by O'Reilly).

JavaMail is actually a generic messaging API, and additional plug-ins are available to support other messaging schemes, such as NNTP, the protocol behind Usenet.

Persistent and nonpersistent messages in JMS

There's another wrinkle worth mentioning before we get to the patterns. While most MOM systems support guaranteed messaging, you can use MOM in guaranteed or nonguaranteed mode. The tradeoff, as usual, is performance: the server can handle more messages in nonguaranteed mode than in guaranteed mode, but there is a chance that a message won't be delivered.

JMS allows outgoing messages to be tagged as either persistent or nonpersistent. A nonpersistent message will be delivered to recipients *at most once*, but possibly never. Marking a message as persistent tells the middleware to use a store-and-forward approach to message delivery, ensuring that a message is delivered *once and only once*. The two delivery mechanisms have different implications depending on the type of message distribution pattern you're using, so we'll touch on this subject a bit more in the next section.

Message Distribution Patterns

Message distribution is built around the concept of a *message channel*, which happens to be the fundamental idiom behind the JMS API. A message channel provides a named destination for messages. Senders can access the channel to send messages, and receivers can read messages off the channel. It's that simple. In the email world, a message channel consists of the combination of SMTP (for sending and transport) and a mailbox (for receipt). In JMS, a channel is represented as either a Queue or a Topic object, for point-to-point or publish-subscribe messaging, respectively. In a MOM environment, channels can be created and destroyed on the fly, or you can preconfigure them within the MOM system.

Point-to-Point Distribution Pattern

The simplest form of messaging is from one actor to one other actor. This situation applies when using messaging to perform remote procedure calls or to deliver document messages for processing by a particular server. In these cases, it is important that a request be sent once and only once, and that the message be received and processed once and only once. The *Point-to-Point Distribution pattern* defines this behavior for our applications.

In the ubiquitous purchasing system example, a purchase order should only be sent once, and should only be fulfilled once. This requirement is particularly important when messaging is used to tie together parts of a process: a message sent by an order handler requesting credit card processing should only bill the card once. There are a number of ways to enforce concurrency in distributed applications (see Chapter 10, if you haven't already), but ensuring that the issues don't arise in the first place is always an excellent start.

Figure 11-2 shows a basic point-to-point messaging system. Application 1 sends a message to the message server, which delivers it (some time later) to Application 2, which acknowledges receipt, preventing the messaging server from trying to deliver again later. After some additional processing, Application 2 sends a reply message, which is delivered back to Application 1 by the server.

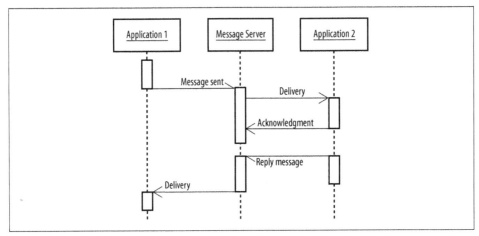

Figure 11-2. Point-to-point messaging

JMS implements point-to-point messaging via the Queue interface. A client places a message on a queue, and another client later removes that message from the queue. Point-to-point distribution can be used to build more complex messaging systems, allowing us to use technology that is intrinsically point-to-point (such as SMTP email) to build more complex systems, as we'll see next.

Publish-Subscribe Pattern

Many enterprise activities require sending the same message, or substantially similar messages, to a large number of recipients. This can certainly be done via point-to-point messaging—as long as the application has a list of recipients for the message, it can loop through and send one to each. But this approach brings its own problems: not only must the application do the work of dispatching a separate message to each individual recipient, it must keep track of the identity of all the recipients. Every application that might send messages to multiple recipients needs a mechanism for tracking the recipient list, and coaxing multiple applications into sending messages to the same list of people becomes a coordination challenge (at best) or nightmare (at worst).

The *Publish-Subscribe pattern* addresses the maintenance and scalability issues of large numbers of recipients. In this scenario, a source application "publishes" a message to a channel. Recipients then register with the channel to receive messages. Recipients can be added or deleted at the message server level rather than the application level. In JMS, a publish-subscribe channel is called a *topic* and is implemented via the Topic interface. Figure 11-3 shows a diagram of publish-subscribe messaging.

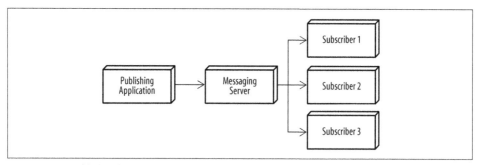

Figure 11-3. Publish-subscribe messaging

In a guaranteed messaging scenario, publish-subscribe can be used to keep a large number of systems synchronized by having each system send a message announcing each change in state. We'll talk more about this with the Control Bus pattern at the end of this chapter. Publish-subscribe can also be used as part of an enterprise management approach: applications publish messages announcing their health (or lack thereof) and respond to command and control messages from a central location. (See the "Control Bus Pattern" section later in this chapter.)

JMS behaviors in a publish-subscribe situation can get fairly subtle. The simple case, where all of the subscribers are connected to the topic at the time a message is sent, is straightforward enough: the subscribers receive the message. But what happens when a subscriber logs on later?

JMS topics can be either persistent or ad hoc; persistent topics are configured at the server level rather than within the Java client itself. Subscriptions to topics can also be configured as either temporary or "durable." Creating a durable subscription allows the client to disconnect and reconnect later without missing the messages sent in between. Normal, nondurable subscriptions only allow a client to receive messages sent while the client is online.

Here's a simple example of connecting to a JMS topic and sending a persistent message to a topic named "greetings".

```
TopicConnectionFactory factory = // retrieve from JNDI

TopicConnection connection =
    factory.createTopicConnection();
connection.start();

TopicSession session = connection.createTopicSession(
    false, Session.CLIENT_ACKNOWLEDGE);
```

```
Topic topic = session.createTopic("greetings");

if (topic == null) {
    System.err.println("Unable to load topic.");
    return;
}

TopicPublisher publisher = session.createPublisher(topic);
TextMessage message = session.createTextMessage("Hello!");
publisher.publish(topic, message, DeliveryMode.PERSISTENT, 2, 0);

publisher.close();
session.close();
connection.close();
```

You will generally use nonguaranteed messaging to implement publish-subscribe for human subscribers. Usenet newsgroups, which are enabled via the NNTP protocol, are a common example. Each newsgroup acts like a JMS topic: a message is sent to the newsgroup itself, and subscribers then connect to the newsgroup and read all of the messages that have been posted. Email-based list servers are an even simpler example: a message is sent to a single address and redistributed to a variety of other addresses.

A private NNTP news server can make a nice, inexpensive publish-subscribe mechanism for interapplication communication, at least where absolute auditability isn't required. News servers have been around for a long time, after all, which means that the underlying software has gotten quite stable.

Malformed Message Channel Pattern

MOM systems usually route undeliverable messages to a *dead letter queue* that can be monitored by the system administrator. When you're writing code that processes incoming messages, the dead letters aren't really your problem: they are undeliverable, so you never even see them (of course, if your application sends a message that turns out to be undeliverable, you should probably have some way of dealing with the consequences). Malformed messages, however, are your problem. A malformed message is deliverable but nonsensical: the application can't successfully process it. This is a bad situation, since a properly reliable application must provide some way to handle messaging related error conditions.

The *Malformed Message Channel pattern* provides a solution by specifying a particular destination to which an application can route all badly formatted messages (Figure 11-4). This step allows you to examine the messages manually and determine the source of the problem. Hopefully, malformed messages will be a relatively rare occurrence, so monitoring the channel will not be too onerous.

To implement a malformed message channel in JMS, simply add a Queue or a Topic to your messaging server, and have your application reroute all unreadable messages

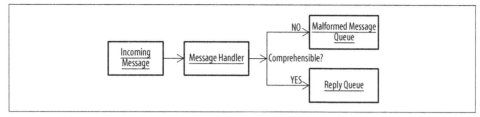

Figure 11-4. Routing messages to a malformed message channel

to the new channel. Most messaging servers provide a mechanism for browsing the contents of a channel, which might be all you need to review the malformed messages. In more complex circumstances, though, you can build an application that alerts the appropriate humans to take corrective action.

The incidence of malformed messages will probably be higher when SMTP is used for messaging. Beyond the ever-present danger of spam (which will manage to find your mailbox if it's anywhere near the Internet), firewalls, strange mail clients, and ill-behaved servers can subtly transform messages. Monitoring these problems becomes correspondingly more important.

Message Types

Within a particular messaging approach, several different types of messages can be sent. Each of these message type patterns can be built on top of the messaging systems discussed in the previous section. They can be implemented using guaranteed or nonguaranteed messaging on a variety of different protocols and with either point-to-point or publish-subscribe delivery.

All message types share a few common elements. A basic message has a sender attribute, a recipient attribute, a set of headers and a set of user-specified attributes. The use of the sender and recipient should be obvious. Headers and attributes serve to further define the message. An email message, for instance, will generally contain headers specifying the subject, the date the message was sent, the email client that was used, the encoding type used for the text, and the various servers that relayed the message.

The JMS APIs break a message up into three major parts: a standard header section, a user-defined header section, and a message body. Only the first of these sections is required, although a message without any user-specified content cannot deliver a whole lot of data. The following message type patterns help determine which data to store in the different parts of a message.

Event Message

Event handling in Java should be familiar to you by now; but on the off chance that it isn't, here's the primer: an object can register itself with another object as an event listener. Once the listener has been registered, the target has a handle to the listener and can use *callback* methods to notify the listening object that a particular event has occurred. This process allows programmers to easily modify runtime behavior by plugging new listeners in at appropriate places. Swing is full of listeners, as is the Servlet API (ServletContextListener, etc.). The Gang of Four identified this behavior as Observer, in which the actor is the object or set of objects performing the main actions, and the observer is the listener.

An *event message* extends the Observer model to a set of distributed applications. The basic informational content of an event message is implicit in the fact that the message has been sent. Event messages can be sent from one system to another to provide notification of lifecycle events within an application, or to announce the status of particular activities. Applications for this pattern include enterprise monitoring (see the discussion of the *control bus* later in this chapter) and centralized logging.

An important characteristic of event messages is that they do not require a reply. In fact, one could go so far as to say there is no requirement that event messages be received, either. In some cases this is true, and in others it isn't: whether events *must* be received should influence your choice of message transport.

In JMS, an event message can be implemented with the user-defined headers of a message. The benefit of this approach is simplicity: applications only need to agree on header names, so there is no need to define a format for the message data. Performance improves, too, since JMS and most MOM packages provide built-in functionality to filter messages based on their headers.

Document Message

Many applications need to share large data files with each other. A *Document Message* allows them to accomplish this via messaging. A document message is a message that contains a substantial payload. Depending on the systems involved, the document might be an XML file, a serialized object, or an actual word processing document.

Designing a document message raises many of the same interoperability questions as any other integration activity. XML-formatted messages can be consumed by a variety of systems, but require more computing power to process than simply reading raw bytes out of a message. Serialized Java objects can only be consumed by other Java systems with the appropriate class libraries installed, but are otherwise very easy to use.

Document messages are generally implemented in JMS by storing the document in the message body. The message headers should be used to store simple information about the document, such as its format and versioning information, while the actual data is put into the body. With Internet email, document messages can be implemented as a file attachment or a series of file attachments. Message headers can still be used to indicate the type of message being sent.

When using Internet email to transmit data, it makes sense to apply some basic security measures. At the minimum, you should include a digest of the data being sent. This record allows you to verify that the message wasn't accidentally tampered with in transit, but will not provide much (if any) security against deliberate sabotage. Encrypting the digest with a public key system allows you to ensure that a message hasn't been tampered with. Encrypting the whole document, of course, prevents it from being tampered with or viewed by unauthorized personnel.*

Command Message

Distributed applications can be a command and control nightmare. Multiple web applications expose different interfaces to the administrator, and actions that affect multiple systems need to be repeated. Tools like JMX (the Java Management Extensions) alleviate this problem to a degree, but only within controlled environments. It can be irritating, but the real challenge comes when disparate applications need to control each other. Since user interfaces are generally not designed to be used by other computers, some kind of remote command infrastructure is required.

A *command message* allows one system to control another application, or a series of other applications, by sending a specially formatted message to that system. A command message includes instructions to perform a specific action, either via headers and attributes, or as part of the message payload. The recipient performs the appropriate action when the message is received. Command messages are closely related to the Command pattern from GoF, which we discussed back in Chapter 3. They can be thought of, in fact, as a remote version of this pattern.

Security is a particular concern with command messages. MOM products provide a variety of mechanisms for securing a message channel. If these products are adequate for your needs (they often are), receipt of a command message can be treated much like an RPC call. If you're using a transport system that doesn't provide security guarantees, such as email, consider the security options we discussed for document messages.

A document message can also be a command message. Many commands require data on which to act; there's no point in sending two messages, what with all the overhead involved in correlation—particularly since neither message will be useful without the other.

---

* Since that's an extremely brief introduction to digital signatures, the user is encouraged to consult *Web Security, Privacy & Commerce* by Simson Garfinkel with Gene Spafford (O'Reilly) and *Java Cryptography* by Jonathan Knudsen (O'Reilly).

Correlating Messages

Asynchronous messaging means that the sender doesn't receive an immediate reply or confirmation of receipt. After sending a message for processing by a remote service, most applications require at least confirmation that the message was received and acted upon, and often require the results of the remote process. Remember—in a normal application, even if a method doesn't return a value, the system at least knows that the method has had a chance to execute.

A *reply message* is a message received in response to another message. Reply messages are generally document or event messages, but are distinguished by being associated with a particular message. Typically, this association is accomplished by assigning each outgoing message a unique identifier (MOM systems do this automatically). If an incoming message is a reply, it includes a reference to the message the remote application is replying to.

JMS includes built-in functionality for associating a reply message with the original. Each JMS message, upon creation, is assigned a message ID, which is accessible via the JMSMessageID property of the Message class. Messages also have a JMSCorrelationID field, not set by default. When composing a reply message, it's standard practice to take the JMSMessageID and store it in the JMSCorrelationID field. Assuming that message and reply are valid JMS messages, and that reply is a response to message, this is how we'd set the correlation:

```
reply.setJMSCorrelationID(message.getJMSMessageID( ));
```

This approach presupposes that the original sender kept track of the message ID. Obviously, reply messages can be linked to their original in whatever manner is appropriate for your application. An identifier with real world significance (purchase orders or database record keys) might make more sense than the ID assigned by the JMS provider.

Sequenced Message Pattern

Message transport systems have limits. These limits frequently have to do with size. Even if the messaging system you're using doesn't impose a strict upward boundary on the size of a message, practical considerations often impose one anyway. Network connections can be interrupted and servers can run out of memory.

As a result, it is sometimes necessary to divide a message into several parts, each of which can be easily digested by the messaging system and the recipient. The *Sequenced Messages pattern* allows you to spread one logical message over a series of actual messages (Figure 11-5). The client must wait until it has received all of the messages in the sequence before it can proceed.

To send sequenced messages in JMS, you need to include at least two additional properties in each message, and usually three. The first is a sequence ID, which

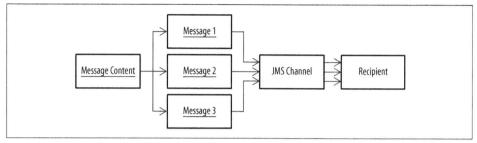

Figure 11-5. Logical message divided into a message sequence

allows the recipient to group messages from particular sequences. The second property is the order of the current message in the sequence. For example, your application might assign a particular message sequence the ID "MSEQ-001", and each of the five messages in the sequence would include a message sequence ID property containing "MSEQ-001" and a message number from 1 to 5. If your application isn't able to determine the length of a message sequence by examining the messages itself, a third property, providing the number of messages in the sequence, is also required.*

Here's a basic example, using two properties. For simplicity, we assume the content is presented as a set of text strings (perhaps an XML file broken up into pieces) created by a getContent( ) method:

```
String sSeqID = "MSEQ-001";
int msgIndex = 1;
String[] contentPieces = getContent(...)

for (int index = 0; index < contentPieces; index++) {
  TextMessage message =
    session.createTextMessage(contentPieces[i]);
  message.setStringProperty("MessageSequenceID", sSeqID);
  message.setIntProperty("MessageNumber", index);
  publisher.publish(topic, message, delivery_mode, priority, 0);
}
```

Since none of the messaging systems we've discussed support sequenced messages natively, error handling in the case of an incomplete sequence is very much in the hands of the client application.

Message Client Patterns

Once a message has been created and dispatched to an appropriate delivery channel, the next step is for the client to retrieve and process it. Retrieval mechanisms for

---

* If the end of the sequence is self-evident from examining the last message, you don't need to specify the number of segments up front; the recipient can look at the message number of the final message in order to determine how many messages were supposed to have been received. This approach can be particularly helpful when it's unclear at the start how large a sequence might end up being.

messages need to balance speed of delivery, reliability, scalability, and ease of use. In this section, we'll look at some patterns for handling messages in client applications. The *Message Handle pattern* shows how to decouple message processing code from message retrieval code. The *Polling Consumer* and *Event-Driven Consumer patterns* explain how to get messages into your application. *Message Façade* demonstrates using messaging to isolate your business logic. *Competing Consumers* shows how to speed up message processing in high volume applications, and *Message Selector* will help you build more efficient client-side message processors.

Message Handler Pattern

All message clients perform two functions: they retrieve and process a message. It's possible to weave these two activities tightly together, but in more complex systems it can result in some pretty complex code. We want to isolate the latter function in a way that lets us share code across different message types. The *Message Handler pattern* abstracts the code responsible for receiving the actual message away from the code responsible for processing the message content.

This pattern allows us to change the method by which we receive a message without changing the code for processing the message. Changing message handling itself becomes easier, since we can drop message handlers in and out without major changes to the rest of the application (we can even do it dynamically). There's also a testing benefit, since you can write standalone test cases for an isolated handler method more easily than for an integrated component.

Example 11-1 shows a simple mail handler interface for incoming JavaMail messages. The code responsible for retrieving the message instantiates the appropriate handler and calls the handleMessage() method, passing in the new message. We'll see the message client code itself when we talk about the Polling Consumer pattern.

Example 11-1. Mail handler interface

```
public interface BlockingMailHandler
{
  /** Process a message, returning true on success, false on failure.
    * Does not return until message is processed. */
  public boolean handleMessage(javax.mail.Message message);
}
```

A more complex application than this simple blocking handler might define a variety of message handler types, such as a threaded handler and a single thread model handler. A JMS example would look similar, but it would accept a javax.jms.Message object instead.

Most applications can get away with a transport-specific handler, since the mechanics of retrieving content from JMS and JavaMail message objects differ widely; most applications only use one transport mechanism for any particular use case. But occasionally, applications need to accept the same kind of message from a variety of different sources. One example of this situation is when some of the applications you're integrated with are separated by a firewall: remote applications can send their messages via email (probably encrypting the content) and local applications can use the MOM backbone. In these cases, you'll either want to provide two handleMessage( ) methods, or descend two different handler classes (one per message type) from the same base class (which contains the logic required for processing the message once it has been extracted from its transport container).

Polling Consumer Pattern

An important reason to use a messaging system is in order to allow one component of an integrated system to go down without immediately affecting all the others. The *Polling Consumer pattern* allows a client to periodically check for messages, rather than maintaining a constant connection to the message server. If the server is unavailable, the client can simply try again later, rather than ceasing all operation. Conversely, if the client goes down, the server will maintain the messages until the client starts up again. In this kind of client crash we still lose time, but we don't lose information.

A polling consumer periodically checks a message channel for new messages, reads them, and processes them. Generally, the consumer is implemented as a thread, which sleeps for a set amount of time before polling for new messages. Polling consumers are the most reliable way to receive Internet mail and are useful for JMS applications where an EJB container isn't used.

Example 11-2 shows the MailMonitor component. MailMonitor is a Java class that can be dropped into a standalone application (by instantiating and running the thread in the main( ) method) or into a web application (started, perhaps, by a ServletContextListener). The mail monitor checks a POP3 mailbox, reads every message, and invokes a BlockingMailHandler to process them. If a message is processed successfully, the client deletes it from the server. Once all messages are processed, the client waits 10 seconds and starts again.

Example 11-2. Standalone MailMonitor

```
import javax.mail.*;
import javax.mail.internet.*;
import java.io.*;

public class MailMonitor extends Thread {
  boolean interupted = false;
  BlockingMailHandler handler = null;
  private static String username = "contentmail";
  private static String password = "poppasswd";
  private static String mailServer = "mail.company.com";
```

Example 11-2. Standalone MailMonitor (continued)

```
public MailMonitor(BlockingMailHandler mh) {
  handler = mh;
}

public void stopRunning( ) {
  interupted = true;
}

public void run( ) {
  Session session = Session.getDefaultInstance(System.getProperties( ));
  Store store = null;
  try {
    store = session.getStore("pop3");
  } catch (NoSuchProviderException nspe) {
    nspe.printStackTrace( );
    return;
  }

  while(!interupted) {
    System.out.println("Looping to collect mail");
    try {
      if (!store.isConnected( )) // should always be true
        store.connect(mailServer, -1, username, password);
      System.out.println("Connected");
      Folder folder = store.getDefaultFolder( );
      folder = folder.getFolder("INBOX");
      if (folder == null) {
        System.out.println("Unable to open INBOX");
        return;
      }

    System.out.println("Opening folders");
    // Try to open read/write. Open read-only if that fails.
    try {
      folder.open(Folder.READ_WRITE);
    } catch (MessagingException ex) {
      folder.open(Folder.READ_ONLY);
    }

    int totalMessages = folder.getMessageCount( );
    int newMessages = folder.getNewMessageCount( );
    System.out.println("Total Messages: " + totalMessages);
    try {
      Message messages[] = null;
      messages = folder.getMessages(1, totalMessages);

      for (int i = 0, i < messages.length; i++) {
        boolean mbDelete = handler.handleMessage(messages[i]);
        // Delete the message
        if (mbDelete) {
          messages[i].setFlag(Flags.Flag.DELETED, true);
        }
```

Example 11-2. Standalone MailMonitor (continued)

```
      } // end for
    } catch (MessagingException e) {
      System.out.println("Unable to get Messages");
    }

    // Close the folder and store
    folder.close(true);
    store.close();

    } catch (MessagingException e) {
      System.out.println(e.toString());
      return;
    }

    try {
      this.sleep(10000);
    } catch (InterruptedException e) {
      System.out.println("Exiting");
      return;
    }
    }
  }
}
```

It's worth noting that in this design the mail handler is responsible for processing a message regardless of its validity. The mail handler implementation is also responsible for error reporting. The only time we want the handler to return false is when a time delay would allow the message to be processed later. Messages that cannot be processed now might be processable later, once other systems come back online or other messages arrive. That said, messaging systems make lousy persistent storage: you really should get the message out as quickly as possible, and deal with queuing in some other context, particularly if you don't have personal control over the mail server in question.

Polling consumers is also useful when an application doesn't need to process a message immediately, or when other factors such as high connection costs create economies of scale for processing multiple messages at once.

Event-Driven Consumer Pattern

Polling for messages can be a lot of work: your application is responsible for waking up periodically, checking for messages, and handling them in a safe fashion. Most of us have been spoiled by event-driven models in various areas of Java development. Servlets, for instance, are event-driven: the service() method is called in response to a specific request. The *Event-Driven Consumer pattern* allows us to forget about most of that code we built up in the Polling Consumer pattern section, in favor of a simple method that is invoked by the environment when necessary. The result is decreased code complexity and increased reuse, since more of the messaging retrieval logic is moved to the server.

Most JMS messages are handed in an event-driven manner. EJB 2.0 supports message-driven beans, which include an onMessage() method that is invoked whenever the application server detects a new message on a topic or queue. The base JMS API supports event-driven messages through the MessageListener interface. MessageListener defines an onMessage() method, which is called by the JMS subsystem whenever a new message is received.

Here's just about the simplest MessageListener class possible:

```
class MyMessageHandler implements MessageListener {

        public void onMessage(Message message) {
          TextMessage msg = (TextMessage)message;
          try {
            System.out.println("Message Received:" + msg.getText());
          } catch (JMSException e) {
            System.out.println(e.getMessage());
          }
        }
    }
```

And here's how we'd associate it with a Topic (assuming we already have a session named session and a topic named topic):

```
    TopicSubscriber subscriber = session.createSubscriber(topic);
    MyMessageHandler handler = new MyMessageHandler();
    subscriber.setMessageListener(handler);
```

Each new message on the topic now triggers a call to onMessage(). This process continues until message delivery on the connection is halted, the session is closed, or the program exits.

The underlying implementation depends on the messaging provider and driver. The driver might very well end up implementing a polling consumer behind the scenes, resulting in some overhead you might not ordinarily expect. Some providers deliver messages over RMI; the driver creates an RMI endpoint, which then delegates to the MessageListener. Check your messaging server documentation for more details.

JavaMail also provides an event-driven consumer via the classes in javax.mail. event, which support listening for changes to folders and message stores. However, we don't advocate the use of these classes: the implementations of the various Internet mail protocols don't support this kind of activity all that well, which means you'll have to test your application even more extensively than usual, and with the same exact infrastructure that you'll be using in production. It's better, in our opinion, to implement a polling consumer: it might be a bit more work, but you'll have tighter control and better visibility when things go wrong.

Message Façade Pattern

The *Message Façade pattern* describes an object that receives and acts on messages from the presentation tier. The message façade receives asynchronous messages from an external source, translates those messages into calls to appropriate business logic methods, executes the calls, and, if appropriate, sends a reply message containing the results. The rationale for isolating business logic behind the message façade is the same as for isolating it behind a business delegate or a session façade: easier maintenance and improved reuse.

Generally, the tradeoff to consider when developing business logic interfaces is whether you want to expose particular functionality in a synchronous or asynchronous manner. Most high-volume applications perform a surprisingly large amount of processing asynchronously; in an application deployed to a large number of users who may or may not have any particular loyalty to your company or institution, any activity that will take more than a second is a good candidate for asynchronous processing.

Message façades, like façades in general, have advantages and drawbacks. Since an application often takes several paths to its business logic (servlets, JMS, web services, and other routes as yet unknown), isolating that business logic behind a façade provides encapsulation and supports reuse. The business logic and domain model components themselves don't need to be aware of the message infrastructure and can be maintained separately. As with any messaging pattern, the business logic can be used asynchronously by the presentation tier. The cost is additional code, more infrastructure, and an additional layer of software between the user and the actual business process.

The Message Façade pattern is the third (and final) pattern in our series of business logic distribution patterns. We used business delegates to provide access to business logic within a JVM, via direct method invocations. We used session façades to provide synchronous access to remote business resources. Now, we'll use message facades to provide asynchronous access to remote resources.

Of course, our simple summary could be a little misleading. There's no reason that different kinds of façades can't, in the course of fulfilling their responsibilities, make calls to each of the others. A business delegate might call out to a remote session façade and fire off a batch of messages to a message façade. In general, creating a business delegate in order to allocate responsibility to the remote façade is a good idea, regardless of the façade type.

Figure 11-6 shows a client accessing a message façade, which in turn unpacks the message and calls a business delegate to do the heavy lifting. The business delegate then calls a DAO to handle persistence.

Implementing a message façade is easy. All you really have to do is implement a consumer. In EJB 2.0, you can create a message-driven bean that includes a JMS `onMessage()` method. Within the `onMessage()` method, you can call your business

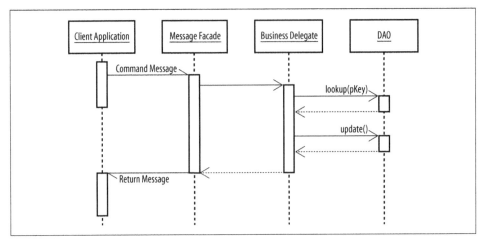

Figure 11-6. Message façade using business delegates and DAOs

objects and assemble a reply message. Using an MDB rather than a regular JMS listener gives you *transactional awareness*: the message-driven bean will participate in any currently running transaction; if a database action fails, the message receipt can be rolled back as well.

You probably won't need to implement message façades with JavaMail all that often, but the process is the same: implement a polling consumer (using the `MailMonitor.java` framework or any other mechanism you wish) and add the business logic functions. When using JavaMail, you'll have to take more care with security, since you won't be able to count on the message server to verify that only authorized parties are sending messages to your application.

Message Selector Pattern

The profusion of message queues and topics is a frequent problem in JMS applications. Designers often establish separate queues or topics for each type of message in the application. Supporting a high number of consumers can eat up a lot of resources, and managing a large number of separate messaging channels can burden IS departments, particularly when each new message type requires the reconfiguration of the message server. Email messaging presents a similar problem, but in the form of multiple target email addresses.

The *Message Selector pattern* allows us to handle multiple message types on a single queue or topic without excessively complex logic because it requires the client to differentiate between the different types of messages on the same channel.

JMS has a fairly powerful selection criteria API, based on a subset of the SQL selection syntax. The selection criteria works against the properties set on a particular message.

A message selector that only retrieves messages in which the MessageType property equals the string "StockCheck" would look like "MessageType = 'StockCheck'".

With the JMS publish-subscribe API, we specify the selector when we create the subscriber—it can't be changed after the fact. The boolean parameter at the end of the createSubscriber() call indicates whether messages originating from the local session should be ignored:

```
TopicSubscriber subscriber = session.createSubscriber(topic,
    "MessageType = 'StockCheck'", true);
```

For point-to-point messaging, we specify the selector in the call to the createConsumer() method, which has the same syntax—except that there is no boolean for ignoring local messages, since that doesn't make sense on a queue.

Using a selector has different consequences depending on the type of messaging used. If a message selector is applied to a queue, the remaining messages stay on the queue and can be read by the same session later on, or by other sessions (see the Competing Consumers pattern, below). When a message selector is used with a topic, the messages that aren't selected are lost to that subscriber, regardless of the durability of the subscription (the alternative would be completely unworkable: thousands upon thousands of undelivered messages, clogging up the middleware for subscriptions that have no intention of ever retrieving them).

Competing Consumers Pattern

Connecting front-line systems with back-office systems via messaging allows the front-line systems to keep on interacting with users, even while performing complex activities. This ability to multitask pushes the delay away from the end user, but it doesn't actually eliminate any bottlenecks. The work is spread out, but messages must still be processed.

Thankfully, there's no rule that says everything in life has to be linear. You can set multiple consumers loose on a single message queue and have them compete for the right to process the messages. Hence, the *Competing Consumers pattern*. Each consumer reads messages off the queue as quickly as it can and processes them in whatever manner is appropriate to the application. If the consumers start to fall behind we can just add more.

Figure 11-7 shows an example of multiple consumers listening to a single JMS queue. The queue is responsible for ensuring that each message is delivered to one and only one consumer. It makes competing consumers easy to implement in a JMS environment. The biggest potential problem is that the messages need to be self-contained: you have no guarantee that the same consumer will retrieve all the messages from a particular client, so using *sequenced messages* is impossible without additional work to coordinate between the consumers.

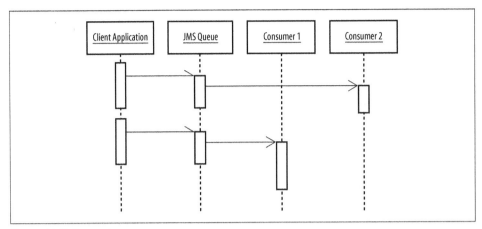

Figure 11-7. Competing consumers

Implementing multiple handlers without a MOM system is a bit more complicated. Since multiple applications cannot reliably access a single Internet email address concurrently, you need to divide the messages between handlers at a central point. Assigning an email address to each of the handlers can accomplish this division. Incoming messages can then be spread across the handlers, either by having one handler that receives all the messages and resends them (which can be much faster than the actual message processing, allowing one client to take care of it), or by configuring the mail server, where possible, to distribute messages in a round-robin fashion. The various handlers can implement polling consumers pointed at the individual addresses.

 When implementing competing consumers with JavaMail, you should never have multiple applications accessing the same mailbox. Most mail servers won't allow it anyway, and those that do won't provide you with sufficient isolation: messages will be read more than once, or might be missed entirely.

Messaging and Integration

For the final section of this chapter, we're going to look at patterns that focus on integrating messaging into an enterprise environment. Of course, all of the patterns in this chapter affect integration to some degree. The Message Façade pattern, for instance, is sometimes known as a *messaging adapter*, allowing nonmessaging-aware applications to participate in message-based data exchanges. The patterns in this section focus on how to route messages between systems, and on what might be done with the content once they've arrived.

Pipes and Filters Pattern

Many applications involve multiple processing. For example, placing an order might require reserving stock at the warehouse, processing payment, and shipping. In a fully integrated enterprise, you might be able to do all of this in one system and at one time, but most companies aren't entirely integrated. Reserving stock might require someone to physically visit the warehouse, and payment processing might involve purchase order approvals or lengthy credit checks. In these cases, it makes sense to decouple the activities into separate components and connect them with messaging.

The *Pipes and Filters pattern* allows us to link a set of message handlers (filters, in this parlance) via a series of pipes. The pattern itself is an old one,[*] and has been applied in a variety of contexts. Anyone who has "piped" the content of one program to another (`cat textfile.txt | more`, for example) should be familiar with the general concept. After each processing stage completes, the message is sent along another channel to the next handler in the sequence (Figure 11-8).

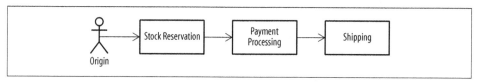

Figure 11-8. Message with intermediate processing

By implementing each stage of the message handler activity as a separate process, you gain a lot of flexibility in the way the steps are performed. New functions can be inserted as additional filters without requiring major modifications. As with stand-alone message handlers, the individual components can be tested much more easily. And, in conjunction with the competing consumers pattern, you can parallelize the more time-consuming elements of message processing. If the payment phase requires dialing out on a modem, for instance, you can buy a few more modems and set up a few more payment servers to help speed up the process.

Neither JMS nor JavaMail provides a simple mechanism to pass one message through a series of processing steps. Instead, each filter needs to pass the message on to the next filter in the sequence. The simplest way to implement this process is to provide each filter with its own channel.

To prevent confusion, it's helpful to provide an external resource, such as a database or XML configuration file, that tells each filter where to send its output. The following XML describes a message chain for the order fulfillment example (you'll need to

---

[*] The pattern was first described in *Patterns Oriented Software Architecture*, Volumes 1 and 2, by Frank Buschmann, et al (Wiley & Sons) for nonmessaging applications, and has been adopted by the messaging community. The filters in this pattern are very similar to what we've been calling handlers, but we didn't want to rename this pattern "Pipes and Handlers."

write your own code in order to parse and use it). All each filter needs to know to determine the next destination is its own name. New filters can be inserted into the XML wherever required.

```xml
<messagechain name="orderfulfillment">
    <filter name="reservation" queue="reservations"/>
    <filter name="payment" queue="payment"/>
    <filter name="shipping" queue="shipping"/>
</messagechain>
```

Look familiar? This is a messaging application of the Service to Worker pattern from Chapter 4.

This technique also makes it easier to use a filter in multiple different pipes and filters chains. As long as the message contains the name of the pipes and filters sequence it's currently passing through, the individual steps can consult the XML to determine the next step for the appropriate chain (so the payment filter can pass to a shipping filter in one chain and a "build a widget" filter in another chain).

To minimize queue profusion, you can also use the publish-subscribe pattern, and have all of the message handlers subscribe to a single queue (see the Competing Consumers pattern, above). Each handler implements a message selector that filters out all of the incoming messages that it doesn't support. Once the handler is done processing, it puts the message back on the queue for handling by the next step. Figure 11-9 shows an example.

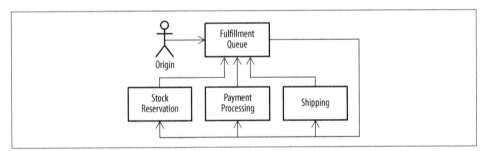

Figure 11-9. Message selector used to distribute messages

This approach works because JMS message selectors, when used with a queue, will leave all unselected messages on the queue for retrieval by other clients. As long as the selection criteria used by each filter are mutually exclusive, you can add as many filters as your MOM server will allow listeners, and you only need to maintain a single queue.

Content-Based Routing Pattern

Developers often face a disconnect between the interface they wish to offer the user and the fundamental reality of their IT environment. This situation often comes up when two organizations merge or when new and legacy environments coexist.

Imagine a large company with three or four expense-management systems. The company wants to introduce a standard, web-based expense report system for all employees. One option is to write some complicated servlets, probably building business delegates for each system and using a business delegate factory to decide, according to the employee, where to dispatch the request. This isn't a bad approach, but it does have a few drawbacks. Maintaining four business delegates isn't too difficult, since you'd have to manage that code anyway, but it's not completely flexible, either. Changing the criteria by which reports are routed to the appropriate system or adding a new system entirely will likely require changes to the core application. If you're using messaging to communicate with the expense-reporting systems, you need to maintain message channels to each system and make sure the web application knows about them. If you don't use messaging, you have to deal with the users' complaints when one system is down and their reports can't be processed.

The *Content-Based Routing pattern* solves this problem by providing a single point of receipt for messages associated with a particular use case. Using this particular pattern allows applications to send a message to a single destination, and have that message routed appropriately, based on its content. In the expense management example, the central recipient receives all expense report requests from every system that needs to send one, examines each request, and then redirects the message to the appropriate system based on the criteria provided. Changes can be centralized with new systems, and plugged in as needed. It's called content-based routing because we route the messages based on their actual content. In the example above, the CBR implementation would be responsible for querying an employee directory to determine which expense report system should receive the message.

Content-based routing can be used in situations where publish-subscribe messaging is too simple-minded. In this case, we could set up a message channel that all the expense systems subscribe to, and just have the systems ignore messages that they can't process. But this provision doesn't guarantee that the message will be processed, since it's conceivable that every system will ignore it. At the individual system level, it becomes difficult to sort out real errors from messages that were intended for other systems. The additional validity check provided by the router allows you to handle unprocessable messages in a clean fashion.

Figure 11-10 shows a system that implements a content-based router to handle expense reports. The web app sends a message to the expense report router, which looks at the message, determines the division that the submitted belongs to, and routes it appropriately. The software division doesn't have a system, so a message is sent to a clerk. Based on our personal experience with expense report systems, it's clear that all of these systems route a certain percentage of reports straight to oblivion, so we implement that, too.

The content-based routing approach can also be used as part of a pipes and filters processing system. In the example illustrated below, the payment processing stage might

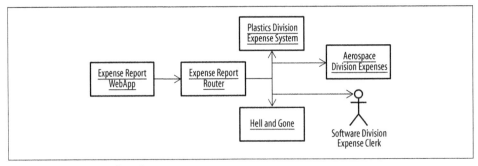

Figure 11-10. Content-based routing

route a message to different destinations based on the success or failure of the payment activity. Figure 11-11 shows a simple example: an order flow process first reserves an item in the warehouse (to prevent concurrency problems if someone else tries to buy it while the transaction is in process); then, it processes payment. The payment processor sends a message to a CBR which, depending on success or failure, either routes the order to the Shipping service or to a Stock Release message façade.

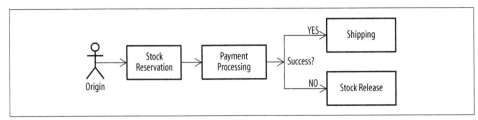

Figure 11-11. Content-based routing and pipes and filters

This approach allows us to easily add or remove payment types from the system—a useful piece of functionality in a changing business environment. It also allows us to reuse the payment component, since we don't have to teach it how to resolve the consequences when payment fails: it just needs to add some information to the message, indicating success or failure, and send it on.

Content Aggregator Pattern

Content-based routing allows applications to send a message to a single address, but what about systems where multiple different types of messages are used to fulfill the same use case? If your message format is standardized, simple messaging, like point-to-point or publish-subscribe, will often do. But things get ugly when you can't standardize on a single message type. Single applications can end up supporting multiple incoming-message formats and even transport mechanisms. The result is a brittle aggregation of difficult to maintain systems.

The *Content Aggregator pattern* is the inverse of a Content-Based Router pattern. When one system is being fed by messages from a variety of other systems, incoming messages are sent to a centralized aggregator, which transforms them into a common format and forwards them to an alternate destination, where the real processing is done. The component doing the heavy lifting only needs to implement a single incoming-message interface.

Consider the expense report example again: the financial systems from the various divisions in the company can send messages to a content aggregator, which standardizes them and forwards them to a centralized, corporate financial-reporting system.

The result is generally less code duplication, since the heavy lifting (processing the message at the target) only needs to be written and tested once. The content transformation components are generally much easier to write; as a result, they are often less error-prone and easier to test.

When the message content is in XML, aggregators can often be implemented using XSL transformations. These transformations make the whole system more flexible and (potentially) easier to maintain. A content aggregator can be used in conjunction with a content-based router, giving a system one way in and one way out.

Control Bus Pattern

The integrated enterprise creates some command and control problems. How do you tell if every system is online? Can you send commands to multiple systems at once? Or rearrange the routing of messages between systems to maximize throughput or deal with capacity problems? These are fairly intractable problems, but we can use a messaging architecture to solve some of them by linking command and control actions via the *Control Bus pattern*.

A control bus implementation consists of one or more message channels spanning a collection of related applications. Administrative clients send command messages to the bus, and either receive responses or monitor the bus for status reports from the various applications involved.

Not every message sent over a control bus needs to be intelligible to every system connected to the bus. Typical uses of a control bus are:

- Sending lifecycle commands (startup, shutdown, idle, and so forth) to a number of related applications
- Receiving still-alive messages from a set of applications
- Remote configuration
- Severe error handling
- Centralized logging

Figure 11-12 shows a simple control bus implementation, which uses two publish-subscribe channels, one for control messages and one for information messages. The applications receive messages on the control channel and send messages on the information channel. In this example, we have an administrative console sending messages and a logging server retrieving them. There's nothing to stop both applications from being a member of both channels.

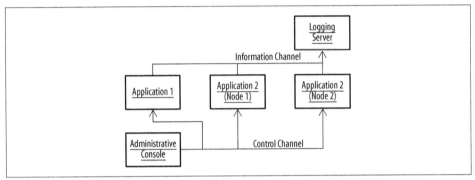

Figure 11-12. Control bus spanning three applications with logging and control channels

Security is important with control buses, particularly when they provide command access to lifecycle activities, or can be interrogated to provide valuable information. It's important not to leave a back door open. Control data, in particular, should never travel over the Internet without encryption. Logging data may (or may not!) be less sensitive.

A control bus can be implemented using MOM or email, depending on the requirements of the current application. Email has the advantage of allowing a human being to control one end of the message exchange, which can lead to dramatic savings in message client development costs.

For Further Reading

If you're new to messaging, the patterns in this chapter should give you some ideas about how to incorporate messaging into your applications. Since this is a topic that deserves further discussion, we suggest the following resources.

Tutorials on the JavaMail and JMS APIs can be found in *Java Enterprise in a Nutshell*, Second Edition, by William Crawford, Jim Farley, and David Flanagan. *Java Enterprise Best Practices* by the O'Reilly Java Authors includes further discussion of advanced techniques with both APIs, and *Java Message Service* by Richard Monson-Haefel and David Chappell provides in-depth coverage of the JMS API. O'Reilly publishes all three books.

On the patterns front, Gregor Hohpe and Bobby Woolf maintain an excellent web site at *http://www.enterpriseintegrationpatterns.com/* which provides a comprehensive resource for enterprise programmers looking to learn about how to incorporate messaging into integration-centric applications.

CHAPTER 12

J2EE Antipatterns

The design patterns we have discussed so far are about learning from what others have done correctly. But often, studying others' mistakes is even more valuable. Skiers, watching the trail from the chairlift above, might point out someone doing a particularly good job getting down the slope. But they always discuss exactly who took a spectacular wipeout and what the hapless victim did to bring it upon themselves. Did he turn a little too fast or put his weight too far back? *Antipatterns* are to patterns what the falling skier is to the successful one: recurring, sometimes spectacular mistakes that developers make when faced with a common problem.

In this chapter, we present a few of the most common antipatterns in the J2EE world. The list is by no means complete. Just like the active community collecting design patterns, there is an equally active community cataloguing antipatterns and their solutions. For a general introduction, the text by William J. Brown, et al, *AntiPatterns: Refactoring Software, Architectures, and Projects in Crisis* (Wiley & Sons), is *the* book on antipatterns; it has a decidedly process-based focus. The current seminal work on Java enterprise antipatterns, which we've relied on heavily, is Bruce A. Tate's excellent resource, *Bitter Java* (Manning).

We will look at the following antipatterns:

Excessive Layering and Leak Collection
   Cover repeated architectural errors that affect performance and extensibility.

Magic Servlet, Monolithic JSP, Compound JSP, and Overstuffed Session
   Cover breakdowns in Model-View-Controller separation.

Everything Is an EJB, Round-Tripping, and Stateful When Stateless Will Do
   Help determine how and how not to use EJBs.

Some of these antipatterns are closely related to the regular patterns we've discussed elsewhere in this book. Since antipatterns are recurring mistakes, and design patterns are recurring solutions, it make sense that most antipatterns have a corresponding pattern or two.

Causes of Antipatterns

Every program, big or small, contains shortcuts, mistakes, and code that could have been thought out a little better. What distinguishes an antipattern from these errors is that, like a design pattern, it is repeated. When we explore the causes of antipatterns, we don't need to look at why they exist—we need to look at why they persist and propagate. The main reasons that antipatterns spread are:

- Inexperience
- Unreadable code
- Cut-and-paste development

Inexperienced developers are the major cause of antipatterns. Obviously, newer developers are less likely to have come across these common mistakes previously, and are less like to recognize when they are making them. The danger of antipatterns is subtler when experienced developers use new technology. This danger is especially pronounced in J2EE technology, which evolves quickly, and in which many of the standard tutorials and code generation tools are full of antipatterns. To combat the problem, most organizations use training as well as code reviews with senior developers. But the best defense against antipatterns is to know your enemy: understanding and recognizing antipatterns is the key to avoiding them.

Unreadable code is another fertile breeding ground for antipatterns. Often, the existence of a well-known antipattern will be hidden because readers have to spend all their mental cycles trying to figure out what the code does, not why it does it. Developers sometimes favor conciseness and optimization over readability without taking into account the maintenance costs. Every shortcut that saves a few keystrokes or a few bytes of memory should be balanced against the costs in terms of developer hours and lost business when a hard-to-find bug is discovered. Unreadable code is best fought with consistency: publishing and enforcing code guidelines, relentless commenting, and aggressive review.

Cut-and-paste development refers to code that is taken from one place and pasted directly into another. Teams sometimes assume that cut-and-paste is a form of reuse: because the code has been used before, it is often considered more robust. Unfortunately, cut-and-paste actually makes code less reliable, since the pasted portion is used out of context. Even worse, bug changes don't propagate: changes to cut-and-paste code must be propagated manually. Cut-and-paste should only be necessary when entire objects cannot be reused. If you find yourself copying a particular piece of code, consider abstracting it and making it available to many classes through inheritance or as part of a separate utility class.

Architectural Antipatterns

The first class of antipatterns we will look at is architectural in nature. These antipatterns are not J2EE-specific: they affect many Java applications and the Java APIs themselves. They are included in a book on J2EE because they affect highly scalable, long-running applications—meaning they are of particular relevance to J2EE developers.

Excessive Layering

If you've read the preceding chapters, you've probably noticed that design patterns tend to suggest adding *layers*. Façades, caches, controllers, and commands all add flexibility and even improve performance, but also require more layers.

Figure 12-1 shows a rough sketch of the "typical" J2EE application. Even in this simplified view, each request requires processing by at least seven different layers. And this picture doesn't even show the details of each individual layer, which may themselves contain multiple objects.

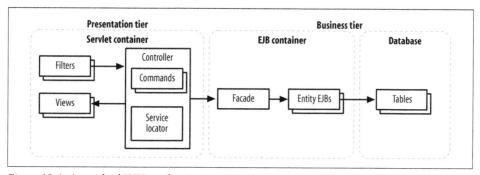

Figure 12-1. A standard J2EE application

Unfortunately, in a high-level, object-oriented environment like J2EE, the layers we add are not the only layers that exist. We've already talked about containers—the servlet and EJB containers are the main ones—and how they provide advanced services, generally through layers of their own. The underlying containers are themselves built on top of Java's APIs; the APIs are still a few layers away from the JVM, which interact through layered system libraries with the operating system—which finally talks to the actual hardware. If you look at stack traces from a running JVM, it is not surprising to see a Java application with a call stack well over 100 methods deep!

It's easy to see how a CPU that can execute billions of instructions a second can get bogged down running the J2EE environment. It's also easy to think that with all these layers, adding a few of our own can't possibly make any difference. That's not the case, however. Think of the structure as a pyramid: every call to a container method requires two or four calls to the underlying Java API, which requires eight

Java instructions, and so forth and so on. The layers we add are far more expensive than many of the preexisting layers.

An example of the *Excessive Layering antipattern* is a common scenario that we call the "Persistence Layer of Doom." While abstracting database access away from business logic has so many benefits that we hesitate to say anything negative about the process, hiding SQL from other components has one serious problem: expensive activities (such as accessing a network or filesystem for a database query) start to look like cheap activities (such as reading a field from a JavaBean). Developers working on the presentation tier will inevitably call the expensive functions frequently, and end up assuming the entire business tier is horribly slow. We'll talk more about this problem later in this chapter when we discuss the Round-Tripping antipattern.

Reducing layers

Because it's easy to add layers to a J2EE application, it's important to understand which ones are necessary and which are excessive. Unfortunately, there's no generic answer, since the correct number of layers depends on the type and expected use of an application.

When deciding whether to add layers, we have to balance the costs with the benefits they provide. The cost of layers can be expressed in terms of design time, code complexity, and speed. The benefits are twofold. Layers that provide abstract interfaces to more specific code allow cleaner, more extensible code. Layers such as caches, which optimize data access, can often benefit an application's scalability.

While we can't provide a generic solution to layering problems, we can offer a few hints as to what level of layering is appropriate for generic types of J2EE applications:

All-in-one application
> For small applications where the entire model, view, and controller always live on the same server (like a single-function intranet application), reduce layers as much as possible. Generally, this will mean condensing the business tier, often using DAO and business delegate objects that interact directly with an underlying database through JDBC. In the presentation tier, you should stick to a simple servlet/JSP model.

Front end
> Often, medium-size applications provide a simple web or similar frontend to a shared data model, usually a legacy application. Examples include airline ticketing systems and online inventory tools. In these applications, the presentation tier is generally the focus of development. The presentation tier should scale across multiple servers, and should be made efficient and extensible with liberal use of layering. Most functions of the business tier will probably be supported by the underlying legacy application and should not be duplicated in a large, deeply layered business tier.

Internet scale application

> The last type of application is the ultimate in J2EE: a large application spread over numerous servers meant to handle thousands of users and millions of requests per day. In these large environments, communication overhead between the many servers, as well as the cost of maintaining a large code base, dwarf the cost of layering. Using all the standard layers and multiple layers of caching in both the presentation and business tier can help optimize network transactions, while layers of abstraction keep the code manageable and extensible.

Communication and documentation are our best weapons. When layers are added for performance, document which calls are expensive, and, where possible, provide alternative methods that batch requests together or provide timeouts. When layers are added for abstraction, document what the layer abstracts and why, especially when using vendor-specific methods (see the "Vendor Lock-In" sidebar). These steps assure that our layers enhance extensibility or improve performance instead of becoming an expensive black hole.

Leak Collection

Automated memory management is one of Java's most important features. It is also somewhat of an Achilles's heel. While a developer is free to create objects at will, she does not control when or how the garbage collector reclaims them. In some situations, objects that are no longer being used may be kept in memory for much longer than necessary. In a large application, using excess memory in this way is a serious scalability bottleneck.

Fortunately, by taking into account how the garbage collector actually works, we can recognize common mistakes that cause extra objects. The Java Virtual Machine uses the concept of *reachability* to determine when an object can be garbage-collected. Each time an object stores a reference to another object, with code like this.intValue = new Integer(7), the referent (the Integer) is said to be reachable from the object referring to it (this). We can manually break the reference, for example by assigning this. intValue = null.

To determine which objects can be garbage-collected, the JVM periodically builds a graph of all the objects in the application. It does this by recursively walking from a root node to all the reachable objects, marking each one. When the walk is done, all unmarked objects can be cleaned up. This two-phase process is called *mark and sweep*. If you think of references as strings that attach two objects together, the mark and sweep process is roughly analogous to picking up and shaking the main object in an application. Since every object that is in use will be attached somehow, they will all be lifted up together in a giant, messy ball. The objects ready for garbage collection will fall to the floor, where they can be swept away.

Vendor Lock-In

Many J2EE vendors offer enhancements to the core J2EE functionality, such as optimized database access methods or APIs for fine-grained control of clustering capabilities. Using these functions, however, ties your application to that vendor's implementation, whether it's a database, MOM, or application server. The more your application depends on a particular vendor's APIs, the harder it is for you to change vendors, effectively locking you into the vendor you started with.

J2EE purists will tell you why vendor lock-in is a bad thing. If your vendor decides to raise their prices, you are generally stuck paying what they ask or rebuilding your application. If you sell software to a customer, they too must buy your vendor's product, regardless of their own preference. And if the vendor goes out of business, you could be stuck with unsupported technology.

From a practical standpoint, however, vendor's enhancements are often just that: enhancements. Using vendor-specific APIs can often make your application easier to build, more efficient, and more robust. So is there a happy middle ground? There is. While using vendor-specific APIs is not an antipattern, vendor lock-in is.

The most important step in avoiding lock-in is understanding which APIs are generic and which are vendor-specific. At the minimum, clearly document all vendor dependencies. Also, make your best effort to avoid letting the structure of the API influence overall design too much, particularly if you think you might have to eventually abandon the vendor.

A better solution is to hide the vendor complexities by defining an interface with an abstract definition of the vendor's methods and then implementing that interface for the particular vendor you have chosen. If you need to support a new vendor, you should be able to simply reimplement the interface using the new vendor's methods or generic ones if necessary.

So how does this knowledge help us avoid memory leaks? A memory leak occurs when a string attaches an object that is no longer in use to an object that is still in use. This connection wouldn't be so bad, except that the misattached object could itself be connected to a whole hairball of objects that should otherwise be discarded. Usually, the culprit is a long-lived object with a reference to a shorter-lived object, a common case when using collections.

A collection is an object that does nothing more than organize references to other objects. The collection itself (a cache, for example) usually has a long lifespan, but the objects it refers to (the contents of the cache) do not. If items are not removed from the cache when they are no longer needed, a memory leak will result. This type of memory leak in a collection is an instance of the *Leak Collection antipattern*.

In Chapter 5, we saw several instances of caches, including the Caching Filter pattern. Unfortunately, a cache with no policy for expiring data constitutes a memory leak. Consider Example 12-1, a simplified version of our caching filter.

Example 12-1. A simplified CacheFilter

```
public class CacheFilter implements Filter {
 // a very simple cache
 private Map cache;

 public void doFilter(ServletRequest request,
   ServletResponse response, FilterChain chain)
 throws IOException, ServletException {
   ...

  if (!cache.containsKey(key)) {
    cache.put(key, data);
  }

  // fulfill the response from the cache
  if (cache.containsKey(key)) {
    ...
  }
 }

 public void init(FilterConfig filterConfig) {
   ...
   cache = new HashMap( );
 }
}
```

Nowhere in this code is there a remove( ) call to match the put( ) call that adds data to the cache. Without a cache expiration policy, the data in this cache will potentially use all the available memory, killing the application.

Reclaiming lost memory

The hardest part of dealing with Java memory leaks is discovering them in the first place. Since the JVM only collects garbage periodically, watching the size of the application in memory isn't very reliable. Obviously, if you're seeing frequent out-of-memory type errors, it's probably too late. Often, commercial profiling tools are your best bet to help keep an eye on the number of objects in use at any one time.

In our trivial example, it should be clear that adding data to the cache and never removing it is a potential memory leak. The obvious solution is to add a simple timer that cleans out the cache at some periodic interval. While this may be effective, it is not a guarantee: if too much data is cached in too short a time, we could still have memory problems. A better solution is to use a Java feature called a *soft reference*, which maintains a reference to an object but allows the cached data to be garbage-collected at the collector's discretion. Typically, the least-recently used objects are collected when the system is running out of memory. Simply changing the way we put data in the cache will accomplish this:

```
cache.put(key, new SoftReference(data));
```

There are a number of caveats, the most important being that when we retrieve data, we have to manually follow the soft reference (which might return null if the object has been garbage-collected):

```
if (cache.containsKey(key)) {
  SoftReference ref = (SoftReference) cache.get(key);
  Object result = ref.get();

  if (result == null) {
    cache.remove(key);
  }
}
```

Of course, we could still run out of memory if we add too many keys to the cache. A more robust solution uses a reference queue and a thread to automatically remove entries as they are garbage-collected.

In general, the most effective way to fight memory leaks is to recognize where they are likely to be. Collections, as we have mentioned, are a frequent source of leaks. Many common features—such as attribute lists and listeners—use collections internally. When using these features, pay extra attention to when objects are added and removed from the collection. Often, it is good practice to code the removal at the same time as the addition. And, of course, make sure to document pairs of adds and removes so that other developers can easily figure out what you did.

Presentation Tier Antipatterns

The Model-View-Controller pattern, covered in Chapter 3, is the fundamental organizing principle for the presentation tier. The building blocks of the MVC pattern create an overall map of the application, making it easier to understand and extend. Preserving the separation of model, view, and controller is essential to maintaining these advantages.

It should be no surprise, then, that the presentation tier antipatterns have to do with the breakdown of model-view-controller separation. While these antipatterns are specific to the presentation tier, be aware that other antipatterns, such as Leak Collection and Excessive Layering, can affect the presentation tier as well.

The Magic Servlet

When servlets were first introduced, developers immediately saw the potential of combining the robust Java environment with an efficient mechanism for serving dynamic content. Server-side Java's killer app was JDBC, a powerful and high-level mechanism for communicating with databases. Over time, technologies like JNDI and JMS were added, allowing J2EE to talk easily and directly to a large number of enterprise information systems.

Because it was suddenly so easy to talk to databases, directory servers, and messaging systems, many developers were tricked into thinking that their applications would be simple, too. Who needed a complicated design when reading a row from a database was a one-line operation? Unfortunately, as applications grew in scope, complexity crept back in—but the design to handle it did not.

The typical symptom of complexity outpacing design is the *Magic Servlet antipattern*, in which a single servlet handles all aspects of a given request. On the surface, the magic servlet seems like a reasonable encapsulation. It captures all the logic needed to handle a request in a single, convenient class. But a magic servlet is also large, complex, difficult to maintain, and impossible to reuse. Typically, these servlets have a huge amount of code in a single doGet( ) or similar method.

Imagine you are given the task of putting an LDAP-based corporate address book on the web. Example 12-2 shows a typical magic servlet solution, using the servlet to read all the names and phone numbers in the LDAP directory.

Example 12-2. A magic servlet

```
import java.io.*;
import javax.servlet.*;
import javax.servlet.http.*;
import javax.naming.*;
import javax.naming.directory.*;
import java.util.*;

public class MagicServlet extends HttpServlet {
  private DirContext peopleContext;

  // setup LDAP access
  public void init(ServletConfig config)
  throws ServletException {
    super.init(config);

    Properties env = new Properties( );
    env.put(Context.INITIAL_CONTEXT_FACTORY, "com.sun.jndi.ldap.LdapCtxFactory");
    env.put(Context.PROVIDER_URL, "ldap://localhost/o=jndiTest");
    env.put(Context.SECURITY_PRINCIPAL, "cn=Manager, o=jndiTest");
    env.put(Context.SECURITY_CREDENTIALS, "secret");

    try {
      DirContext initalContext = new InitialDirContext(env);
      peopleContext = (DirContext)initalContext.lookup("ou=people");
    } catch (NamingException ne) 2{
      ne.printStackTrace( );
      throw new UnavailableException("Error inializing LDAP", ne);
    }
  }
}
```

Example 12-2. A magic servlet (continued)

```java
// close LDAP
public void destroy( ) {
  try {
    peopleContext.close( );
  } catch(NamingException ne) {
    ne.printStackTrace( );
  }
}

// "magic" function is model, view and controller
protected void doGet(HttpServletRequest request,
            HttpServletResponse response)
throws ServletException, IOException {
  // view logic
  response.setContentType("text/html");
  java.io.PrintWriter out = response.getWriter( );
  out.println("<html>");
  out.println("<head>");
  out.println("<title>Servlet</title>");
  out.println("</head>");
  out.println("<body>");
  out.println("<table>");2

  // model logic
  try {
    NamingEnumeration people = peopleContext.list("");
    while(people.hasMore( )) {
      NameClassPair personName = (NameClassPair)people.next( );
      Attributes personAttrs = peopleContext.getAttributes(personName.getName( ));
      Attribute cn = personAttrs.get("cn");
      Attribute sn = personAttrs.get("sn");
      Attribute phone = personAttrs.get("telephoneNumber");

      out.println("<tr><td>" + cn.get( ) + " " +
          sn.get( ) + "</td>" +
          "<td>" + phone.get( ) +
          "</td></tr>");
    }
  } catch(Exception ex) {
    out.println("Error " + ex + " getting data!");
  }

  // back to view logic
  out.println("</table>");
  out.println("</body>");
  out.println("</html>");
  }
}
```

The doGet( ) method talks directly to the data source, LDAP. It also writes directly to the output. This example is relatively simple, since it doesn't handle input validation or any kind of error handling, for starters. Adding those functions would make the servlet even more complicated and specialized.

The problem with a magic servlet is not a lack of encapsulation, but rather *improper* encapsulation. The first rule of objects is that they should perform a single function well. The scratch test is whether you can describe what an object does in one phrase. For our magic servlet, the best we could say is "it reads phone numbers from a database and formats the results as HTML." Two phrases at least, and awkward ones at that.

Refactoring the magic servlet

To fix the Magic Servlet antipattern, we need to break our servlet into multiple objects, each with a specific task. Fortunately, we already have a pattern for solving just this type of problem: the Model-View-Controller. MVC is covered extensively in Chapter 3, so we won't go into too much detail here. The salient point is the separation of the interaction into (at least) three pieces.

The model is responsible for all interactions with persistent storage. We will create a simple JavaBean, Person, with accessor methods for fields firstName, lastName, and phoneNumber. Then we create a class, LdapPersonCommand, to read from LDAP and expose the values as a collection of class Person. The command implements a generic PersonCommand interface:

```
public interface PersonCommand {
  // initialize the command
  public void initialize(HttpSession session) throws NamingException;

  // execute the query
  public void runCommand( );

  // get the result of the query as a List of class Person
  public List getPeople( );
}
```

The view, a simple JSP page, uses an instance of class PersonCommand placed in request scope and the Java Standard Tag Libraries to generate a table of names and phone numbers. *PersonView.jsp* is shown in Example 12-3.

Example 12-3. PersonView.jsp

```
<%@page contentType="text/html"%>
<%@taglib uri="/jstl/core" prefix="c"%>

<html>
<head><title>Addresses</title></head>
<body>
<jsp:useBean id="personCommand" scope="request"
      class="PersonCommand" />
<table>
 <c:forEach var="person" items="${personCommand.people}">
  <tr><td><c:out value="${person.firstName}"/></td>
```

Example 12-3. PersonView.jsp (continued)

```
    <td><c:out value="${person.lastName}"/></td>
    <td><c:out value="${person.phoneNumber}"/></td>
  </tr>
 </c:forEach>
</table>
</body>
</html>
```

As you can see, our JSP is entirely focused on view management. It contains only the minimal amount of JSTL code needed to handle looping and output.

All this abstraction leaves us with a very simple servlet, as shown in Example 12-4.

Example 12-4. PersonServlet.java

```java
import javax.servlet.*;
import javax.servlet.http.*;
import java.IO.*
import javax.naming.*;

public class PersonServlet extends HttpServlet {
  protected void doGet(HttpServletRequest request,
            HttpServletResponse response)
  throws ServletException, IOException {
    try {
      PersonCommand personCommand = new LdapPersonCommand( );
      personCommand.initialize( );
      personCommand.runCommand( );

      request.setAttribute("personCommand", personCommand);
    } catch(NamingException ne) {
      throw new ServletException("Error executing " + "command", ne);
    }

    RequestDispatcher dispatch =
      getServletContext( ).getRequestDispatcher("/PersonView.jsp");
    dispatch.forward(request, response);
  }
}
```

This servlet is responsible for coordinating the response but not for performing the dirty work of reading LDAP or generating HTML. The major advantages of this solution are in extensibility. We could easily replace LdapPersonCommand with a class that reads from a database or legacy system. Writing a separate JSP to output to WAP or WML or a different language would also be easy and require no modification of the servlet. All of this should be familiar from previous chapters. The point is that the problem can be solved. You can resolve this antipattern a piece at a time. In this case, you might want to isolate the view first, and come back and separate the model and controller when you have time.

Monolithic/Compound JSPs

When JSPs were first introduced, some developers recognized their potential to replace the awkwardness of embedding HTML output in a servlet with the convenience of scripting. Many decided that since JSPs were parsed into servlets internally, they were just a new syntax for servlets. So they built servlets—including access to models, control logic, and output—as JSPs. Example 12-5 shows a worst-case JSP design.

Example 12-5. LoginPage.jsp

```
<%@page contentType="text/html"%>
<%@page import="antipatterns.LoginManager" %>
<html>
<%
  LoginManager lm = new LoginManager();
  ServletRequest req = pageContext.getRequest();
  if (!lm.doLogin(req.getParameter("username"),
        req.getParameter("password"))) {
%>
<head><title>Login Page</title></head>
<body>
 <form action="/LoginPage.jsp" method="post">
  User name: <input type="text" name="username"><br>
  Password: <input type="password" name="password"><br>
  <input type="submit">
 </form>
</body>
<% } else { %>
<head><title>First Page</title></head>
<body>
 Welcome to the page!
<% } %>
</body>
</html>
```

This example has the same problems as a magic servlet. It performs operations belonging to the model, view, and controller. The example above combines the functionality of JSP and servlets, but represents the worst of both worlds from the point of view of maintenance. The HTML is confusing, often duplicated, and spread throughout the file in an opaque way. The Java code is embedded awkwardly—again, hard to find and follow.

There are actually two common antipatterns in Example 12-5. The *Monolithic JSP antipattern* occurs when JSP pages do more than their fair share of the work, often acting as both view and controller. While this example doesn't interact directly with the model via JNDI or JDBC, it would be a logical extension, further destroying the separation of model and controller.

A closely related antipattern is the *Compound JSP antipattern*, in which multiple JSP files are crammed into one using Java conditionals. In the example above, our code tests the return value of a call to doLogin( ) and displays different pages based on the result.

Fixing monolithic and compound JSPs

JSP's advantage is its simplicity. As a tag-based language, it should be familiar to web designers who no longer need to understand the complexities of Java development in order to build web pages. It is also meant to integrate easily into existing tools, such as WYSIWYG HTML editors.

Monolithic and compound JSPs take away those advantages. It would take a pretty sophisticated editor to separate the two pages contained in Example 12-5. And web designers working with it would have to understand the embedded code, at least enough so as not to break it.

Since monolithic JSPs are really just another type of magic servlet, the solution is pretty much the same. The JSP should be refactored into three separate pieces, with a servlet acting as the controller, the JSP as the view and JavaBeans as the model. We won't go through the whole exercise of converting our monolithic JSP to MVC, since the result is so similar to the previous example and those in Chapter 3.

Compound JSPs present a slightly different problem, but again a similar solution. In Example 12-5 we effectively have two pages: the login page and the welcome page. We should separate these into two separate JSP pages (in this case, HTML pages would work as well). The selection logic should go in the controller servlet, which contains code like:

```
if (lm.doLogin(username, password)) {
    nextPage = "/welcome.jsp";
} else {
    nextPage = "/login.jsp";
}

RequestDispatcher dispatch =
  getServletContext( ).getRequestDispatcher(nextPage);
dispatch.forward(request, response);
```

Overstuffed Session

The session, which tracks users as they navigate a web site, is a major feature of the J2EE presentation tier. Objects like the user's security permissions can be stored in the session when a user first logs in, and used several pages later to determine what the user can access. While maintaining session information is quite convenient, it is not without its pitfalls. Putting too much data or the wrong kind of data into the session leads to the *Overstuffed Session antipattern*.

The first danger of this antipattern is from data with a short lifespan. Since the session is implemented as a collection, we have to be on the lookout for a variant of the Leak Collection antipattern. Putting objects in the wrong scope, as we have done in Example 12-6, can lead to a pseudo memory leak.

Example 12-6. The LeakyServlet's doGet() method

```
protected void doGet(HttpServletRequest request,
          HttpServletResponse response)
throws ServletException, IOException {
  HttpSession session = request.getSession( );

  // create the bean
  AddressBean address = new AddressBean( );
  address.setFirst(request.getParameter("first"));
  address.setLast(request.getParameter("last"));

  // pass the bean to the view
  session.setAttribute("antipatterns.address", address);

  // instantiate the view
  RequestDispatcher dispatcher =
    getServletContext( ).getRequestDispatcher("/View.jsp");
  dispatcher.forward(request, response);
}
```

As the snippet shows, we have placed a bean called AddressBean (which contains state data that is only used in this request) in session scope. This bean, however, will be kept around in the user's session for as long as the user is connected.

It's hard to see this kind of scenario as a real memory leak. The user's session expires when they log out, and the memory is reclaimed. But each object adds up, and if lots of users store lots of irrelevant beans in session scope, the total number of users that can connect at any one time will be reduced.*

The second danger is from data with a long lifespan. It is very common to store complex state data—such as shopping carts or user preferences—in the user's session, assuming the session will stay alive for as long as the user is using the site. Unfortunately, this is not always the case: if the user takes a break to respond to email or read another web page, or if the web server crashes, the user may unexpectedly lose all the data. This can be a real problem: just ask anyone who has painstakingly selected all the components for his new computer system only to have them disappear while he is looking for his credit card.

---

* If you use Struts or a similar web application framework, pay particular attention to this issue. The default Form Bean scoping in Struts is to the session, rather than to the request, so it's easy to end up with a large number of extra objects in memory for each active user.

Unstuffing the session

Fortunately, as far as antipatterns go, fixing an overstuffed session isn't too difficult. For short-lived data, make sure you default to request scope for all your objects, and only use session scope when it is explicitly required. Also, remember that it is possible to remove items from the session if you know they will no longer be used.

Long-lived data should generally be migrated to the business tier. This precaution has a number of advantages, including persistence between logins and across server restarts and transactions. Recently, there has been a trend toward applications with a database solely used by the presentation tier. While it may be overkill, this method provides a convenient (and usually high-speed) place to store user and session information without affecting the design of the business tier.

EJB Antipatterns

Our final set of antipatterns deal with Enterprise JavaBeans. EJBs are a powerful technology, but can also be complicated and heavyweight. Two of our antipatterns deal with the complexity of EJBs: the *Everything Is an EJB antipattern* describes when EJBs are appropriate to use at all, while the *Stateful When Stateless Will Do antipattern* describes when stateful session EJBs should be used. The *Round-Tripping antipattern* covers common performance problems in client-server applications, and often turns up when you're using remote EJBs.

Everything Is an EJB

There is a common antipattern called the *golden hammer*. A golden hammer starts life as a good solution to a recurring problem—the kind of solution that design patterns are made from. Eventually, however, the golden hammer starts getting used because it is the most familiar to developers, not because it's the best solution. Like a carpenter with only one saw, the golden hammer may get the job done, but it doesn't give the cleanest or easiest cut.

In many cases, EJBs are just such a golden hammer. Developers—especially developers with a history of database development—tend to see entity EJBs as the solution to every problem. Need security? Create a username and password bean. Need an address? Create an address bean.

Unfortunately, EJBs are not the solution to every problem. Like any other technology (and EJBs are a complex technology, at that), EJBs have both costs and benefits. EJBs should only be used when *their benefits outweigh the costs in solving the problem at hand.* This is an important concept, so let's look at each aspect separately.

The first part of applying this concept is to understand the benefits of EJBs. The central idea behind Enterprise JavaBeans, particularly entity beans, is to create an "abstract persistence mechanism." EJBs provide a generic, object-oriented way to manage data without worrying about the details of what's underneath. So we describe the data we want to store, along with transaction characteristics, security mechanisms, and so on, and the EJB container worries about translating it into whatever database or other storage mechanism we happen to use. On top of that, the container makes the beans available remotely, enforces the security constraints, and optimizes access to the beans using pools and other mechanisms. It seems like a pretty good deal.

The other significant aspect of the benefit/cost concept involves understanding that there are also substantial costs to using EJBs. EJBs add significant complexity to an application. EJBs must be created, looked up, and referenced using JNDI, and a dizzying array of home, remote, and local interfaces. While containers use caching and pooling to help, EJBs are often a memory and performance bottleneck. And, of course, you often need to negotiate with the purchasing department to buy the container.

Choosing whether to use EJBs comes down to one key issue: solving the problem at hand. EJBs are a great solution when their benefits line up with the features you need. If you don't need to use an existing database, using container-managed persistence can be quite efficient.* If you need to add transactions to otherwise transactionless storage, or add secure remote access to your data, EJBs are also a good idea. Too frequently, however, EJBs are used when none of these features are needed.

For example, let's go back to our web-based address book application based on an LDAP database. At the under-designed extreme, we have the magic servlet we saw earlier. While the magic servlet is not robust or extensible enough, solving the problem with entity EJBs is overkill. Figure 12-2 shows a sketch of the EJB solution: an address command in the presentation tier uses an address EJB, which in turn communicates with the underlying LDAP directory.

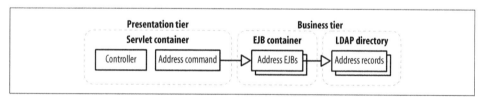

Figure 12-2. A poor use of entity beans

What are the EJBs adding? Chances are, the LDAP directory already provides some of the basic EJB features, such as remote access to the data, security, and maybe even transactions. If the AddressCommand is well defined, it will provide a level of abstraction between the controller and the underlying LDAP. Since we're stuck with the

---

* Contrary to popular belief, CMP can be far more efficient than BMP in recent EJB implementations, due to built-in pooling and caching. Advanced database concepts like views and indexes, however, are still not fully matched with CMP, and mapping existing schemas to CMP can be painful, particularly when there's a lot of data normalization involved.

existing LDAP database anyway, the EJBs are not really protecting us from changes to the underlying storage. In the end, there are no real advantages to using EJBs in this case, and the costs in terms of development and performance outweigh the benefits.

Escaping EJBs

What are our options, if EJBs are out of the picture? If it's entity beans we gave up, usually the answer is just plain JavaBeans. A command interface looks a whole lot like an EJB, anyway: there are usually setter methods to describe the arguments to the command, business methods to perform the actual command, and getter methods to read the results. We simply build a Command like we would a BMP entity bean, by communicating directly with a database. Since the fundamental bean structure is preserved, it's usually a simple task to switch back to EJBs if we need the features later.

There are, of course, other alternatives. For instance, storing data in XML files or as serialized objects works for simple applications. In more complex cases, Java Data Objects (JDO) provide a simple way to persist arbitrary Java objects without many of the complexities of EJBs.* A flexible but more complicated option is to use a variation of the Service Locator pattern (described in Chapter 9) in conjunction with façades to hide whether beans are local or remote at all.

On the system logic side, consider turning stateful session beans to stateless session beans (see the section "Stateful When Stateless Will Do"), and evaluate your stateless session beans to determine whether they should be EJBs. If not, think about replacing them with business delegates.

The following criteria can help determine whether you can safely convert your session beans into business delegates:

- Transaction management is locally controlled, such as with a transaction wrapper (see Chapter 10).
- Entity beans are not being used.
- The session bean is just a gateway to an additional remote service (such as a DAO or PAO).
- A small number of clients (such as a presentation tier) will be using the business component.
- Business processes all have to run in the same environment.

If most or all of these conditions are true, there won't necessarily be much of a benefit to using session beans. Transaction management, in particular, is often a simpler problem than it is sometimes portrayed as: EJBs make it easy to distribute transactions across multiple resources, including databases and MOM middleware, but if all

---

* In fact, some developers have suggested that using JDO in conjunction with session EJBs provides a better architecture than BMP entity EJBs, but we'll leave that debate for a different book.

your transaction management needs are focused on simple database calls (or invoking DAOs), a transaction wrapper is often sufficient.

If your session bean is acting as a session façade (see Chapter 9), look carefully at what it is providing access to. One of the prime advantages of a façade is that you can run a lot of your code much closer to the entity beans it acts on. If you aren't using entity beans, you lose this benefit. The same applies if the session façade spends most of its time dealing with resources that are themselves remote: if all the façade does is forward requests to a database, you might as well have the presentation tier connect to the database directly.

Clustering is frequently cited as a reason for using both session and entity EJBs, but you'll often find in these cases that it's either entirely unnecessary or can be done more cheaply. Pointing multiple instances of a web app at the same data store might be frowned upon, but is often the easiest solution. This is particularly true if the number of total clients is small: you don't need to worry about creating infrastructure that can handle 10,000 connections at once if all you really need is to provide business services to a couple of web servers.

Round-Tripping

Compared to the speed of local execution, using a network is extremely slow. That may sound like the sales-pitch for huge SMP servers, but it's not. Distributed architectures are essential to providing applications that scale to Internet demands. But even within a distributed architecture, performance can be dramatically improved by doing work locally.

The communication between the presentation and business tiers is a common source of performance problems within distributed architectures. Whether it's remote EJBs, directories, or databases, the cost of maintaining and using remote data is easy to lose track of, especially when development takes place on a single machine.

The *Round-Tripping antipattern* is a common misuse of network resources. It occurs when a large amount of data, like the results of a database lookup, needs to be transferred. Instead of sending back one large chunk of data, each individual result is requested and sent individually. The overhead involved can be astonishing. Each call requires at least the following steps:

1. The client makes the request.
2. The server retrieves the data.
3. The server translates the data for sending over the network.
4. The server sends the data.
5. The client translates the data from the network.

Round-tripping occurs when this sequence is repeated separately for each result in a large set.

The Round-Tripping antipattern is most often seen with remote entity EJBs. One of the features of EJBs is that they can be moved to a remote server, more or less transparently.* This power, however, is easy to abuse. Example 12-7 shows a command that reads addresses from a set of entity EJBs and stores the results locally.

Example 12-7. A PersonBean client

```
import java.util.*;
import javax.ejb.*;
import javax.rmi.*;
import javax.naming.*;
import javax.servlet.http.*;

public class EJBPersonCommand implements PersonCommand {
  private List people;
  private EJBPersonHome personHome;

  public void initialize(HttpSession session) throws NamingException {
    InitialContext ic = new InitialContext();
    Object personRef = ic.lookup("ejb/EJBPerson");

    personHome =
      (EJBPersonHome) PortableRemoteObject.narrow(personRef, EJBPersonHome.class);

    people = new Vector();
  }

  // read all entries in the database and store them in a local
  // list
  public void runCommand() throws NamingException {
    try {
      Collection ejbpeople = personHome.findAll();

      for(Iterator i = ejbpeople.iterator(); i.hasNext();) {
        EJBPerson ejbPerson = (EJBPerson)i.next();
        people.add(new Person(ejbPerson.getFirstName(),
                  ejbPerson.getLastName(),
                  ejbPerson.getPhoneNumber()));
      }
    } catch(Exception ex) {
      ...
      return;
    }

  }

  public List getPeople() {
    return people;
  }
}
```

---

* Whether it's more or less usually depends on which EJB container you are using.

The code looks innocuous enough. The `PersonHome` interface is used to find all people in the database, which are returned as instances of the `EJBPerson` EJB. We then loop through all the people, reading their various attributes and storing them in a local `List`.

The problem is that when this client and the `Person` EJB are not on the same machine, each call to `EJBPerson.getXXX()` requires a call across the network. This requirement means that, in this example, we're making $3n$ round trips, where n is the number of people in the database. For each trip, we incur the costs of data marshalling, the actual transfer, and unmarshalling, at the very least.

Reducing round-tripping

Fortunately, round-tripping is not hard to recognize. If you suddenly find performance problems when you move an application onto multiple servers, or find your intranet saturated, chances are round-tripping is to blame.

To reduce round-tripping, we need to combine multiple requests into one. Our options are to modify the client or modify the server. On the client side, we can implement caches to make sure we only request data once, not hundreds of times. Obviously, this will only benefit us if the data is read more often than it is changed.

A more robust solution is to modify the server, letting it make many local calls before returning data over the network. In the EJB case, this involves two patterns we have already seen, the Data Transfer Object and the Façade. We replace our many remote calls to `EJBPerson.getXXX()` with a single call to a façade, which returns the data in a custom data transfer object. If it sounds complicated, don't worry, it's actually quite simple, as you can see in Figure 12-3.

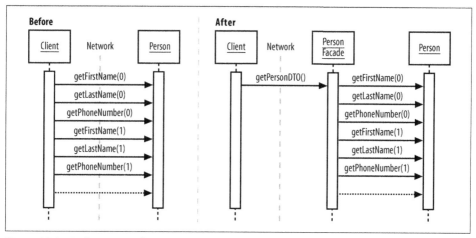

Figure 12-3. Reducing round-tripping

The first step is to define a DTO that encapsulates our data:

```
public class PeopleDTO implements Serializable {
  private List people;

  public PeopleDTO() {
    people = new Vector();
  }

  public List getPeople() {
    return people;
  }

  public void addPerson(Person person) {
    people.add(person);
  }
}
```

The next step is our façade. The façade in this case is a full-fledged, stateless session bean. The business methods of the façade match the finder methods of the original bean. Since we got the list of people in the original bean using the findAll() method, we will create a matching findAll() method in our session bean, which is shown in Example 12-8.

Example 12-8. A façade for EJBPerson

```
import javax.ejb.*;
import java.util.*;
import javax.naming.*;

public class PersonFacadeBean implements SessionBean {
  private SessionContext context;
  private LocalEJBPersonHome personHome;

  public void setSessionContext(SessionContext aContext) {
    context=aContext;
  }

  public void ejbActivate() {}
  public void ejbPassivate() {}

  public void ejbRemove() {}

  // find the local bean
  public void ejbCreate() {
    try {
      String beanName = "java:comp/env/ejb/local/Person";

      InitialContext ic = new InitialContext();
      personHome = (LocalEJBPersonHome) ic.lookup(beanName);
    } catch(Exception ex) {
      throw new EJBException("Error looking up PersonHome", ex);
    }
  }
}
```

Example 12-8. A façade for EJBPerson (continued)

```
  // find all entries and store them in a local DTO
  public PeopleDTO findAll()
  throws FinderException {
    Collection c = personHome.findAll();
    PeopleDTO dto = new PeopleDTO();

    for (Iterator i = people.iterator(); i.hasNext();) {
      LocalEJBPerson ejbPerson = (LocalEJBPerson)i.next();

      dto.addPerson(new Person(ejbPerson.getFirstName(),
                ejbPerson.getLastName(),
                ejbPerson.getPhoneNumber()));
    }

    return dto;
  }
}
```

The session bean basically performs the same loop as we did in our original client. Notice how the session bean uses the LocalEJBPerson interface instead of the EJBPerson interface. The local interface is a feature of EJB 2.0 that allows far more efficient operation for EJBs that are known to be in the same container. Using the LocalEJBPerson interface guarantees that round-tripping will not occur while we build the DTO.

The final step is the replace the original client with one using the DTO. As with the other steps, this is quite straightforward. We just replace the previous loop with a call to the façade:

```
  public void runCommand() throws NamingException {
    try {
      PersonFacade facade = personFacadeHome.create();
      PeopleDTO peopleDto = facade.findAll();
      people = peopleDto.getPeople();
    } catch(Exception ex) {
      ex.printStackTrace();
      ...
    }
  }
```

This method traverses the network just once, no matter how big the database is. The performance improvements from reduced round-tripping can be substantial. In one unscientific test of the example above, the time to transfer 1,000 addresses was reduced from over 4 minutes to 14 seconds.

In addition to the DTO pattern, you should also consider using a *data transfer row set* (see Chapter 7) to address these issues.

Stateful When Stateless Will Do

It is a common misconception that stateful and stateless session EJBs are basically the same thing. It makes sense: they're both types of session EJBs. As their name implies, stateful EJBs maintain a conversational state with clients, like a normal Java object, while stateless beans must be given all their state data each time they are called.

The major difference between stateful and stateless beans, however, is how they are managed by the container. A stateless bean is relatively simple to manage. Since operations on the bean do not change the bean itself, the container can create as many or as few beans as it needs. All the copies of a stateless bean are essentially equal. Not so with stateful beans. Every time a client makes a request, it must contact the same bean. That means that every client gets its own bean, which must be kept in memory somehow, whether the client is using it or not. The necessary management and storage makes a stateful session bean far more expensive for the container to manage than a stateless one.

Since stateful EJBs work more like normal objects, it's a common mistake to use them when stateless beans could be used to achieve the same effect at a much lower cost. For example, we could build an AddressBookEntry entity EJB with local home interface:

```
public interface AddressBookEntryHome extends EJBLocalHome {

    // required method
    public AddressBookEntry
        findByPrimaryKey(AddressBookEntryKey aKey)
        throws FinderException;

    // find all entries in owner's address book
    public Collection findAll(String owner)
        throws FinderException;

    // add a new entry to owner's address book
    public AddressBookEntry create(String owner,
        String firstName, String lastName,
        String phoneNumber) throws CreateException;
}
```

To access this bean, we might decide to use a session bean as a façade, much like in the previous example. Unlike our previous example, however, this new façade must store the owner's name so that only entries in that user's personal address book are retrieved. We might therefore choose to build a stateful session bean, like the one shown in Example 12-9.

Example 12-9. A stateful façade

```
import javax.ejb.*;
import java.util.*;
import javax.naming.*;
```

Example 12-9. A stateful façade (continued)

```
public class AddressBookBean implements SessionBean {
  private SessionContext context;
  private String userName;
  private LocalAddressBookEntryHome abeHome;

  public void setSessionContext(SessionContext aContext) {
    context=aContext;
  }

  public void ejbActivate( ) {
    init( );
  }

  public void ejbPassivate( ) { abeHome = null; }
  public void ejbRemove( ) { abeHome = null;}

  public void ejbCreate(String userName) throws CreateException {
    this.userName = userName;
    init( );
  }

  public PeopleDTO findAll(String firstName, String lastName)
  throws FinderException {
    Collection c = abeHome.findAll(userName);
    PeopleDTO dto = new PeopleDTO( );

    for (Iterator i = people.iterator(); i.hasNext( );) {
      LocalAddressBookEntry entry =
        (LocalAddressBookEntry) i.next( );

      dto.addPerson(new Person(entry.getFirstName( ),
                entry.getLastName( ),
                entry.getPhoneNumber( )));
    }

    return dto;
  }

  private void init( ) throws EJBException {
    try {
      String name = "java:comp/env/ejb/local/Address";

      InitialContext ic = new InitialContext( );
      abeHome = (LocalAddressBookEntryHome) ic.lookup(name);
    } catch(Exception ex) {
      throw new EJBException("Error activating", ex);
    }
  }
}
```

As it stands, this façade must be stateful, because the userName variable is set by the initial call to create( ). If it were stateless, each call to findAll( ) could potentially be dispatched to a bean that had been created with a different username, and chaos would ensue.

Unfortunately, because this bean is stateful, it requires more container resources to maintain and manage than a stateless version of the same thing. As with any stateful session bean, we have to wonder if there is a stateless bean that could do the same thing.

Turning stateful into stateless

Our example is admittedly trivial, so it should be pretty obvious that a slight change to the façade's interface could allow it to be stateless. If the username was passed into each call to findAll( ), instead of the create method, this bean could be made stateless.

For simple cases, it usually suffices to simply pass in all the relevant state data with each call. On more complex objects, however, this method becomes prohibitively expensive in terms of managing all the arguments and sending them over the network with each call. For these complex scenarios, there are a number of different solutions, depending on the nature of the data:

Use a client-side adapter
> When simply keeping track of arguments becomes difficult, it is often useful to build a simple helper on the client in order to store the arguments. Generally, this helper presents the same interface as a stateful session bean would and stores the arguments on the client side. This allows the helper to adapt the stateful calls into stateless ones by passing in the stored arguments.

Use a stateless façade and entity EJBs
> Entity EJBs are often the best choice for storing state data, even if the data is not permanent. A good example of this is a shopping cart, which is often implemented using stateful session beans. Using entity EJBs instead can give a number of benefits, including better performance, the ability to refer to data from multiple servers (useful with load-balanced web servers), and better resiliency when the server crashes.

Cache data in the client
> Stateful session beans are used as a server-side data cache, much like the HttpSession object on the client side. Often, developers prefer the server-side cache because it is considered more robust. In fact, a stateful session bean that stores data in server memory is no more reliable than storing the data in client memory, since the stateful bean will be destroyed if its client goes away anyway. In a web application, it is usually better to cache data locally in the HttpSession object than it is to cache the data remotely, since HttpSession is equally reliable and much faster.

If you've considered all these solutions and stateful beans still seem most appropriate, go ahead and use them. Stateful beans can provide a big performance boost when the beginning of a multiple-request session involves creating expensive resources that would otherwise have to be reacquired with each method call. There are a whole slew of problems that stateful session beans solve. They can be a powerful tool when used properly.

In this chapter, we have seen a number of common mistakes in application architecture, the presentation tier, and the business tier. While the specifics might differ, the same few principals apply to every case. Know your enemy: recognize and fix anti-patterns as early as possible in the design process. Know your tools: understand how the costs and benefits of technologies relate to the problem at hand—don't use them just because they are new and cool. And of course, document, document, document.

Presentation Tier Patterns

Architectural Patterns

Decorator

Also Known As

Decorating Filter

Goal

Dynamically add functionality to the front controller (Figure A-1).

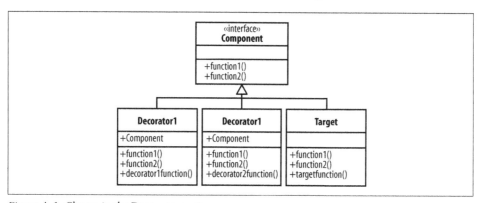

Figure A-1. Classes in the Decorator pattern

Participants

Component

    A common interface implemented by both decorators and the target.

Decorators

Encapsulate a piece of common functionality, such as decryption or logging, while presenting the same interface as the target.

Target

The final object in the request processing chain, coordinates all specific activities such as input handling. Typically the front controller (Figure A-2).

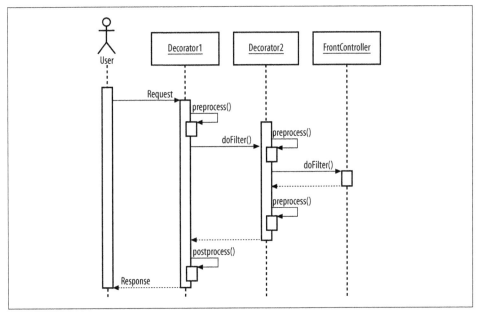

Figure A-2. Interactions in the Decorator pattern

Interactions

The decorator intercepts all requests destined for target and performs a common function such as logging or decryption. The decorator then forwards the request to the next decorator in the chain, or the target if there are no more decorators.

Notes

In the J2EE presentation tier, decorators are typically implemented as servlet filters with a servlet as the target. Note that filters have a slightly different API than servlets.

Front Controller

Goal

Create a single, central component to perform common functions (Figure A-3).

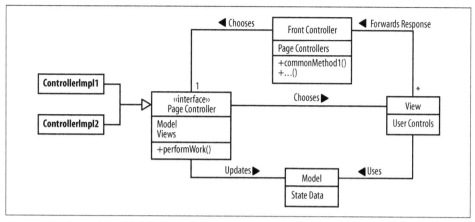

Figure A-3. Classes in the Front Controller pattern

Participants

Front controller
    Singleton object that intercepts all requests and performs common functions.

Page controllers (or Actions)
    Process user input, update the model, and choose views.

Model
    Store application state data.

Views
    Transform model data into a form appropriate for display to the user (Figure A-4).

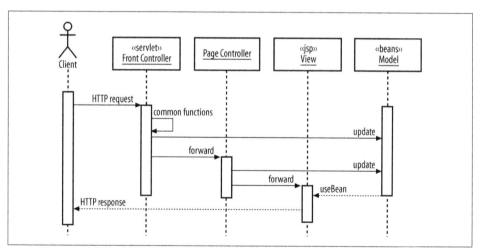

Figure A-4. Interactions in the Front Controller pattern

Interactions

The front controller intercepts all requests and performs common functions such as logging or decryption. The front controller chooses and forwards the request to a page controller. The page controller parses user input, and translates it into appropriate updates to the model. The model applies business rules and stores the data persistently, either locally, in the business tier, or using some other remote persistence mechanism. Based on the model changes and user input, the page controller chooses a view. The view transforms the updated model data into a form suitable for the user.

Notes

In J2EE, the front controller is typically implemented as a servlet, although in some cases it may be implemented as a servlet filter.

Model-View-Controller

Also Known As

MVC, Model 2

Goal

Separate presentation tier into self-contained, reusable pieces (Figure A-5).

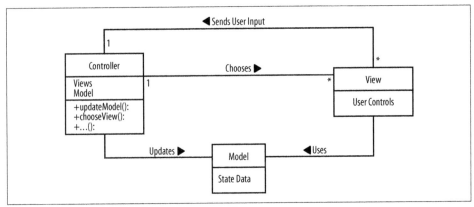

Figure A-5. Classes in the MVC pattern

Participants

Model

Stores application state data.

Views

> Stateless pages that transform model data into a form appropriate for display to the user, such as HTML, WAP or XML.

Controllers

> Process user input, update the model, and choose views (Figure A-6).

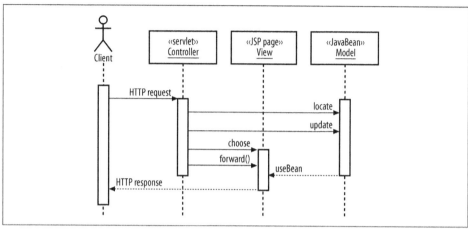

Figure A-6. Interactions in the MVC pattern

Interactions

The controller receives the user input, and translates it into appropriate updates to the model. The model applies business rules and stores the data persistently, either locally, in the business tier, or using some other remote persistence mechanism. Based on the model changes and user input, the controller chooses a view. The view transforms the updated model data into a form suitable for the user.

Notes

In J2EE, the model is typically implemented as JavaBeans or EJBs. The views may be JSPs, static HTML pages, or even servlets. The controller is usually a servlet.

Advanced Architectural Patterns

Composite View

Goal

Building a view from multiple reusable subviews (Figure A-7).

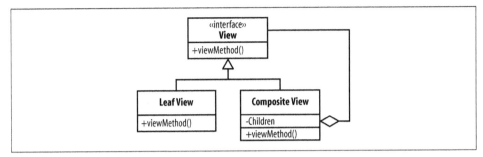

Figure A-7. Classes in the Composite View pattern

Participants

View
> A common interface implemented by both composite and leaf views.

Leaf view
> A view responsible for data that is actually displayed.

Composite view
> A view responsible for managing other views, including both leaves and other composites (Figure A-8).

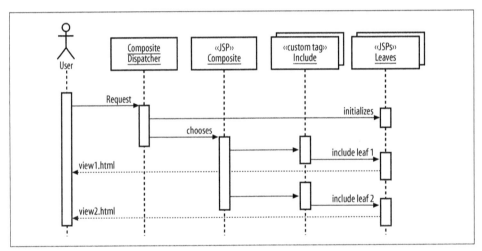

Figure A-8. Interactions in the Composite View pattern

Interactions

The dispatcher initializes a set of leaf views based on request or navigation data. The dispatcher then forwards control to a composite view, which includes multiple elements with generic names, such as leaf1. The correct leaf view, for example view1.html, is substituted for each generic name. The composite passes control to each leaf view in turn, each of which generates a portion of the final view.

Notes

Simple composite views can be implemented in a number of ways, including JSP `include` directives. A more flexible approach is to use templates that refer to leaves by generic names, allowing reuse of the template with different sets of leaves. JSP custom tags are usually the best way to implement templates. Templates are also included in the the Apache Struts "tile" mechanism.

Service to Worker

Also Known As

Dispatcher View

Goal

Decouple navigation from the front controller (Figure A-9).

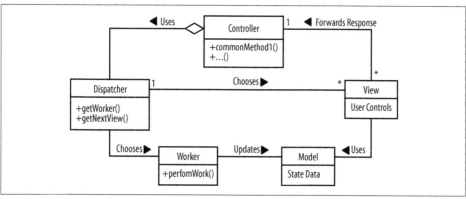

Figure A-9. Classes in the Service to Worker pattern

Participants

Service (front controller)
   Singleton object that intercepts all requests and performs common functions.

Dispatcher
   Encapsulates worker and view selection based on request information and/or an internal navigation model.

Workers (actions)
   Process user input and perform a specific update on the model.

Model
   Stores application state data.

Views

Stateless pages that transform model data into a form appropriate for display to the user (Figure A-10).

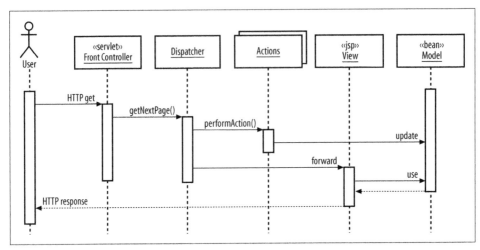

Figure A-10. Interactions in the Service to Worker pattern

Interactions

The front controller intercepts all requests and performs common functions using decorators. The front controller passes request information to the dispatcher, which uses the request and an internal model to chooses and execute appropriate actions. The actions process user input, translating it into appropriate updates to the model. The model applies business rules and stores the data persistently. Based on the user input and results of the actions, the dispatcher chooses a view. The view transforms the updated model data into a form suitable for the user.

Notes

Actions are typically implementations of the GoF Command pattern. The amount of functionality in the dispatcher, especially whether there is an internal navigation model, varies from application to application.

The Service to Worker pattern is the basis of many presentation tier frameworks, including Apache Struts and Java Server Faces.

View Helper

Goal

Avoid over-specialization in views.

Participants

View
> Stateless page that transforms model data into a form appropriate for display to the user.

Helper
> Encapsulates transformation of a specific type of data, such as stock quotes, from model data into presentation data.

Model
> Stores application state data (Figure A-11).

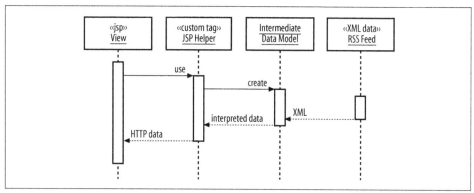

Figure A-11. Interactions in the View Helper pattern

Interactions

The view uses a set of view helpers to translate from model data into an intermediate data model. Either the view or the view helper can translate the intermediate data into a form suitable for presentation to the user, such as HTML, WAP, or XML.

Notes

In J2EE, view helpers are generally implemented as JSP custom tags. The tag may directly generate HTML, or it may expose scripting variables or JavaBeans that can be formatted into HTML by the JSP page.

Scalability Patterns

Asynchronous Page

Goal

Cache remote data as it is generated.

Participants

Publishers

Remote entities that generate new data at some interval. May also notify subscribers when new data is available.

Subscriber

A singleton object responsible for retrieving, formatting, and caching remote data either as it is generated or at some interval.

Models

Store state data for applications.

Views

When requests are received, translate model data into a format appropriate for display to the user (Figure A-12).

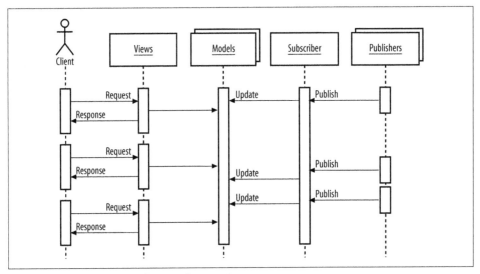

Figure A-12. Interactions in the Asynchronous Page pattern

Interactions

The subscriber retrieves data from the publisher either when it has changed or at some predefined interval. The subscriber processes the data and updates all appropriate models. When requests are received, the view translates current model data into a format suitable for the user.

Notes

The most effective use of this pattern is when a single subscriber downloads dynamic data and uses it to generate static HTML pages on each web server. It is also useful in situations where multiple web servers use separate data models that must be kept up to date.

Caching Filter

Goal

Minimize repeated page generation by caching dynamic pages when they are generated (Figure A-13).

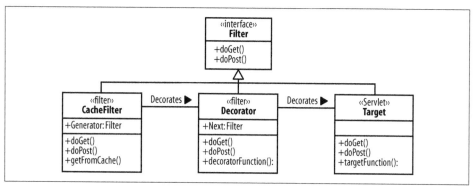

Figure A-13. Classes in the Caching Filter pattern

Participants

Filter

A common interface implemented by the cache, decorators and target.

Cache filter

Intercepts all requests and replies efficiently with cached pages if available. If no cached data is available, caches the results of generating the page.

Decorators

Encapsulate a piece of common functionality, while presenting the same interface as the target.

Target

The final object in the request processing chain. Coordinates all specific activities, such as input handling. Typically the front controller (Figure A-14).

Interactions

The cache filter intercepts all requests destined for target and determines if the page has been cached. If it is cached, data is returned from the cache. If not, the remaining decorators in the chain and the target are executed to generate the page, and the results are cached.

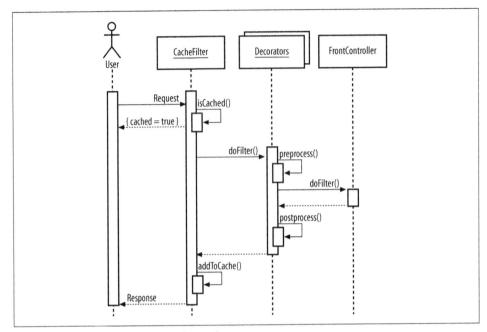

Figure A-14. Interactions in the Caching Filter pattern

Notes

The caching filter is a variation of the decorator pattern. To ease implementation of filters such as the caching filter, the servlet API allows you to decorate the HTTPServletResponse object in order to store the results of request processing.

Resource Pool

Goal

Decrease costs of instantiating and maintaining large objects using a pool of pre-generated objects (Figure A-15).

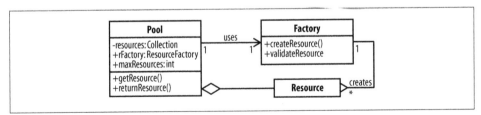

Figure A-15. Classes in the Resource Pool pattern

Participants

Pool

A limited collection of pre-generated objects that can be loaned out and returned.

Factory

Used by the pool to generate new instances of a resource or validate a returned resource.

Resource

An object that will be loaned out by the pool (Figure A-16).

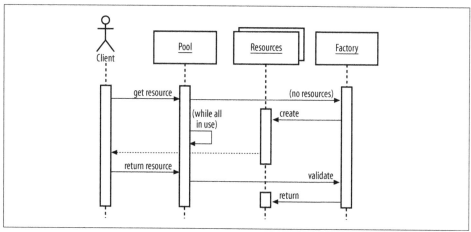

Figure A-16. Interactions in the Resource Pool pattern

Interactions

The client requests objects from the pool, which returns a resource if one is available. If no resources are available, but the pool is not at capacity, a new instance is generated using the factory. If all resources are loaned out, the client waits until one becomes available. When the client has finished using the resource, it returns it to the pool, which uses the factory to validate the returned resource.

Notes

A resource pool can easily be implemented based on the Java collections APIs.

Business Tier Patterns

Business Tier Patterns

Composite Entity

Also Known As

Entity Façade

Goal

Efficiently represent a particular entity within the domain model, aggregating value from multiple sources or objects, in order to reduce complexity and communications overhead.

Notes

A composite entity aggregates data from a variety of sources into a single object. This is particularly useful in EJB environments, since it prevents a profusion of EJBs throughout the application.

Domain Object Model

Goal

Create a java object that represents the concepts underlying the application.

Participants

Data objects
    Track data within a system.

Interactions

Objects in the domain model are connected to each other in ways that represent the underlying business relationships.

Notes

See Chapter 6.

Data Transfer Patterns

Data Transfer Hash

Goal

Reduce coupling between objects communicating via DTOs (Figure B-1).

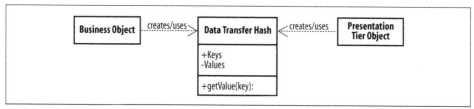

Figure B-1. Data transfer hash classes

Participants

Business objects
    Create hashes for sending data, or use values in received hashes.

Data transfer hash
    Stores data for transport between layers as a set of values associated with well-known keys.

Presentation tier objects
    Create hashes for sending data, or use values in received hashes.

Interactions

A presentation tier object requests data from the business tier. The business object reads the data, and inserts the values into a hash table with well-known keys for transport. The presentation tier object retrieves the data in the received hash by key. The presentation tier object modifies the received hash or creates a new one to transport data back to the business tier.

Notes

Data transfer hashes may be implemented as simple hash tables (or `HashMaps`). A more robust implementation uses a container object to hold the hash, as well as identifying information, type-safe data retrieval methods, and well-known keys.

Data Transfer Object (DTO)

Goal

Improve performance by reducing the number of objects passed between tiers (Figure B-2).

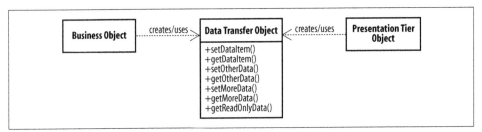

Figure B-2. Classes in the DTO pattern

Participants

Business objects
    Create DTOs for sending data, or use values in received DTOs.

DTO
    Stores data for transport between layers.

Presentation tier objects
    Create DTOs for sending data, or use values in received DTOs.

Interactions

A presentation tier object requests data from the business tier. The business object reads the data and copies it into a DTO for transport. The presentation tier object uses the data in the received DTO. The presentation tier object modifies the received DTO or creates a new one to transport data back to the business tier.

Notes

DTOs may be data objects used within the business objects themselves, or dedicated classes for transporting data. DTOs often follow JavaBean semantics, but this is not a requirement.

Row Set DTO

Goal

Minimize overhead while transporting the results of a database query.

Participants

Business objects
  Perform database query and formats results as row set DTO.

Row set DTO
  Stores data for transport between layers in database columns and rows.

Presentation tier objects
  Use data from rows and columns.

Interactions

A presentation tier object requests data from the business tier. The business object performs a database query and stores the resulting rows and columns in a row set DTO for transport. The presentation tier object accesses the data in the received DTO as rows and columns.

Notes

In many instances, it is easiest to simply send the JDBC ResultSet object directly to the client. When this is not desirable, a separate class implementing the ResultSet interface can be used, or a lighter-weight interface can be defined.

Database Patterns

DAO Factory

Goal

To hide the process of selecting an appropriate persistence layer or set DAO objects from the business tier, and to allow configuration of DAO features at runtime in a centralized manner (Figure B-3).

Participants

Client
  Includes a business tier or a presentation tier object.

DAO factory
  Determines how to create the DAO object.

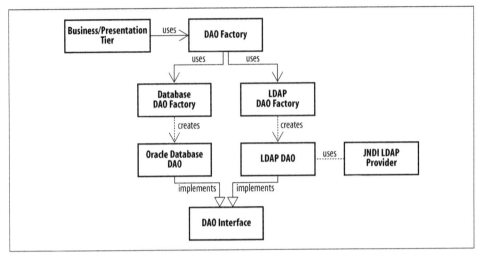

Figure B-3. DAO factory with two DAO types

Implementation-specific factory
    Responsible for creating the DAO objects.

DAO implementation
    The implementation itself.

Interactions

The client, a business tier or presentation tier object, calls a method on a DAO factory object, requesting a DAO object. The DAO factory is responsible for determining how to create the DAO object. This may involve implementation-specific DAO factories responsible for creating the DAO objects.

Data Access Object

Goal

Separate code for accessing data from a persistence mechanism from code used for processing data (Figure B-4).

Participants

Business object/presentation object
    Implements business logic for an application.

Data access object (DAO)
    Provides access to the persistence layer via a Java interface.

Data object
    Represents the data in the persistence layer as a Java object.

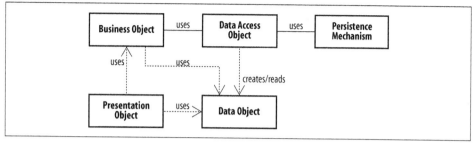

Figure B-4. Data access object

Persistence mechanism
    Provides a method for saving and restoring application data.

Interactions

A business object or presentation tier object obtains an instance of a data access object (DAO), which it uses to save and retrieve data objects. The DAO is responsible for all interactions with the persistence mechanism (database, raw files, etc.) used to store the application data. A data object independent from the persistence layer (see the Data Transfer Object pattern) is used to exchange data between the business objects and the DAO.

IsDirty

Goal

To prevent writing data to the database unnecessarily.

Participants

Data object (EJB or Plain Old Java Object)
    Makes data available to the application and notes when the data changes.
DAO
    Provides access to the persistence layer.

Interactions

A DAO is used to create a data object. When the data object is updated, it records the fact. When the DAO is used to update the database with the changed values, it can use this information to avoid writing to the database when the underlying data hasn't changed.

Notes

The obvious benefit of this pattern is to eliminate the performance overhead of doing the write operation in the first place. There's also a hidden benefit when running against databases that perform auditing: the database is spared the overhead of storing huge quantities of unnecessary change tracking. Since in an active database the volume of audit trail information can far exceed the actual volume of data, the performance and storage benefits of this pattern can be huge.

Lazy Load

Goal

To avoid delays created by excessive and unnecessary database access (Figure B-5).

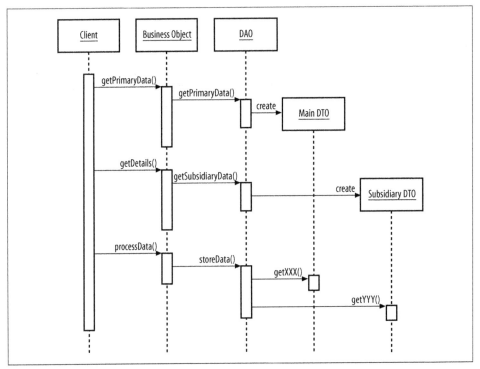

Figure B-5. Lazy load sequence

Participants

Client
Presentation tier or other system component.

Business object
Business delegate, session façade or other business logic related object.

DAO
Provides access to the persistence layer.

DTOs
    Objects for exchange of data between participants.

Interactions

The client calls methods on a business object, requesting specific data. The business object calls a DAO method to retrieve only the data required for the current method. If the client needs additional data, the business object performs an additional request to the DAO.

Notes

Implementing the Lazy Load pattern intelligently requires a bit of analysis of your application. If your application can retrieve several kinds of data with a single database query, it will generally be more efficient to do that then to retrieve each piece separately. If multiple queries would be required anyway, and different use cases require different data, the Lazy Load pattern can improve performance by limiting queries to only those strictly necessary.

Procedure Access Object

Goal

Leverage stored procedures in the database by providing a transparent Java interface (Figure B-6).

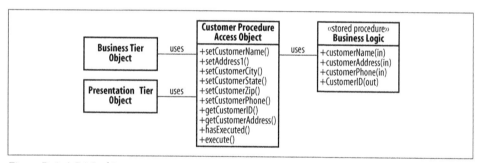

Figure B-6. A PAO object

Participants

Business tier or presentation tier object
    Executes business logic.

PAO
    Provides Java code with access to a database stored procedure.

Database stored procedure
    Implements business logic within a database system.

Interactions

A business or presentation tier object (the client) creates an instance of a PAO and optionally sets properties. The client calls the PAO's execute( ) method. The PAO then accesses the database and invokes a stored procedure using the properties passed in by the client. The PAO may perform transformations of the parameters set by the client to match the expectations of the stored procedure. After the stored procedure completes, the client may read additional properties on the PAO to retrieve the results of the stored procedure.

Notes

A PAO can also be implemented using a method-return syntax, in which all input parameters are passed into a single, possibly static, method call on the PAO object. In this case, return values are provided to the client via a DTO object. Also see the GoF Command pattern.

PK Block Generator Pattern

Goal

Efficiently generate a block of unique numerical identifiers, supporting distributed applications and eliminating risk of duplicate identifiers.

Participants

Sequence block object
   An object that provides unique primary keys to other objects upon request.

Database sequence
   A database feature that allows production of a series of unique identifiers.

Interactions

The application maintains an object responsible for handing out identifiers. The object maintains a block of identifiers and hands them out one at a time. When the current block is exhausted, the object accesses the database and reads a new unique value from a database sequence. The new value is used as a seed to generate a new block of sequences.

Notes

Since the database maintains the seed values used to generate each sequence block, there is no problem with duplicate identifiers, even if the application is running across multiple JVMs. The worst that will happen in this case is that identifiers may not be contiguous and may be assigned out of order.

Serialized Entity Pattern

Goal

To easily persist Java objects to the database.

Participants

Data object
    An object representing some data that we want to store.

DAO
    Uses Java object serialization to translate the object into a set of bytes.

Database table
    Stores the set of bytes.

Interactions

The client passes a data object to a DAO. The DAO uses Java object serialization to translate the object into a set of bytes, which are stored directly in the database. When the client needs to retrieve the object, the DAO reads the bytes back from the database and reconstitutes the object.

Notes

Using serialization has two major drawbacks: the data cannot be queried directly in the database, and the data must be converted if the structure of the underlying objects changes. Using objects that can write themselves to XML alleviates both these concerns.

Stored Procedures for Primary Keys Pattern

Goal

Efficiently assign primary keys to new entities, using the database's key management techniques without performing multiple queries.

Participants

Data object
    Tracks data within a system.

DAO
    Handles persistence for objects within the system.

Stored procedure
    Creates new rows in the database table to represent the data object.

Database table(s)
    Stores the data associated with the data object.

Interactions

The client passes the data object to a DAO object to be used in the creation of a new entity in the database. The DAO passes this information to a stored procedure, which generates a new primary key and inserts the data into the target table, or inserts the data into the target table and allows the database to assign a primary key, which the stored procedure can then retrieve. The DAO then passes the new key back to the application.

Table Inheritance Pattern

Goal

Provide a simple mapping between a class hierarchy and a set of database tables.

Participants

Domain object model
   Provides an object representation of the data a system must deal with.

Database schema
   Provides a method to store and query against the data in the domain object model.

Interactions

Concrete table inheritance
   Each concrete class in the domain object model has a corresponding table in the underlying database schema. When the object model is persisted to the database, each object is written to a row in the corresponding table.

Class table inheritance
   Each class in the domain object model, whether abstract or concrete, has a corresponding table containing the data items defined in that class. Tables associated with a subclass are linked within the database, via primary key relations, with the table associated with their superclass.

Tuple Table Pattern

Goal

To automatically store an object in a database in a way that is human-readable and easily extensible.

Participants

Data object
An object representing some data that we want to store.

Tuple table DAO
Takes a data object and converts its properties to name=value pairs.

Database table
Stores the rows of pairs.

Interactions

The tuple table DAO takes a data object and converts its properties to name=value pairs. It then writes those pairs into multiple rows of a database table. Each row of the table contains the object's primary key, a field name, and a value. When the client needs to retrieve the data from the table, the DAO reads the name=value pairs and uses them to reconstitute an instance of the object.

Notes

The tuple table approach makes it easy to add new fields to the database, since you only need to extend the data object.

Business Tier Interface Patterns

Business Delegate

Goal

Encapsulates knowledge of how to locate, connect to, and interact with business objects in the presentation tier (Figure B-7).

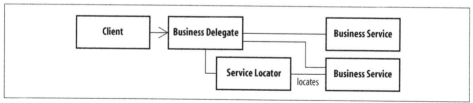

Figure B-7. Classes in the Business Delegate pattern

Participants

Client
> Manipulates business tier data using a delegate. Usually part of the presentation tier's model.

Business delegate
> Locates, connects to, and interacts with business services.

Business service
> Controls access to business objects.

Business objects
> Store business data.

Interactions

A client calls a business method of the business delegate. The delegate locates the correct business service and connects to it. The business service grants the business delegate access to the relevant business objects. The business delegate manipulates the business objects and returns the result to the client.

Notes

Business delegates are part of the client's data model, not the business tier. In non-EJB implementations, delegates often use service adapters to connect to business services. In an EJB implementation, delegates may perform JNDI lookups and manipulate EJB home objects directly, or may use service locators or data access objects.

Business delegates may be stateful or stateless. Business delegates may also be nested, allowing one delegate to use other delegates.

Business Delegate Factory

Goal

Simplify instantiation and configuration of business delegates.

Participants

Client
> Manipulates business tier data using a delegate.

Business delegate factory
> Configures and instantiates business delegates.

Business delegates
> Locate, connect to, and interact with business services (Figure B-8).

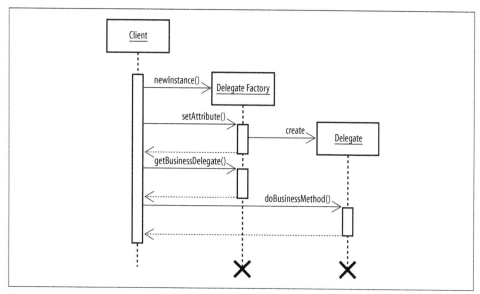

Figure B-8. Interactions in the Business Delegate Factory pattern

Interactions

A client creates a new instance of a business delegate factory. The client sets attributes of the factory that control the type and options of the desired delegate. The factory generates a new instance of the requested delegate with the relevant parameters and returns it to the client. The client uses the delegate to interact with the business tier.

Notes

A business delegate factory may be stateful or stateless. If the factory is stateless, each call must contain all the required configuration parameters, but the factory can be a singleton.

Service Adapter

Goal

Simplify access to remote business data by adapting the data into Java objects.

Participants

Client
    Manipulates business data using an adapter.

Service adapter
    Adapts business data into a convenient Java implementation.

Business service

Stores and controls access to business data (Figure B-9).

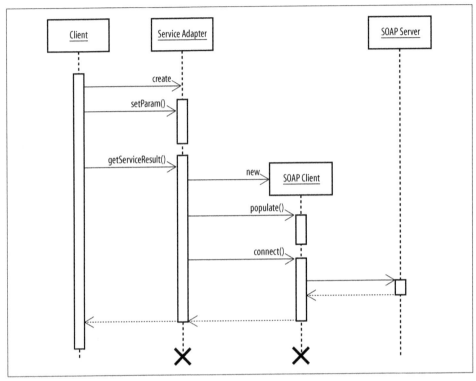

Figure B-9. Interactions in a SOAP service adapter

Interactions

The client creates and initializes the service adapter. The client requests business data from the adapter, passing in Java objects as arguments. The adapter connects to the remote service using an appropriate protocol and translates any arguments to the correct form. The adapter receives the results and translates them into Java objects, which are returned to the client.

Notes

Service adapters are most useful when business data is stored in a non-Java format. Adapters may also be used to impose desired semantics such as transactions onto services. For EJBs, service locators are usually more appropriate than service adapters.

Service Locator

Goal

Simplify and centralize connections to remote services (Figure B-10).

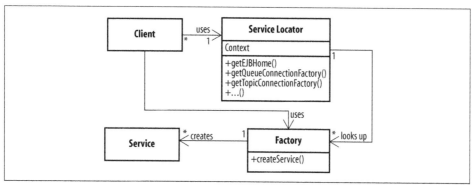

Figure B-10. Classes in the Service Locater pattern

Participants

Client
> Locates business services using a service locator.

Service locator
> Looks up and maintains connections to remote service factories.

Service factory
> Instantiates business services.

Business services
> Control access to business data (Figure B-11).

Interactions

The client instantiates and configures the service locator. The client requests a remote service factory from the locator. The locator looks up and optionally caches the service factory. The client uses the factory to generate an instance of the business service. The client uses the business service to manipulate business data.

Notes

In J2EE, service locators can be used to encapsulate interactions with the JNDI directory. The service factories are EJB home objects, or JMS connection factories. EJB service locators frequently cache results of JNDI lookups such as EJB home objects.

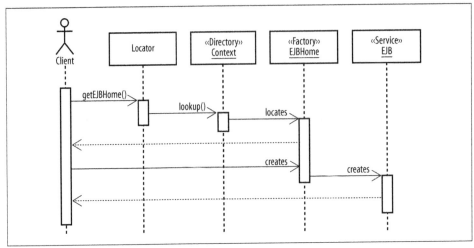

Figure B-11. Interactions in the Service Locator pattern

Session Façade

Goal

Increase performance by organizing remote business data in the most efficient manner (Figure B-12).

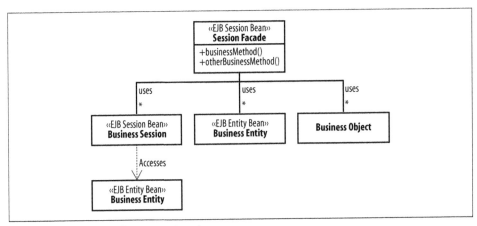

Figure B-12. Classes in the Session Façade pattern

Participants

Client
    Manipulates business data using a façade.

Session façade
    Remote object that provides access to business data.

Business objects
    Stores business data (Figure B-13).

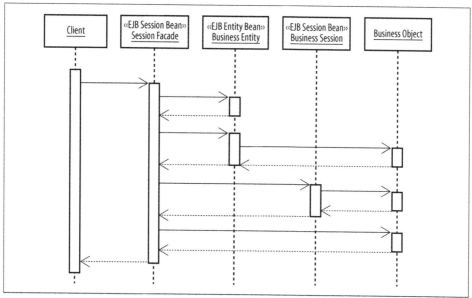

Figure B-13. Interactions in the Session Façade pattern

Interactions

The client calls a business method of the remote session façade. The façade locates and manipulates business objects locally and returns the result to the client.

Notes

Session façades are most effective when using Session EJBs and EJB local home objects. This combination allows the façade to manipulate EJBs locally, significantly reducing network overhead. Façades usually communicate with clients using DTOs.

Concurrency Patterns

ACID Transaction Pattern

Goal

To perform multiple actions on a set of resources while ensuring that the underlying resources always remain in a correct state (Figure B-14).

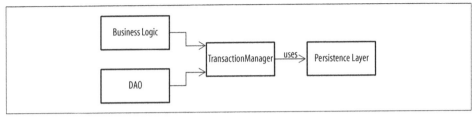

Figure B-14. Classes in a managed transaction environment

Participants

Business logic
Provides the application with its underlying constraints and process flow.

Transaction management layer
Provides code for coordinating the business logic and data access logic to ensure that all transactions meet a set of requirements.

Persistence layer
Responsible for storing data in persistent storage, usually (but not necessarily) a database.

Interactions

All business and data-access logic route any changes to data via a transaction manager object. The transaction manager acts as a gateway either to the persistence layer of the application or to the domain object model itself. It is responsible for ensuring that all permanent changes to the data underlying the application are atomic (treatable as a single unit rather than a set of individual changes), consistent (consistent with its business rules and constraints at the end of each transaction), isolated (do not interfere with other simultaneous transactions), and durable (changes made in the course of a successful transaction become part of the permanent state of the system).

Notes

In an EJB environment, the transaction manager is embedded within the application server. When using regular objects with a database, the database itself can assume some transaction management responsibilities, and the other patterns in this section, such as Lock Manager, can be used to fill in the gaps.

Lockable Object Pattern

Goal

Implement simple locking within a single JVM (Figure B-15).

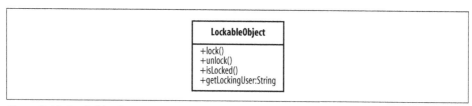

Figure B-15. Lockable object

Participants

Business delegate
Provides access to business logic.

Lockable object
Provides a data object that can be locked for exclusive use by a business delegate.

Interactions

When a business delegate needs to modify an object, it calls the object's lock( ) method. If a lock can be obtained, the business delegate updates the object and releases the lock.

Lock Manager Pattern

Goal

Provide a central point for managing lock information without requiring individual data objects to be locking-aware (Figure B-16 and Figure B-17).

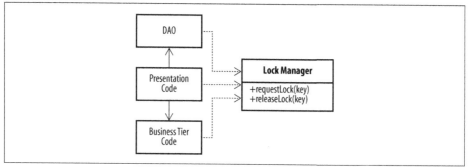

Figure B-16. Lock manager

Participants

Business delegate
Provides access to business logic.

DAO
Provides access to the persistence layer.

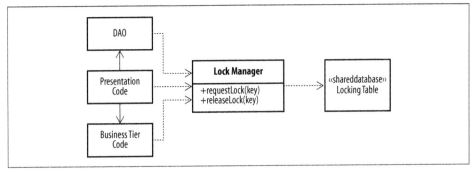

Figure B-17. Offline lock manager

Lock manager
    Coordinates access to resources for different objects.

Database (offline variant)
    Provide a centralized location to store locking information for use by many clients or by a clustered application.

Interactions

When a business delegate or a DAO needs to lock a resource, it requests a lock on the object via a lock manager object. The lock manager takes a primary key and determines if the entity associated with the key is already locked. If it is not, it locks the resource on behalf of the user requesting the lock. When the user is done, he releases the lock.

The *offline lock manager* variant stores lock information "offline," in a database. This allows multiple JVMs to share locking information in a distributed environment.

Notes

As with pessimistic concurrency in general, applications must take care to ensure that locks are released, and ensure that abandoned locks are released after a timeout period.

Optimistic Concurrency Pattern

Goal

To allow multiple users safe access to shared resources in environments in which there is minimal risk that two users will simultaneously edit the same data (Figure B-18).

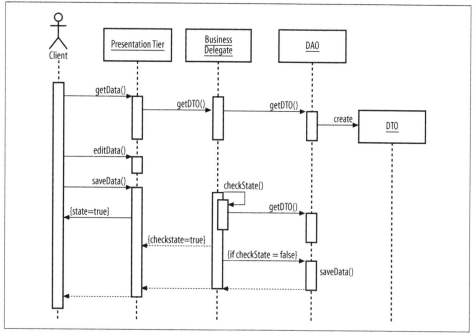

Figure B-18. Optimistic concurrency sequence

Participants

Presentation tier
> Presents the end user with an interface to the application.

Business delegate
> Provides access to business logic.

DAO
> Provides access to the persistence layer.

Interactions

A user interacting with the presentation tier requests data to edit. The user performs edits and requests that the edits be saved by the system. The system checks to see if the data has been changed externally since the user began the edit process (possibly by retrieving the data a second time and comparing). If the data was changed externally, the system provides the user with an error message. If the data has not been changed, the system applies the user's changes.

Notes

Optimistic concurrency works best in situations where there is little opportunity for collision between users, because when collision occurs, one user will have to rekey their data.

Pessimistic Concurrency Pattern

Goal

Allow multiple users to access shared resources in an environment where the possibility of collision is high, without forcing users to discard work (Figure B-19).

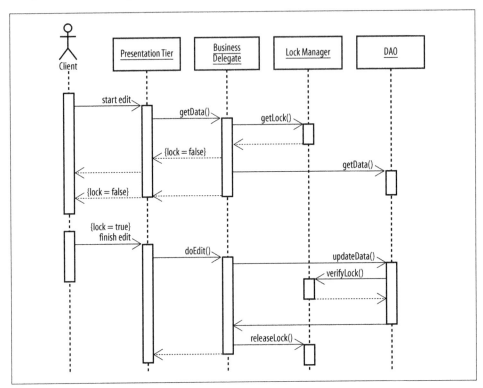

Figure B-19. Pessimistic concurrency pattern

Participants

Presentation tier
  Provides a user interface to the end user.

Business delegate
  Provides access to business logic.

Lock manager
  Coordinates resource locking across multiple objects.

DAO
  Provides access to the persistence layer.

Interactions

A client connects to the presentation tier and initiates a data edit session. The presentation tier contacts a business delegate to retrieve the data the user wants to edit. The business delegate contacts a lock manager object and requests a lock on the specific data the user wants to edit. If a lock is unavailable, the business delegate returns a message to the presentation tier. If a lock is available, the business delegate retrieves the data from a DAO and passes it back to the presentation tier. The user makes their edits and submits them back to the presentation tier. The presentation tier submits the changes to the business delegate, which submits them to the DAO. The DAO verifies the lock and writes the changes to the persistence layer. The business delegate then releases the lock.

Notes

Pessimistic concurrency prevents users from having their edits rejected by the system due to concurrent changes. However, it can be much more difficult to implement properly: if locks are not released properly, the entire system can gradually become unavailable.

Transactional Context Pattern

Goal

Allow multiple objects to participate in a single transaction without imposing a large amount of overhead on the programmer (Figure B-20).

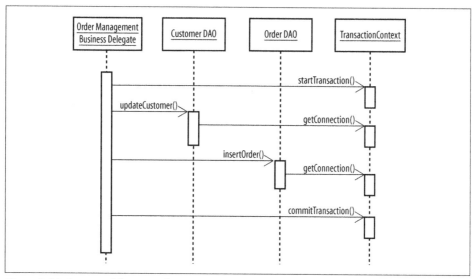

Figure B-20. Business delegate and DAOs using the Transactional Context pattern

Participants

Business delegates
> Provide access to business logic.

Data access objects
> Provide access to persistence resources, such as a database.

Transactional context object
> Coordinates activities between business delegates, data access objects, and the underlying database.

Transaction-aware database
> Provides system level transaction support.

Interactions

When an application needs to begin a transaction, it obtains a transactional context object from the system and initiates a transaction with the context. All classes with access to the context use it to access transaction-sensitive resources, such as database connections, allowing multiple objects to share a single database transaction.

Notes

This pattern is particularly useful when building servlet-based applications with business delegate and DAO objects. You can associate a transactional context with each request, allowing business delegates to easily manage a transaction involving multiple DAOs and even multiple business delegates. See Chapter 10 for extensive examples.

Version Number Pattern

Goal

Provide a simple way to detect when an object has changed (Figure B-21).

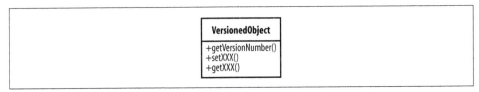

Figure B-21. Versioned object

Participants

Versioned object
> Provides an object representation of data subject to change control, and tracks the changes that occur to the data.

Business tier code
   Uses the version number to determine when to persist the versioned object.

Interactions

When an application modifies a property on a versioned object, a version number associated with the object is incremented. Other code can record this version number and use the information to resolve concurrency problems, such as change detection in an optimistic concurrency implementation.

Notes

See related patterns IsDirty and Optimistic Concurrency.

Messaging Patterns

Message Distribution Patterns

Malformed Message Channel

Goal

Provide a procedure to handle messages that can be successfully delivered but cannot be properly processed due to invalid or corrupted message data.

Participants

Message client
> Monitors a message delivery channel, receives messages, and processes correctly-formatted messages according to a set of business rules.

Malformed message channel
> A messaging destination used for messages that cannot be processed.

Message server
> Responsible for routing messages to a delivery channel and receiving messages from a client.

Interactions

The messaging server delivers messages to a client. If the client cannot properly process the message, it routes a copy to a special messaging destination configured within the messaging server. A human can monitor this *malformed message channel* and delete or act upon the messages it contains.

Notes

In JMS, use a specially designated Queue or a Topic in your messaging server as a malformed message channel. You use your message server's tools to periodically examine the channel to identify unprocessed messages. The incidence of malformed messages will probably be higher when using SMTP for messaging.

Point-to-Point Distribution Pattern

Goal

Send a message once and only once to a destination known to the sender.

Participants

Sender
> Originates a message and is aware of the destination.

Recipient
> Receives a message.

Messaging server
> Relays a message from a sender to a recipient.

Interactions

The sender dispatches a message to a messaging server, which is responsible for relaying the message to a particular recipient. The messaging server may proactively deliver the message (by contacting the recipient directly), or hold the message until the recipient connects to retrieve it.

Notes

In a JMS environment using an enterprise message queue product, point-to-point messaging is implemented via the Queue interface. In an SMTP environment with JavaMail, all messaging is point-to-point.

Publish-Subscribe Pattern

Goal

Send a single copy of a message for delivery to multiple recipients who may or may not be individually known to the sender.

Participants

Sender
> Originates a message of a particular type.

Messaging server
> Accepts a message from a sender and delivers it to zero or more recipients.

Recipients

Register to receive (subscribe to) a particular type of message.

Interactions

Rather than identify a particular recipient, the sender identifies a message as being of a certain type. Recipients may then register with the messaging server as being interested in receiving all messages of a particular type. When a sender creates a new message, all recipients who have expressed interest in receiving messages of that type will receive a copy.

Notes

In a JMS environment, publish-subscribe is implemented via the Topic interface. In an SMTP/JavaMail environment, implementing publish-subscribe requires additional infrastructure, either within your application or within your mail server.

Message Client Patterns

Competing Consumers Pattern

Goal

To distribute message processing across multiple consumers, allowing multiple messages to be processed in parallel (Figure C-1).

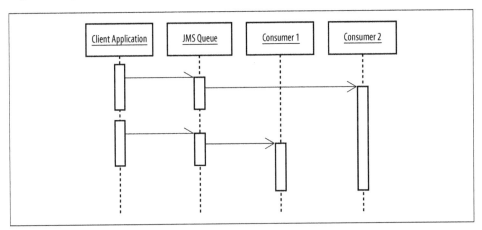

Figure C-1. Competing consumers

Participants

Message originators
> One or more applications sending messages.

Queue
> List of messages.

Multiple consumers
> Consumers with access to read and process the messages in the queue.

Interactions

One or more applications send messages to a queue. Multiple consumers access the queue, each reading different messages and processing them. Each message is read from the queue by one and only one consumer.

Notes

The Competing Consumers pattern is best implemented using JMS, as Internet mail providers generally do not support multiple readers on a single mailbox terribly well.

Event-Driven Consumer Pattern

Goal

To deliver messages to a client as quickly as possible, while minimizing the complexity of the code, the developer must assemble to handle messages.

Participants

Message server
> Receives incoming messages.

Application server
> Communicates with the message server and retrieves new messages.

Client code
> Performs the actual processing, based on calls from the application server.

Interactions

Incoming messages are delivered to the message server. The application server communicates with the message server and retrieves new messages destined for a particular client. When new messages arrive, the application server calls appropriate client code to process them.

Notes

Message-driven EJBs implement the Event-Driven Consumer pattern. JMS also supports implementing event-driven consumers directly. JavaMail supports event-driven consumers via the FolderListener interface, although we do not recommend it. Most event-driven consumer implementations simply push implementation to the application server/application framework level, while still implementing a polling consumer behind the scenes.

Message Façade Pattern

Goal

To hide business logic behind a standard façade that can be accessed asynchronously and maintained independently (Figure C-2).

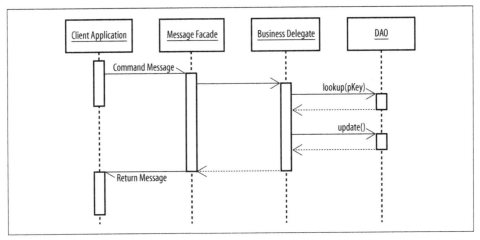

Figure C-2. Message façade

Participants

Client application
> Creates a command message.

Command message
> Carries information from the client to the façade.

Message façade
> Uses the command message to access the business tier code.

Business tier code
> Performs the actual processing to fulfill a use case.

Interactions

The client creates a command message and sends it to the message façade using any sort of message transport. The façade receives the message (using a polling consumer or an event-driven consumer) and uses the information it contains to access business tier code to fulfill a use case. Optionally, a return message is sent to the client confirming successful completion of the use case and returning data.

Notes

Also see the Business Delegate and Session Façade patterns.

Message Handler Pattern

Goal

Decouple the code responsible for the processing of messages from the code responsible for receiving messages. Provide a simpler framework for testing message-handling code.

Participants

Message client
    Responsible for receiving messages from a messaging server.
Message handler
    Responsible for processing individual messages after they have been received.

Interactions

The message client is responsible for retrieving messages from a transport mechanism, via JavaMail, JMS, or other technologies. Once a message is received, it is handed off to a separate message handler object, which is responsible for processing the message content.

Notes

The message handler design is a building block for more complex client designs.

Message Selector Pattern

Goal

To manage multiple types of messages on a single message channel.

Participants

A client
    Reads the channel and selects messages.
One or more senders
    Transmit messages.

A message channel
> A single channel managing messages.

Interactions

Senders transmit messages to a single message channel. Each message includes identifying information, such as headers, that can be used to determine the purpose of the message. The client reads the channel and selects the messages it is capable of handling.

Notes

Message selectors can be implemented in JMS using the built-in selection criteria API, which allow you to add SQL-like selection criteria to a Queue or a Topic.

Polling Consumer Pattern

Goal

Allow an application to participate in a messaging exchange without requiring that the application be running 100% of the time and without requiring a continuous two-way connection with the messaging server.

Participants

Message client
> A particular client receiving messages.

Message server
> Transmits messages to the client.

Interactions

As messages for a particular client arrive at the message server, the server stores each incoming message in a holding area. The client periodically contacts the message server and issues a request for all new messages intended for it. The message server transmits all of the held messages to the client, which processes them.

Notes

All consumers working with POP3 implement the Polling Consumer pattern. JMS consumers have a wider variety of options, including the Event-Driven Consumer pattern.

Messaging Integration Patterns

Content Aggregator Pattern

Goal

To allow a single handler to easily process messages from a variety of sources that have similar content but different formats.

Participants

Multiple senders
  Send messages to the content aggregator.

Content aggregator
  Reads each message and creates a new message in a common format.

Message handler
  Processes the messages.

Interactions

Senders send messages to the content aggregator. The aggregator reads each message and creates a new message in a common format. The new message is sent on to a single handler.

Content-Based Routing Pattern

Goal

Provide a single point of receipt for messages associated with a particular use case, even if the use case will be handled by different backend systems depending on the content of the request (Figure C-3).

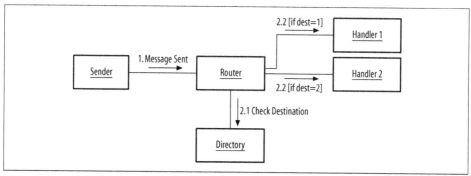

Figure C-3. Content-based routing

Participants

Sender
> Sends the message to the router.

Message
> Contains the content.

Content router
> Examines the content and determines which handler should be used.

Handlers
> Process the message.

Interactions

The sender sends a message to the router. The router examines the message content and determines which handler should be used to process it. This check may be assisted by an external resource, such as a directory server. The router then dispatches the message to the appropriate handler.

Control Bus Pattern

Goal

To provide a centralized interface for asynchronously managing multiple systems and multiples nodes of single systems (Figure C-4).

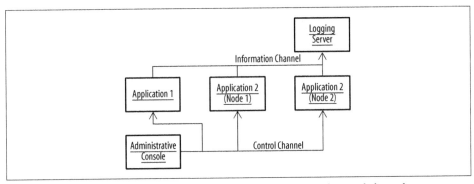

Figure C-4. Control bus spanning three applications with logging and control channels

Participants

Administrative clients
> Read event messages.

Control bus channel
> Sends event messages and receives control messages.

Applications
    Share a single control bus channel.

Interactions

The applications being controlled share a single control bus channel to send event messages and receive control messages. Event messages are read off the channel by administrative clients, which include administration consoles and logging servers. The controlled applications monitor the control bus channel for command messages.

Notes

Command messages on the channel can take two forms: *global* and *targeted*. All applications must be compatible with the command message format used on the bus. This compatibility allows an administrative application to send global commands as well as commands to individual applications. Event messages, likewise, must share a common format, allowing administrative and logging clients to easily process the information provided by each application.

Pipes and Filters Pattern

Goal

To spread processing of a message across multiple consumers, allowing flexible workflow, distribution of processing, and easy reuse (Figure C-5).

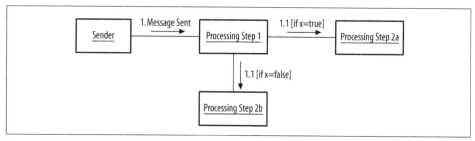

Figure C-5. Pipes and filters collaboration

Participants

Sender
    Sends the message.
Message
    Contains the content.
Multiple message handlers
    Examine and process the message.

Interactions

The sender transmits a message to the first message handler in the processing chain. The first handler in the chain examines the message and performs whatever processing is required. It then forwards the message to another handler for further processing. Each handler is required to determine the appropriate next destination.

Notes

For more on implementing flexible workflows, see the Service to Worker pattern.

J2EE Antipatterns

Architectural Antipatterns

Excessive Layering

Mistake

Unnecessary layers make application inefficient and bloated.

Watch for It When

Adding layers to *any* application, developing a small application that does not need to scale, or building adaptors to external programs that duplicate functionality of the external program.

Solution

Understand the costs and benefits of each layer in the system. Layers generally have a benefit in terms of either extensibility (providing a reusable interface) or scalability (caching data).

Match the use of layers to the general application type. For example, do not build a complex, multilayered business tier for a small application that simply accesses a local database.

Leak Collection

Mistake

Objects with a short lifespan cannot be garbage-collected because an object with a long lifespan refers to them, resulting in a memory leak.

Watch for It When

Using objects with mismatched lifespans (usually collections), using objects that use collections internally, such as listeners, and using caches.

Solution

Put adds and removes close to each other in the code. If you have a cache, define an expiration policy. Where possible, use weak references to allow garbage collection.

Presentation Tier Antipatterns

Magic Servlet

Mistake

A single servlet performs duties of model, view, and controller, making the servlet large and difficult to maintain.

Watch for It When

Servlets are large and complicated, servlets output HTML directly, or servlets are directly connected to databases or other external resources.

Solution

Refactor into the MVC architecture. Separate all output generation into JSP pages or separate servlets. Separate calls to business data into reusable actions. Coordinate input processing, actions, and views with servlets.

Monolithic/Compound JSPs

Mistake

A single JSP page performs duties of model, view, and controller, making the page large and difficult to maintain.

Watch for It When

JSP pages are large and complicated, JSP pages contain a large amount of embedded logic, JSP pages directly connect to databases or other external resources, or JSP pages contain lots of if/then statements.

Solution

Refactor into the MVC architecture. Separate all output generation into JSP pages or separate servlets. Separate calls to business data into reusable actions. Coordinate input processing, actions, and views with servlets.

Overstuffed Session

Mistake

Data with too short or long a lifespan is stored in the HTTP session, leading to excessive memory use and potential loss of important data.

Watch for It When

Data stored in the session is only used in a single request, data stored in the session is used over a long period of time and should survive web server crashes.

Solution

Store short-lived data in request scope. Store long-lived data in the business tier or other persistence mechanism. Make sure that data added to the session is removed when it is no longer relevant.

Business Tier Antipatterns

Everything Is an EJB

Mistake

EJBs are used when they provide few benefits, leading to an unnecessarily bloated or complex application.

Watch for It When

EJB features such as CMP, transactions, or security are not needed, few clients access the business tier, entity beans are simply a wrapper to an existing database, session beans are used as a gateway to other remote services, or business services do not need to be distributed.

Solution

Often entity beans can be replaced with local commands or JavaBeans working in conjunction with DAOs. Direct database access, flat files, and JDO can also provide lighter-weight persistence mechanisms than entity EJBs.

Session EJBs can often be replaced with business delegates or other, non-EJB façades.

Round-Tripping

Mistake

Frequent calls to remote EJB getter and setter methods slow down the entire application and saturate the network.

Watch for It When

Remote entity EJBs are used directly, get or set methods of remote EJBs are called frequently, especially when iterating over a collection of EJBs (Figure D-1).

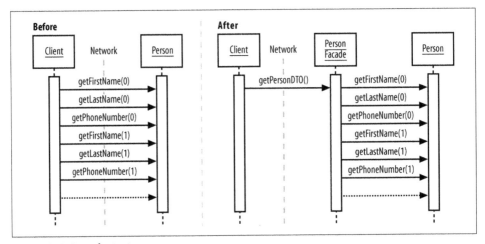

Figure D-1. Round-tripping

Solution

Refactor remote entity EJB calls to use a facade and a DTO. Use a session EJB as a façade to copy the entity EJBs into DTOs before they are sent across the network. Set values by sending back modified DTOs.

Stateful When Stateless Will Do

Mistake

A stateful session EJB is used unnecessarily, causing much higher overhead for the EJB server.

Watch for It When

Using *any* stateful session EJBs, arguments are passed into the create method of a session EJB to avoid passing the data later, or session EJBs are used specifically to store state, such as in a shopping cart.

Solution

Convert stateful into stateless by passing all state with every call to the bean. If there are too many arguments, consider using a client-side adaptor to store them. Store other persistent data (even if it is not permanent) using entity EJBs.

Index

non-EJB database components, performance gains in, 151
nonguaranteed messaging, 234
nonpersistent messages, 235
nonrepeatable read (transactions), 201
normalized data structure, 126

O

object diagrams, 29
object model, building, 120–125
Object Oriented Software Engineering (OOSE) method, 18
object-relational mappings, 159–171
objects, difference between classes and, 25
offline lock management, 219, 221–226
online lock management, 219–221
optimal pool sizes, 111
Optimistic Concurrency pattern, 215, 320
Overstuffed Session antipattern, 272, 339

P

packages, 29
Page scope, 44
PAOs (Procedure Access Objects), 152–154
PartnerUser class, 26
pathways, 3
PatientDAO interface, 144
patterns
    ACID Transaction (see ACID Transaction pattern)
    antipatterns (see antipatterns)
    architectural, 287–295
    Asynchronous Page (see Asynchronous Page pattern)
    Business Delegate Factory (see Business Delegate Factory pattern)
    Business Delegate (see Business Delegate pattern)
    business tier, 300–325
    business tier interfaces, 311–317
    Caching Filter (see Caching Filter pattern)
    catalogs, 4
    Competing Consumers (see Competing Consumers pattern)
    Composite Entity Bean, 188
    Composite Entity (see Composite Entity pattern)
    Composite View (see Composite View pattern)
    concurrency (see concurrency patterns)
    Content Aggregator (see Content Aggregator pattern)
    Content-Based Routing (see Content-Based Routing pattern)
    Control Bus (see Control Bus pattern)
    Decorator (see Decorator pattern)
    description, 3
    design (see design patterns)
    Domain Object Model (see Domain Object Model pattern)
    Entity Façade (see Entity Façade pattern)
    Event-Driven Consumer (see Event-Driven Consumer pattern)
    Front Controller (see Front Controller pattern)
    Gang of Four Adapter, 184
    IsDirty (see IsDirty pattern)
    Lazy Load (see Lazy Load pattern)
    Lock Manager (see Lock Manager pattern)
    Lockable Object (see Lockable Object pattern)
    Malformed Message Channel (see Malformed Message Channel pattern)
    Message Façade (see Message Façade pattern)
    Message Handler (see Message Handler pattern)
    Message Selector (see Message Selector pattern)
    messaging (see messaging, patterns)
    Model-View-Controller (MVC) (see Model-View-Controller (MVC) pattern)
    Optimistic Concurrency (see Optimistic Concurrency pattern)
    Pessimistic Concurrency (see Pessimistic Concurrency pattern)
    Pipes and Filters (see Pipes and Filters pattern)
    PK Block Generator (see PK Block Generator pattern)
    Point-to-Point Distribution (see Point-to-Point Distribution pattern)
    Polling Consumer (see Polling Consumer pattern)
    presentation tier (see presentation tier patterns)
    Procedure Access Object (see Procedure Access Object pattern)
    Publish-Subscribe (see Publish-Subscribe pattern)

User class, 26
user experience, 36
user interfaces, 38

V

validateResource( ) method, 106
Value Objects, 132
vendor lock-in, 264
Version Number pattern, 226–228, 324
View Helper pattern, 63, 294
view helpers, 75–81
views, 38, 39, 46
    advanced, 75–88
    composite (see composite view)
    Service to Worker pattern, 68
visible business tier, 116

W

web services
    session façade, 192
    versus asynchronous messaging, 231
WebRowSet, 139
Woolf, Bobby, 258
workflow, 67
write lock, 215
WSDL definition files, 185

X

XML-based serialization approach, 166
XMLParserFactory, 109

About the Authors

William Crawford has been developing web-based enterprise applications since 1995, including one of the first web-based electronic medical record systems (at Children's Hospital Boston) and some of the first enterprise-level uses of Java. He has consulted for a variety of institutional clients, including Children's Hospital Boston, Harvard Medical Center, numerous startups, and several Fortune 500 companies. Prior to an acquisition he was CTO of Invantage, Inc., in Cambridge, Massachusetts. He received a degree in history and economics from Yale University. He is the co-author of *Java Servlet Programming* and *Java Enterprise in a Nutshell*.

Will is currently Principal Software Architect at Perceptive Informatics, Inc., in Massachusetts, a provider of software and services to the pharmaceutical industry. He can be reached at *http://www.williamcrawford.info*.

Jonathan Kaplan has been a software developer at Sun Microsystems since 1997. Before joining Sun, he worked on a web-based electronic records system at Children's Hospital Boston. At Sun, he has focused on system management, including early Java- and browser-based applications. Jonathan received his Bachelor's and Master's degrees in Computer and Information Science from the University of Pennsylvania. He currently lives with his wife Tracy in Cambridge, Massachusetts.

Colophon

Our look is the result of reader comments, our own experimentation, and feedback from distribution channels. Distinctive covers complement our distinctive approach to technical topics, breathing personality and life into potentially dry subjects.

The animal on the cover of *J2EE Design Patterns* is a mollusk. Oysters, squid, and snails all belong to this group of invertebrates (phylum *Mollusca*), which can be found in streams and oceans as well as on land. There are herbivorous, carnivorous, scavenging, and parasitic mollusks. Most possess a *mantle*, a layer of tissue that protects the animal's gills or lungs, and often produces a calcareous shell. They have a powerful, muscular foot section that they use for moving around.

Aquatic mollusks breathe through gills, and filter water for their food, which includes plankton and other single-cell plants and animals. Scientists have found that filter-feeding mollusks can serve as a benchmark of the degree of pollution in a body of water. The contaminants are a health hazard to the mollusks, and also to the people who may eat them.

There are three main classes of mollusks: the bivalves, the gastropods, and the cephalopods. The bivalve class is made up of mollusks with two hinged shells, such as oysters, clams, and scallops. Snails and slugs are members of the largest class of mollusks, the gastropods, which includes over 40,000 species. Gastropods often have a single, spiral-shaped shell, although some species have none. Cephalopods usually do not have shells; this group includes octopus and squid. The shells of mollusks are strong and enduring, and provide a meaningful fossil record of these creatures.

Colleen Gorman was the production editor and the copyeditor for *J2EE Design Patterns*. Marlowe Shaeffer was the proofreader, and Jane Ellin and Darren Kelly provided quality control. Julie Hawks wrote the index.

Hanna Dyer designed the cover of this book, based on a series design by Edie Freedman. The cover image is a 19th-century engraving from the Dover Pictorial Archive. Emma Colby produced the cover layout with QuarkXPress 4.1 using Adobe's ITC Garamond font.

David Futato designed the interior layout. This book was converted by Julie Hawks to FrameMaker 5.5.6 with a format conversion tool created by Erik Ray, Jason McIntosh, Neil Walls, and Mike Sierra that uses Perl and XML technologies. The text font is Linotype Birka; the heading font is Adobe Myriad Condensed; and the code font is LucasFont's TheSans Mono Condensed. The illustrations that appear in the book were produced by Robert Romano and Jessamyn Read using Macromedia FreeHand 9 and Adobe Photoshop 6. The tip and warning icons were drawn by Christopher Bing. This colophon was written by Colleen Gorman.

Lightning Source UK Ltd.
Milton Keynes UK
UKOW05f0828020915

257915UK00003B/75/P